PETROTURFING

PETROTURFING

Refining Canadian Oil through Social Media

JORDAN B. KINDER

MIN NE SO TA University of Minnesota Press | Minneapolis | London

Portions of chapter 1 were previously published in a different form in "From Dirty Oil to Ethical Oil: Petroturfing and the Cultural Politics of Canadian Oil after Social Media," *Journal of Environmental Media* 1, no. 2 (2020): 167–83, https://doi.org/10.1386/jem_00014_1. Portions of chapter 5 were published in a different form in "Sustaining Petrocultures: On the Politics and Aesthetics of Oil Sands Reclamation," in *Energy Culture: Art and Theory on Oil and Beyond,* edited by Imre Szeman and Jeff Diamanti (Morgantown: West Virginia University Press, 2019), 93–103.

Published by the University of Minnesota Press
111 Third Avenue South, Suite 290
Minneapolis, MN 55401-2520
http://www.upress.umn.edu

ISBN 978-1-5179-1432-5 (hc)
ISBN 978-1-5179-1433-2 (pb)

A Cataloging-in-Publication record for this book is available from the Library of Congress.

CONTENTS

INTRODUCTION

IN LATE FEBRUARY 2020, representatives from the pro-oil group Rally 4 Resources flew from Alberta to Toronto, Ontario.[1] These representatives did so to covertly attend a demonstration against the Prospectors & Developers Association of Canada (PDAC) Convention. PDAC is the largest minerals and mining conference in the world, taking place annually in Toronto's Financial District as a sort of trade show celebrating Canada's central role in the global mining industry; it draws considerable crowds of protestors each year. Rally 4 Resources attended for this reason, to "witness one of these radical demonstrations with [its] own eyes," gather intel on the anti-extraction movement in Canada, and report the experience back to its followers, which was done through a blog post. The post offers descriptions of participants and some actions taken throughout the day; it also takes stock of the demonstration's perceived racial demographics: "Out of the 200–300 participants, only six–twelve were First Nations, and the majority of them were guest speakers and their companions." "The rest of the attendees," the post continues, "were mostly fresh, young urbanites or hippie type folks with grey hair." In closing, the post describes the event as "a meticulously organized charade by obviously paid professionals" whose "militant type tactics disrupt and inconvenience everyday, innocent Canadians." The takeaway from attending the event, the post concludes, "is that there is nothing grassroots about this [anti-extraction] movement."[2]

Rally 4 Resources understands itself as fueled by grassroots energies. In the organization's own words, it is "a volunteer movement that involves grassroots Canadians" who "[protect] and promot[e] our resource based jobs, families, and communities."[3] Founded sometime in 2016, the Red Deer, Alberta-based group emerged in the latter part of the 2010s as an active voice in the pro-oil movement in Canada, which first took shape in the early 2010s. Since then, the movement transitioned from a largely social media–based phenomenon with deep ties to right-wing media ecologies and think tanks into one that stages relatively well-attended on-the-ground demonstrations. Rally 4 Resources played a role in this transformation by spearheading a number of demonstrations in support of the oil and gas industry.

I begin *Petroturfing: Refining Canadian Oil through Social Media* with a reflection on Rally 4 Resources' account of the 2020 PDAC demonstration not only because the group's preoccupation with authenticity and legitimacy highlights a number of key themes addressed throughout this book. I begin here also because I was at this demonstration on a chilly late-winter's afternoon. Here, I felt the contours of a pressing energetic moment wherein a number of resistance efforts coalesced to challenge the very machinations of extractive capitalism whose allies I examine in this book.

My experience tells a much different story of the PDAC event. That my version does so brings into relief some representational conflicts that have emerged in recent years over questions of authenticity surrounding movements both for and against Canada's extractive apparatuses. In Rally 4 Resources' account of the PDAC protest, metrics of legitimacy are applied in order to call into question the motivations of protestors. The group's emphasis on authenticity as determined by visible Indigeneity reveals a strategy that defines legitimacy and authority in terms of race and ethnicity. Perceived race and ethnicity are highlighted to separate those with real grievances against extraction from those who are construed as outside agitators. Accusations of demonstrators being paid only add more fuel to the proverbial fire, as if global social and ecological injustice, deepening climate change, and politically or economically motivated murders of Indigenous activists in Latin America were not on their own terms enough to bring together genuine, coherent protest among diverse peoples.[4]

Many more features of Rally 4 Resources' account betray my experience in direct ways. I am a white-skinned Indigenous person. I was not paid to attend. And among those "six-twelve First Nations," young urbanites, and hippies were also children and toddlers in strollers who remained undisturbed even as alleged "militant type tactics" were deployed. A central aspect of the demonstration left out of Rally 4 Resources' account was the staging of a sobering collective memorial art piece. The piece asked participants to tie red ribbons representing victims of extractive violence in Latin America and elsewhere to a long string, which was then carried as a street-wide banner. These unreported moments offer a kinder version of events than is described in the post. To represent the events as violent, however, was precisely the point. When Rally 4 Resources circulated the blog post through its Facebook page, this representational goal was achieved. One commenter called the action "terrorism" while another claimed the demonstrators to be "just a bunch of paid protestors."[5] In setting sights on demonstrators in terms of their supposed legitimacy, Rally 4 Resources delineated what counts as the currency of activist engagement.

Rally 4 Resources' version of events was told through a blog post hosted on a website built with NationBuilder, which was circulated across popular social media platforms. This circuit is pertinent in identifying the architectures of the contemporary web that groups like Rally 4 Resources mobilize to build their own legitimacy. NationBuilder is a tech start-up that provides software solutions and online communication platforms that allow customers to build a large database of subscribers and communicate to them in sophisticated ways. Its services are largely geared toward political campaigns, advocacy organizations, and nongovernmental organizations (NGOs)—those who, as NationBuilder's promotional slogan says, seek to "build the future."[6] An exemplar of what political theorist Nick Srnicek calls "platform capitalism," or an enmeshment of digital technologies and capitalism, NationBuilder is an enterprise whose product is a kind of database management.[7] This management enables smooth communicative access to a set of subscribers en masse—subscribers who constitute the *Nation* in NationBuilder's parlance. Rally 4 Resources' use of the platform lends tacit credence to its self-presentation as a grassroots advocacy organization. Through this mode of self-presentation, the disingenuous premises of Rally 4 Resources emerge, beginning with the group's founding gesture: Canada's oil and gas industry is marginalized and in need of grassroots advocacy. Already dominant relations, particularly those that relate to what Andreas Malm, Bob Johnson, and others call the "fossil economy," or an economy motivated by endless growth powered by the burning of fossil fuels, are recast as underdog ones in order to rationalize grassroots support of this economy.[8] The future Rally 4 Resources is rallying for is, in other words, a future much like the present.

Rally 4 Resources' efforts represent some of the most recent interventions in what I understand as the twenty-first-century *oil culture wars,* phrasing I employ as a riff on the painfully ubiquitous concept of culture wars that has been used to describe tensions between progressive and conservative ideological visions for the future as they manifest in political arenas and public spheres.[9] These wars over how we collectively understand our relationship to oil, I argue, occur in tandem with material disputes over the expansion of the fossil economy. On one side are those who see an urgent necessity of nurturing good relations beyond those tied to the fossil economy in order to transition away from its socially and ecologically destructive inertia. On the other side are those who hope to maintain and expand the fossil economy through the building of new fossil fuel infrastructure. Planetary in character and consequence, the oil culture wars manifest as a deeply localized phenomenon that has, in North America and elsewhere, brought into view the relationship between fossil fuels and the far right that has in turn been stoked through social media. As the effects of global warming continue to be increasingly (if unevenly) felt, fossil fuels have become a vehicle through which right-wing political identities have formed. This movement of support for fossil fuels that this book takes as its subject of study seeks to fortify the stronghold of the fossil economy in the hearts and minds of a broader public at a time when consensus on the necessity of a swift energy transition to avoid catastrophe continues to grow.

My wager is that the realization of a more equitable future beyond the fossil economy will be further delayed if the conflict at the heart of the oil culture wars intensifies. Motivated to provide a deeper understanding of the contours of this conflict and hasten the realization of a more equitable future, this book investigates the pro-oil movement in Canada first to challenge the terms and conditions of the oil culture wars, and then to call into question how the architectures and infrastructures of social media have nurtured the disingenuous modes of presentation upon which groups such as Rally 4 Resources rely. By architectures of the contemporary web, I mean protocols and other structures such as algorithms; by infrastructures, I mean material foundations, like data centers or undersea network cables. Canada is a pertinent site from which to examine how the oil culture wars have taken shape, since it is home to the third-largest proven oil reserves on the planet: 97 percent of Canada's reserves are located in Alberta's oil sands, and, as of 2018, 96 percent of Canada's oil exports go to the United States.[10] In 2019, Canada supplied the United States with 56 percent of all its crude oil imports, making Canada its largest source of energy imports.[11] To increase the presence of Canadian oil on the global market rather than just the U.S. one, industry and government have aggressively pursued the construction of pipelines over the past decade, making the oil sands into what journalist Chris Turner calls "the first major battleground in a global conflict over the future of energy in the Anthropocene epoch."[12] Turning to Canada's pro-oil movement as it emerged through social media over the course of the 2010s, *Petroturfing* details how new media is currently being used to sustain an old energy regime.

Given the overrepresentation of Canadian oil in the U.S. energy mix, Canada's fossil economy is deeply enmeshed with that of the United States, as is its ideological relationship to fossil fuels. Koch Industries has played a key role in nurturing this relationship. One of the largest and most lucrative private companies on the planet, Koch Industries owes much of its success to Alberta's oil sands. As journalist Jane Mayer details, when Charles Koch took over the family company after his father's passing, he put the company into overdrive by acquiring a majority share of a legacy refinery equipped to process heavy crude in Rosemount, Minnesota, in 1969. Koch Industries purchased the low-quality bitumen on the cheap and upgraded it in Rosemount to turn massive profits.[13] Although Koch Industries transferred or abandoned its oil sands assets in 2019, journalists Steven Mufson and Juliet Eilperin noted in 2014 that Koch Industries was at the time "the biggest foreign lease holder in Canada's oil sands" if not the single largest one.[14] But Mayer's book is less about how the Koch brothers became some of the richest people on the planet than it is about how the brothers, especially Charles, employed that wealth to strategically promote far-right political agendas through the creation and funding of shadowy front groups with innocuous names similar to those in Canada's pro-oil movement, such as Americans for Prosperity. For the Kochs, these groups served a dual financial and ideological function made possible by efforts to "weaponize philanthropy."[15] First, these groups diverted funds that would otherwise be paid to the government as taxes by lowering taxable income. Second, through a host of front groups that used sophisticated methods to evade violations of campaign-finance laws, these groups aimed to shape public consciousness in favor of tenets that serve the architects and agents of the fossil economy—such as lower corporate taxes and fewer environmental regulations. The strategies used by the pro-oil movement owe a great deal to those pioneered by the Kochs in both form and content as the pro-oil movement, for instance, weaponizes the environmental nongovernmental organization (ENGO) form in the service of the fossil economy.

Investigating the pro-oil movement in Canada, this book follows two interwoven paths. First, the book tells the story of the emergence of self-styled grassroots Canadian organizations, groups, and campaigns that use popular social media platforms to promote Canadian oil and its infrastructures from positions presented as distanced from government and industry. Second, I offer a critique of the oil culture wars and interrogate the ambivalence underwriting the architectures and infrastructures of the contemporary web that help fuel these wars. To this end, *Petroturfing* serves a kind of historical, archival function as much as it does a critical one.

I trace the origins of this phenomenon to the 2010 launch of Ezra Levant's book *Ethical Oil: The Case for Canada's Oil Sands,* which can be read as a response to journalist Andrew Nikiforuk's 2008 book *Tar Sands: Dirty Oil and the Future of a Continent.*[16] While I provide a more detailed account of this emergence in chapter 1, *Ethical Oil*'s larger purpose was to provide counterclaims to notable arguments from campaigns against the oil sands that enshrined the notion of "dirty oil" into popular public consciousness. Through his counterclaims, Levant recast the production and consumption of Canadian oil as ethical.

Levant is a well-known, controversial figure in the Canadian political mediascape. A lawyer by trade who previously worked as a lobbyist for Big Tobacco and Oil, he has since become a public media figure of the far right.[17] Levant's career culminated in the 2015 cofounding of Rebel Media, a primarily YouTube-based media group reminiscent of the U.S. alt-right media outlet Breitbart News. The book *Ethical Oil,* as I show in chapter 1, is a manifesto for the pro-oil movement in Canada, whereas the media campaign that followed in the book's wake is the pro-oil movement's playbook. As a broader online media campaign centralized on the EthicalOil.org home page paired with an active presence on Facebook, Twitter, and YouTube, the Ethical Oil media campaign served as a test run of media strategies for the promotion of Canadian oil from a grassroots subject position before social media was what we understand it to be today. These media strategies would become a prototype for the pro-oil movement in Canada over the 2010s.

The rough temporal scope of *Petroturfing* covers the 2010s, a time of considerable activity and contestation surrounding proposed oil sands infrastructure developments, including several pipeline construction and expansion projects. Enbridge's Northern Gateway Pipeline, for instance, was initially proposed in 2006 and shelved in 2014. TC Energy's Energy East Pipeline was announced in 2013 but experienced a similar fate as the Northern Gateway and was canceled in 2017. TC Energy's Keystone XL expansion project was recently moving ahead after first being rejected by the Barack Obama administration in 2015, later revived by former president Donald Trump in 2017, only to be effectively quashed by President Joe Biden in 2021. And the Trans Mountain Expansion (TMX) project, purchased from Texas-based Kinder Morgan by the Canadian federal government, was first announced in 2012 and approved in 2016. Together, these pipeline projects form a dense network of almost 6,500 miles that, if built, would bisect territories, bind nations, and project Canada's fossil economy further into our shared planetary energy future (see Figure 1). Though many projects are canceled, the current status of these pipelines only says so much about their potentiality. A canceled pipeline project may never be truly dead. Uncertainty underwrites the speculative nature of the fossil economy. The same uncertainty that challenges large-scale projects creates inertia that helps keep the fossil economy afloat. In this book, I look at the period of 2010 to 2020 as an instrumental moment when the speculative expansion of Canada's fossil economy through pipeline projects established media strategies that became the cultural counterpart of this speculative expansion.

In tracing the emergence of the pro-oil movement in Canada, a larger question this book asks is how the ambivalence of new and social media, like oil, fuels the status quo—what climate justice scholars and activists often refer to as "business as usual." Business as usual describes the dominant logics and impulses that constitute the present, that is, an extractive capitalism that binds platform and fossil economies.[18] These processes are baked into the system, and their courses must be disrupted to avoid intensifying the myriad social and ecological crises that mark the present. Recognizing the necessity for moving away from business as usual into systems and relations beyond extractive capitalism, I see the media produced by the pro-oil movement as an intensification of an ideological struggle over our collective energy imaginaries in the service of already dominant relations that have produced the conditions for the ongoing climate crisis. By energy imaginaries, I mean the ways in which we collectively understand and imagine our relationship to energy beyond its role as a one-way input of everyday life. These imaginaries are generated out of and negotiated within lived experiences and the broader cultural narratives that shape such experiences.

Figure 1. The approximate routes of the Northern Gateway (*top left horizontal*), Trans Mountain Expansion (*top left diagonal*), Keystone XL (*center-downward*) and Energy East (*center-rightward*) pipelines. Map created by the author.

Put another way, energy imaginaries can be understood in terms of what literary and cultural theorist Raymond Williams describes as a "structure of feeling," that is, "the culture of a period" that "operates in the most delicate and least tangible parts of our activity."[19] Structures of feeling related to energy, or energy imaginaries, are shaped by conscious and unconscious processes, through banal, taken-for-granted contexts and relations, as well as those that elide total understanding. In examining how Canadian pro-oil energy imaginaries are constructed, expressed, and circulated through social media, I interrogate how, in the case of the pro-oil movement, the media ecology of social media—its architectures and infrastructures—tends toward a reproduction of the ideologies of extractive capitalism presented as though these relations were new or different. I do this by looking at how groups such as Rally 4 Resources shape what I call *energy consciousness* through a process of *legitimation through circulation,* two concepts I develop throughout the book that serve both descriptive and critical ends that I will define shortly. Such conscious attempts from the pro-oil movement to shape the meaning of Canadian oil primarily through affective registers bring into view how specific mythologies of oil inform more general cultures of energy that do not quite square with the material context to which they are bound, particularly as they relate to the fiction repeated by industry and its allies that oil is marginalized in Canada.

A brief empirical illustration underscores the stakes of interrogating the politics of oil's cultural and social life alongside its material one. At a material level, oil production in Canada has generally *increased* over the decade or so that I focus on in this book. In 2010, for instance, Canadian oil production totaled roughly 3.4 million barrels per day; in 2019, it reached 5.6 million.[20] Despite this growth, which signals widespread support for the oil and gas industry that culminated in $3.3 billion in subsidies in 2015, it is clear that industry and governments perceive public support as waning or, at least, believe it has the potential to wane.[21] As Canadian oil's material life enjoys record-breaking production, its cultural life remains contentious. In recent years, several strategies from industry and government have intervened directly in the cultural politics of Canadian oil through media that, for instance, stoke a mutually reinforcing relationship between pipeline projects and nationalism. I follow these strategies as they have been taken up by groups, organizations, and campaigns that formed over the 2010s. I show how in order to construct the argument that oil production is under threat, which is their condition of possibility, they tap in to deeply held settler mythologies of frontierism and extraction. By doing so, they employ affective appeals to nationalism wherein perceived threats to Canadian oil from Indigenous and environmental activists are simultaneously threats against the nation and its settler citizenry.

Approaching the Pro-oil Movement

To refer to these mutually informing efforts as a singular phenomenon, I offer the portmanteau *petroturfing.* Petroturfing describes the actions of often well-connected organizations, groups, and campaigns that disingenuously or suspiciously claim grassroots origins or character to promote oil and other fossil fuels by producing and circulating claims that the oil industry, its workers, and its supporters are unfairly targeted by allegedly dominant liberal, environmentalist voices. Put simply, petroturfing refers to the activities of these groups, organizations, and campaigns that resemble advertising strategies that have come to be called "astroturfing." As a critical term, petroturfing foregrounds the high stakes of promoting oil using these strategies, underscoring that hydrocarbons are a constitutive component of astroturf itself. Coined by American politician Lloyd Bentsen in the 1980s, astroturfing identified industry-funded lobbying efforts that were framed as grassroots, popular movements. As John C. Stauber and Sheldon Rampton argue, the practice is historically tied to the tobacco industry, notably when "Burson-Marsteller (the world's largest PR firm) created the 'National Smokers Alliance' to mobilize smokers into a grassroots lobby for 'smokers' rights.'"[22] Such efforts have also been leveraged to "defeat environmentalists" by "creat[ing] green-sounding front groups such as 'The Global Climate Coalition' and 'British Columbia Forest Alliance.'"[23] Moving beyond the metric of direct corporate funding as a determining characteristic, more expansive notions of what qualifies as astroturfing in the internet age have been theorized by sociologist Philip N. Howard, who defines astroturfing as the creation of an image of consensus or support in disingenuous, exaggerated ways that can end up gaining support from "genuine people with sincere grievances and legitimate demands."[24] I follow this wider approach in order to analyze how the practices that comprise petroturfing serve to channel collective economic concerns and anxieties into support for an abstract entity—industry—that arguably benefits the architects and agents of the fossil economy far more than its workers or consumers.

What counts as petroturfing? My findings reveal a set of defining characteristics, which I have used as a loose guide for establishing which groups, organizations, and campaigns to approach on these terms. These characteristics are crystallized as powerful animating fictions, the lynchpins of which are, first, the claim that the oil and gas industry is a marginalized political and economic force in Canada and, second, a refiguration of oil and its infrastructures of progressive forces. Alongside claims to marginalization and a refiguring of oil and its infrastructures as progressive forces, a populist claim to represent the voice of the people as a sort of silent majority underwrites media in the petroturfing project. And through this claim to broader representation, audiences are asked to show support through pledges and other modes of thinly veiled data gathering. The affordances offered by architectures and infrastructures of new and social media, I argue throughout this book, help provide legitimacy to these animating fictions. Many of these dimensions track with what Canadian communications scholar Shane Gunster and others have described as "extractive populism." For Gunster, extractive populism contains three major tenets: extraction benefits all, future extraction is under threat by environmental and Indigenous groups, and a collective counterforce of support for extraction is necessary.[25] Petroturfing is part of this counterforce and shares these tenets. However, I hesitate to employ populism as a primary heuristic for reasons I outline later.

In terms of origins, these groups, organizations, and campaigns are often established by an individual with suspect claims to distance from the oil and gas industry or, in some cases, as a grassroots offshoot of existing lobbying groups. And while I do not claim that all the groups, campaigns, and organizations that I situate under the banner of the petroturfing project collude with one another or receive direct funding from industry, in many cases they have clearly articulated relationships with one another and, as investigative journalists have found in at least one case, received funding from industry. More work should be done to uncover these links where they exist, but uncovering precisely how these groups, organizations, and campaigns are funded is not the purpose of this book. There is no "smoking gun" in this book that financially links the petroturfing project with the oil and gas industry. But to find a financial smoking gun isn't the point of this book. As a media and cultural studies theorist interested in the politics of energy and environment, I am less concerned with uncovering immediate financial relations than I am with excavating how dominant mythologies of oil are repackaged as marginalized for circulation in the social media age. I am, instead, interested in how these groups, campaigns, and organizations symbolically *refine* Canadian oil to shape *energy consciousness* by means of *legitimation through circulation.* After following how the petroturfing project has taken shape over the past decade, it is clear to me that its voices will only become more prominent; by better understanding the petroturfing project's origins and messaging strategies, we will be better equipped to disrupt its influence.

Framing such groups as artificial is contentious. In a 2018 article on the "Canada's Energy Citizens" campaign overseen by the Canadian Association of Petroleum Producers (CAPP), communications scholar Tim Wood challenges Greenpeace's dismissal of the campaign as "astroturfing."[26] The campaign gathers signatories in support of Canada's energy sector. The campaign also hosted a series of profiles for users to "Meet Citizens Like You," which were removed from the larger campaign in 2019. Wood argues that the campaign hinges upon characteristics like transparency rather than, as critics suggest, opacity. Against charges of artifice, Wood uses the framework of "subsidized publics" to describe how "institutional actors enlist allies by providing training, resources, or mediated forums to make advocacy less burdensome for supporters."[27] His motivation to challenge frameworks of artifice is to nuance perceptions of participation in these efforts and to move beyond what he perceives as divisive rhetorics. He concludes with a call for researchers to "examine the tactics companies use to earn the consent of their allies" and to "attend to patterns in oil industry PR practice."[28] *Petroturfing* shares this drive to attend to these patterns. But part of attending to such patterns requires comparative analysis that examines the larger media environment in which these efforts circulate. CAPP's status as a lobbying group makes its campaigns particularly amenable to Wood's approach. But CAPP's campaign is part of a larger mediascape that often relies on dubious claims and positioning. From Levant's history as an oil lobbyist to Canada Action's receipt of $100,000 from ARC Resources in 2019, throughout the history of these media efforts, leaked documents continue to reveal suspicious relations to industry by those who claim distance.[29] Industry efforts to create doubt surrounding scientific consensus on climate change are outlined by historians of science Naomi Oreskes and Erik M. Conway, who show how the opacity of which Wood absolves CAPP's campaign is performed elsewhere.[30]

Far from "treat[ing] citizens as dummies, lumps of raw material that can be enlivened at a whim," as Wood asserts perspectives that rely on astroturfing frameworks do, the critical position that *Petroturfing* adopts interrogates how these efforts mobilize the affordances of social media to imbue Canadian oil with positive signifiers.[31] The fossil economy is steeped in contradiction, and the capacities that the extracting, refining, and burning of fossil fuels unevenly generate also generate affective attachments. Historian Bob Johnson argues that the combustion of fossil fuels generates a paradox—one that "prop[s] up the rich emancipatory qualities that many of us, especially in the upper and middle classes, expect from modern life in the West," even as it serves as "the fuel for widespread social injury and limited horizons."[32] *Petroturfing* recognizes this paradox as it takes aim at the architects and benefactors of the fossil economy, such as executives and politicians, in solidarity with and support of the peoples, communities, and ecosystems that experience the negative consequences of extraction most sharply. These peoples, communities, and ecosystems remain relatively absent from Wood's account, appearing in a way that suggests the voices that resist the continued expansion of Canada's fossil economy are uncritical and lack nuance.

Legitimately grassroots movements exist to challenge dominant relations, not reproduce them. Perhaps more important to emphasize is the related fact that as petroturfing has continued to enjoy apparent legitimacy over the past decade, dissent and resistance, especially Indigenous resistance, has become increasingly criminalized. As Andrew Crosby and Jeffrey Monaghan detail, at the same time pro-oil interests have been posturing as grassroots movements, the extractive industry has benefited from efforts to surveil genuine grassroots groups, like Indigenous land defenders and water protectors, under the guise of protecting so-called critical infrastructure.[33]

My intervention draws out generalizable characteristics, strategies, discourses, and rhetorics across the petroturfing project to better understand how oil and its infrastructures gain meaning in the twenty-first century. By focusing on Canadian oil, I am not suggesting that these kinds of astroturfing phenomena do not exist elsewhere or in other industry contexts. In the United States, for instance, similar efforts emerged in the context of the Appalachian coal industry, performing what environmental communications scholars Peter K. Bsumek, Jen Schneider, Steve Schwarze, and Jennifer Peeples call "corporate ventriloquism," wherein voices of opposition are appropriated and co-opted through various means.[34] These means include astroturfing and "aggressive mimicry," a form of appropriation that sees an "entity . . . [co-opt] an opposing organization's structure and discourse in order to sow doubts about their opponent's identity, with the intended effect of distracting or destroying the opponent."[35] For Bsumek et al., these efforts are enabled by the dominant discourse of the neoliberal moment that, following the work of communications and media theorist Nick Couldry, "limits the possibilities of what can be said, frames political controversies as primarily economic in nature, and reproduces neoliberal ideology, like the idea of a free market, as 'common sense.'"[36] My account of petroturfing shows that such aggressive mimicry is made possible not only by neoliberal capitalism's dominant narratives and affects but by social media's architectures and infrastructures as well.

There are unique aspects to the scope, reach, and persistence of petroturfing in Canada that serve as fertile grounds in disentangling petroturfing's form and content in order to initiate a practice of critique against it. Scholars and researchers who have studied these groups, organizations, and campaigns have applied a range of critical perspectives that provide my analysis with insight into how what I call petroturfing mythologizes Canadian oil and its infrastructures in terms of, for example, gender, economy, and nationalism.[37] Rather than focus on a singular media effort through a singular mode of analysis, I offer a sustained, interdisciplinary analysis of petroturfing across an expanded mediascape—from op-eds in conventional news media to content circulated on popular social media platforms such as Facebook, Twitter, and YouTube, each of which offer the petroturfing project a particular set of affordances. "Affordances," literary theorist Caroline Levine writes, "is a term used to describe the potential uses or actions latent in materials and designs."[38] In other words, affordances name the constraints and possibilities enabled by the tendencies of a given media form.

Due to the ephemeral nature of these media, I cite archived versions through the Internet Archive's Wayback Machine wherever possible and draw upon archives of, for instance, tweets that I have gathered during my research through application programming interface (API) access. As recent history has shown, the legacy of social media platforms is subject to the whims of CEOs.[39] Using these public sources, both persistent and disappeared or discarded, I show how petroturfing strategies *saturate* the broader mediascape with rhetorical and discursive positions on Canadian oil and its infrastructures that are irrefutably dominant yet appear as marginal. If the increasingly visible modes of Indigenous and environmentalist resistance to the continued expansion of Canada's fossil economy signify a counterdiscourse and counterpolitics to dominant petrocultural mythologies and ideologies, then petroturfing is a self-construed counter-counterdiscourse that strategically denies the dominance of its positioning in order to envelop the discursive field in the service of Canada's fossil economy.

Through these trajectories, this book offers two major contributions to the fields it is writing with and into: the energy humanities and media studies. To the energy humanities—a burgeoning field that uses humanities methods to address the social and cultural dimensions of energy—it offers an interrogation of the ways in which oil and its infrastructures are consciously signified in late petrocapitalism. To media studies, it builds on existing critical voices who bring into view the limitations of new and social media in effectively supporting material change. *Petroturfing* contributes to this line of thought by investigating the ease through which disingenuous positioning is structurally supported by social media platforms. Once celebrated by many as a revolutionary and democratizing technology (now an arguable cliché), the contemporary web has often been perceived as a de facto site for horizontal participation, a space that through its very operation enables alterity rather than deepening or reproducing existing relations of inequity.

Dissident voices, however, recognized that the web was not quite what it promised early on. These positions have been expressed through accounts from media theorists such as Nick Dyer-Witheford and Darin

Barney.[40] Two decades into the twenty-first century, business as usual seems not only to be the dominant mode but one that is presented under the guise of innovation, disruption, or change. It is not my intention here to cynically dismiss the possibilities of new and social media for effective organizing; nor is it my aim to undermine the important movement-building work that has originated within and been enabled through such organizing—for instance, the ongoing Idle No More movement. But, in the same breath as outlining the importance of social media in shaping the movement, even Michi Saagiig Nishnaabeg theorist Leanne Betasamosake Simpson, a preeminent activist voice of Idle No More, has cautioned against an overreliance on social media and the internet in organizing.[41] Tracing how this tension between revolution and reproduction plays out in the context of Canadian oil and its infrastructures, I explore the consequences of how new and social media operate ambivalently in terms of the systems and structures fueling the destruction of ecosystems and the human and more-than-human relations that rely on these ecosystems.

Canadian Oil between the Settler Colonial and the Technoscientific

Western Canada has arguably been the epicenter of conflict over the national fossil economy in the twenty-first century and, in turn, a primary battleground of the oil culture wars. Yet the episodes and relations accounted for in this book reverberate at a planetary level and, accordingly, exceed regional and temporal specificities. After all, the oil economy is a world economy, and, as scholars and activists continually remind us, climate change does not respect borders. One might ask, then, in a time when the planetary has taken precedence over the nation-state as a privileged site of critical attention, why foreground Canada? What does Canada offer for addressing the ways in which oil and its transnational infrastructures are negotiated in the twenty-first century? As gestured to previously, Canada is a major global oil producer and, while other regions such as Newfoundland and Labrador's offshore produce oil, most of its reserves are in Alberta's oil sands. But oil sands production remains "landlocked" due to limited transportation infrastructure that largely goes to the United States.

Until recently, these sands were colloquially and apolitically referred to as "tar sands." And due to the scale and resources required for extraction and refinement, activist Tzeporah Berman argues that they represent "the single largest and most destructive industrial project on earth."[42] The unique material properties of bitumen in the oil sands demand intensive processes to render it into oil as such. To turn the goopy, tar-like substance into oil requires modes of technoscientific innovation that consume resource inputs such as water and liquefied natural gas in massive quantities. The politics of land are central to the political economies and political ecologies of the oil sands life cycle. Crown land—that is, land owned by the state—is leased in parcels to companies with the clause that the land will eventually be reclaimed and returned to the province of Alberta in a state equivalent to its pre-extractive condition. But what constitutes equivalence remains murky, and as of today, only one mine project has fully completed this cycle. These political economies and ecologies are particularly significant given that, as a nation, Canada is simultaneously the product of imperialism and, as landscape architect Pierre Bélanger reminds us, a participant in and sanctioner of imperialism at home and abroad.[43]

Canada's well-established image on the world stage as a social and environmental leader obfuscates how it relies on the persistent dispossession of Indigenous peoples. As resistance to oil sands infrastructure projects motivated by questions of dispossession and environmental impacts continues to be waged, this image is fading. Urban theorist Martín Arboleda offers an extensive critique of accounts of extractivism that center on the nation-state as a primary site of analysis, an orientation he identifies as methodological nationalism. In Arboleda's view, those who employ this method consciously or unconsciously exaggerate the role of the nation-state both in reproducing extractive capitalism and in serving as a key site for political transformation. He joins a chorus of voices that call for a focus on the planetary, seeing in the nation-state a layer of mediation that performs the bidding of a larger totality—global extractive capital. As a result, the *totality* deserves our critical and political attention.[44] This is why nationalizing narratives such as the ones petroturfing strategies leverage must be exposed for the ideological work they do, not only in reproducing relations of inequality and exploitation in Canada but in obscuring the planetary nature of the system that produces such relations globally and undermines the planetary solidarities necessary to address these challenges. The introduction to a recent issue of the *South Atlantic Quarterly* intervenes upon these questions surrounding extraction, the nation-state, territoriality, and dispossession by exploring how Canada's dubious claims of jurisdiction undermine Indigenous sovereignty and obscure generative Indigenous economies outside and against settler colonial capitalism. In the issue's introduction, editors Shiri Pasternak and Dayna Nadine Scott detail how "Canada's claim to exclusive territorial authority across all the lands and waters is a failed project."[45] Alex V. Green takes this point further in a think piece on Canada's dubious jurisdictional claims in the context of pipeline politics, declaring, "Canada is fake."[46]

Such high-stakes questions of jurisdiction and territory are not the only features that make oil sands development stand out in terms of unique intersections of political economies and ecologies. The oil sands life cycle includes the deployment of new methods of extraction to building and operating transmission infrastructures such as pipelines and, as a final stage, reclaiming affected landscapes to be returned to the state. At the stage of extraction and refinement, the material properties of the bituminous sands notably resist refinement into a substance with the expansive use value we have come to expect from oil, and, as a result, have required significant technological innovation to make it viable in these terms. Above and below the surface of the oil sands as we know them today is an entanglement of technoscientific knowledges and extractive capitalist frontiers.

What are now the Athabasca oil sands have always been an important geologic formation. Dene peoples, for instance, used bitumen in its raw form for purposes such as sealing leaks on canoes. More recent histories express how the bitumen that bubbles across the shores of the Athabasca River was noticed by early colonizers as a potentially valuable material. In 1776, fur trader Peter Pond, allegedly the first European settler to enter the region, speculated on the value of bitumen in ways that anticipated the sands' political–economic status today.[47] But it was not until the mid-twentieth century when Dr. Karl Clark, a chemist who made a name for himself by working for the Geological Survey of Canada and later as a professor at the University of Alberta, fine-tuned a process to separate usable bitumen from the sands that the viability of the economic exploitation of the sands became feasible. Promotional lore, like that on display at the Oil Sands Discovery Centre in the municipal epicenter of the oil sands, Fort McMurray, Alberta, frames this techno-scientific pursuit as an entrepreneurial endeavor.

Following this entrepreneurial momentum, a more efficient method was refined to access deposits that are unreachable through strip mining: steam-assisted gravity drainage (SAGD). Pioneered in the 1970s by who the Canadian Petroleum Hall of Fame describes as the "father of steam assisted gravity," Dr. Roger M. Butler, SAGD offers access to bitumen deposits that lay deeper than strip mining can reach, ultimately increasing prospective deposits.[48] Like hydrofracturing, or "fracking," SAGD disrupts geological formations well below the surface, leaving aboveground landscapes looking undisturbed. SAGD in turn plays a central role in oil and gas industry promotional materials, as it retains visible features of the affected landscape that reflect dominant Western perceptions of natural value. The landscapes of SAGD offer those undisrupted lines of sight that are inextricably bound to what cultural anthropologist Macarena Gómez-Barris calls the "extractive view"—the very view that renders ecosystems into resources in the first place.[49]

This is all to say that innovation as such is constitutively entangled with the oil sands imaginary in ways that exceed the technical processes that these technologies perform. This entanglement arguably explains why alongside such material–economic processes of extraction and upgrading that render bitumen into oil, the cultural and symbolic life of Canadian oil is likewise carefully managed by vested interests and actors. Throughout this book, I build an account of petroturfing that ties it to these modes of innovation as a kind of cultural technology itself that refines Canadian oil to generate positive energetic structures of feeling. If the persistence of the fossil economy in Canada and the petroculture it mediates relies on these positive energetic structures of feeling, then examining how these structures of feelings are shaped now and what they aim to accomplish in the future is an important task.

Refining Canadian Oil

The oil and gas industry has been effective in leveraging communication technologies toward corporate image making. Pamela Vang's expansive cultural semiotic study of twentieth-century oil industry print advertising describes the industry's construction of a mythology in which oil as a substance and the oil industry itself are agents for good. In her aptly titled book *Good Guys*, Vang examines advertisements from transnational oil companies such as BP, Royal Dutch Shell, and ExxonMobil, showing how they presented themselves as heroic benefactors—that is, the "good guys"—and oil as a magical substance.[50] Alongside innovations in communication technologies, the oil and gas industry has continuously employed contemporary media forms to construct and disseminate these representations and narratives.

From exhibitions to documentary films, the oil and gas industry has strategically mobilized media forms for promotional ends since its inception. Staging an exhibit at the British Empire Exhibition of 1924–25, for instance, the Anglo-Persian Oil Company (now BP) mounted what historian Ian Wereley describes as an "oil spectacle" in order to curate a positive public image.[51] As media historian Mona Damluji details, under the Anglo-Iranian Oil Company moniker at that point, the company also produced documentaries, including 1952's *Persian Story*, which "attempted to shape perceptions of modernity in the oil city of Abadan."[52] Likewise, Royal Dutch / Shell has had a dedicated "Film Unit" since the 1930s.[53] These are only a small sample of a much longer media history that highlights one dimension of the mutually entangled history between oil and media. And this history reveals a commitment to the performance of a kind of cultural work that is achieved by one of the most influential industries on the planet.

Shaping Energy Consciousness

As I argue throughout *Petroturfing*, the oil and gas industry's media efforts are attempts to shape *energy consciousness*. In the energy humanities, there has been a tacit privileging of the ways in which energy imaginaries are shaped, expressed, or registered unconsciously at a subterranean level. Energy consciousness excavates to show how these imaginaries are *also* shaped on the surface. As literary and cultural theorist Patricia Yaeger's seminal contribution to the field outlines, the "energy unconscious" identifies latent energy imaginaries and relations that undergird literary and cultural production. Following Fredric Jameson's articulation of the political unconscious, which describes how cultural production contains within it subterranean political imaginaries and horizons, Yaeger argues that cultural production also contains energy imaginaries in these ways. Yaeger turns to Jack Kerouac's *On the Road* as an emblematic, illustrative text on these terms. This quintessentially American road novel is marked by signifiers of petrocultural abundance; yet, despite the narrative propulsion made possible by automobility, a key infrastructural base of petroculture—the gas station—remains a marginal site, and petroleum itself is unmentioned in the text despite fueling the narrative. In the energy unconscious, Yaeger argues, abundance of one cultural object creates the representational absence of others, and the energy fundamental to the habits and rituals of contemporary everyday life gets buried. The dynamic of the energy unconscious can be scaled out as a diagnosis of the American or, indeed, Western cultural imaginary of the latter half of the twentieth century.[54]

Yet, like broader operations of ideology, the political–energetic unconscious tells only part of the story of how energy imaginaries are expressed, negotiated, and shaped. If *literary* texts are so dense with meaning that excavating their political–energetic unconscious offers broad lessons in how energy operates historically and culturally, then more popular or commercial forms of cultural production must do so as well, perhaps with less nuance. Advertising, for instance, hinges upon a primary directive of promotion, which Vang describes as attempts to "protect and nurture capital," that taps into conscious and unconscious registers in ways that continue to evade comprehensive psychological understanding.[55] Without wading too far into the psychological and psychoanalytic implications of these processes, my point is simply that a critical eye looking to uncover a latent energy unconscious in literature does just as well by training that eye on to the latent *and* manifest energy imaginaries across an expanded field of media and cultural production. Energy consciousness, then, is not a critique of the energy unconscious so much as it is an extension. By privileging manifest imaginaries, *Petroturfing* is invested in more deeply understanding these structures of feeling in terms of how the embodied experiences of those attached to Canada's fossil economy—especially workers who see in the maintenance of the fossil economy the sustenance of their livelihood—are negotiated to generate support for the oil and gas industry.

The methodological orientations that inform this book, which I will elaborate further shortly, emerge from the premise that material infrastructures are mutually entangled with energetic structures of feeling.

Capitalism as we know it today came to fruition in large part due to the capacities that the burning of fossil fuels enables at the base, or infrastructural level, as those working at the intersections of geography, political economy, and political ecology, including Elmar Altvater, Matt Huber, and Andreas Malm, have argued. It follows that the superstructural relations are likewise shaped by fossil fuels.[56]

In this way, the kinds of mythologies that petroturfing puts forward are part of broader efforts to reinscribe an intimately bound nexus of culture and fossil fuels. To make this point, I draw upon Marxist theorist Louis Althusser's influential argument that for capitalism to persist as a dominant form, it must continually reproduce itself infrastructurally *and* superstructurally in the face of perpetual antagonism across these levels, in order to argue that for fossil fuels to remain dominant, fossil fuels and their relations must be reproduced similarly.[57] Situating Althusser in this context generates a theory of mediation between infrastructures and superstructures that centers energy's role in fueling modes of production and social relations while identifying how ideological and repressive state apparatuses maintain these relations. Such methodological orientations are the conceptual infrastructure of my analysis, which is performed with an eye toward the possibilities of living otherwise—in a media ecology otherwise, and with energetic–infrastructural relations otherwise.

Legitimation through Circulation and the Political Economy of Dis- and Misinformation

The oil and gas industry's massive public relations efforts testify to its own recognition of the importance of curating social and cultural imaginaries as they relate to energy. But this book is not about *corporate* image making through advertising, public relations, or corporate social responsibility—at least not on the surface. I turn instead to media produced and circulated by groups, organizations, and campaigns that claim grassroots status or distance from industry, to those cultural objects that claim to be based on a populist foundation, working from "below"—on behalf of the allegedly everyday Canadian—rather than from "above," where conventional advertising or government communiqués are situated. Yet, as I show throughout this book, the narratives these groups put forward indeed come to the same conclusions and support the same relations.

Ultimately, my interest resides in examining how the form of social media tends toward the nurturing of dominant petrocultural views, narratives, and relations while these views are claimed as marginal, and in tracing the consequences of this animating point of petroturfing.

A number of media critics and theorists have diagnosed the contemporary mediascape, which is underwritten by connectivity enabled by networks and ubiquitous access to communication technologies like the smartphone, as one that nurtures the status quo ideologically and economically. While a proliferation of networks enabled by new media technologies once promised emancipation, evidence that these new networks reinforce older networks of power continues to emerge. From political economies to cultural studies of media, theorists have generated an emergent vocabulary for confronting the frontiers of capital made possible by new and social media. As part of a broader project on the mutations of contemporary capitalism since the turn of the millennium, media theorist McKenzie Wark argues that shifts in the nature of wealth accumulation vis-à-vis platform capitalism have ushered in a fundamentally new mode of production—not quite capitalism as such but, as the title of her 2019 book *Capital Is Dead* provocatively suggests, something worse. This "something worse," Wark argues, emerges in part due to an objective shift from an economy in which the majority of wealth is accumulated by those who own the means of production, that is, the bourgeoisie, to one in which such wealth is being accumulated by those who control means of information and communication, a class Wark names vectoralist.[58] This reconfiguration of class antagonism from the bourgeoisie–proletariat dyad to the vectoralist–hacker one was first proposed in Wark's 2004 book *A Hacker Manifesto* and has since only become more pronounced.[59]

Political and media theorist Jodi Dean identifies something similar to Wark through the notion of "communicative capitalism," which describes "the materialization of ideals of inclusion and participation in information, entertainment, and communication technologies in ways that capture resistance and intensify global capitalism."[60] The resonance between Dean's and Wark's formulations shapes my approach to the political economy of the contemporary mediascape in *Petroturfing.* In an extended, generous response to *Capital Is Dead,* Dean proposes instead that the condition of networked or communicative capitalism is giving rise to neofeudalism.[61] Without getting hung up on debates surrounding what precisely marks a new mode of production, I want to draw attention to the fact that together these interventions signal that objective shifts in the accumulation of wealth have occurred, which demand attention in the context of new and social media. How these political–economic changes have shaped communicative relations continue to play out in real time as the internet's role in stoking fissures rather than solidarity or, for instance, in nurturing various fascisms cannot be overstated. A recent report by the Tech Transparency Project, for instance, shows how Facebook has profited off recruitment advertisements by U.S.-based right-wing militias on the platform by "routinely [being] behind the curve in cracking down on domestic extremists."[62]

The atmosphere generated in this political–economic context nurtures the concentration of power vis-à-vis representation and circulation. The structural mechanisms at play here have been recently outlined by media theorists Nick Couldry and Ulises Mejias, who show how new and social media enabled new modes of appropriation or extraction by capital through social quantification and other algorithmic means comprising what they call "data colonialism," or "the capture and control of *human life itself* through appropriating the data that can be extracted from it for profit."[63] While I have elsewhere criticized the arguably unintended consequences of Couldry and Mejias's employment of an expanded digital colonialism in settings where historical colonialism persists, their sharp theorization of how digital capitalism operates through quantification and appropriation remains pertinent. As they argue, the recent scandal over "fake news," for instance, "is just one example of what happens when this abstracted model of the social world collides with the contextualized expectations of real people."[64] Controversy surrounding dis- and misinformation in the contemporary mediascape came to the fore during former president Donald Trump's 2016 campaign, in which he waged an ideological battle against mainstream media sources by accusing them of being "fake news."[65] While this is not the place to rehearse these dramatic, well-documented episodes of recent media history, it is difficult to deny the impact that these moments have had on day-to-day engagement with media as well as in media and communication studies as a critical discipline. My concept of *legitimation through circulation* captures and condenses these recent critical interventions by highlighting a *process* of valorization achieved through the affordances of new and social media. Legitimation through circulation, in other words, is a shorthand invocation of the political economic and media theoretical criticisms of processes underwritten by the architectures and infrastructures of new and social media that fuel dis- and misinformation so prescient in today's media environment.

Critique in a Warming World

The larger stakes of this book are located in the limits and possibilities of pursuits of making change, particularly those pursuits oriented toward the toppling of the fossil economy, within the contemporary media environment in a time marked by mutually intensifying social and ecological crises. I follow the insights of Indigenous thinkers, including Potawatomi theorist Kyle Powys Whyte and Sisseton Wahpeton Oyate theorist Kim TallBear, who trouble the universalizing and flattening effects of identifying today's crises as somehow "recent," a particularly egregious characterization given the perpetual social and ecological crises of settler colonialism experienced by Indigenous peoples in, for instance, what is now called Canada and the United States. However, I also see critical purchase in the social conditions that allow such contemporary crises to be seen as unprecedented.[66] The temporal and collective registers in which environmental and economic disasters play out speak to the urgency of building futures otherwise, even if that urgency is unevenly experienced. I locate petroturfing squarely in this urgent moment, arguing that it serves as a central strategy in mitigating and disavowing the urgency that, however unevenly, all are now feeling or seeing. As literary and cultural theorist Mark Simpson argues of Ethical Oil in particular, we can view petroturfing as an effort to "smooth" out the "political frictions" of oil in the name of fortifying impasse and delaying transition.[67]

The methods I employ in this book are interdisciplinary, yet they remain committed to a materialism that sees the entanglements of fossil fuels and communicative capitalism as a recipe leading toward an increasingly destructive present and future. I am informed by disciplines including political economy, political ecology, media studies, feminist theory, critical Indigenous studies, and science and technology studies in order to bring to readers the historical and theoretical foundation necessary to confront the archive of petroturfing. Memes, which petroturfing employs as a primary communicative strategy, condense meaning and rely on embodied and situated knowledges that are embedded in particular communities, serving in part to interpellate audiences and create shared, community-based collective experiences. The larger task I have set for myself is to historicize and contextualize these communicative acts and events in ways that clarify their stakes and critique their consequences.

Though my primary mode of analysis is rhetorical and discursive in nature, I take into account and respond to the myriad insights that materialist media studies have generated in recent years regarding the necessity to think the materials of media and their ecological impacts as analytics or heuristics. There is, in other words, a larger question of media ecologies and media materialities that animates the encounter between oil and social media that this book examines. Literary and cultural theorist Stephanie LeMenager's observations on "petroleum media" make the point directly: "Oil itself is a medium that fundamentally supports all modern media forms concerned with what counts as culture—from film to recorded music, novels, magazines, photographs, sports, and the wikis, blogs, and videography of the Internet."[68] By approaching oil and its infrastructures as media, the ways energy imaginaries are produced and negotiated in relation to the material dimensions of energy and infrastructure come more clearly into view.

Through deeper critical engagement with the NationBuilder platform in my contribution to *Digital Energetics,* I describe this relationship between the energetic and infrastructural imaginaries circulated through media platforms and the material, ecological, and energetic relations of platforms themselves as constituting a kind of "platform energetics."[69] Platform energetics takes cues from Nick Couldry and Anna McCarthy's dialectical formation of MediaSpace, which names the spatial relations created by media as well as the "effects that existing spatial arrangements have on media forms as they materialize in everyday life," including, in my view, the cultural narratives that circulate about space through media.[70] Likewise, platform energetics names the concrete, material–energetic dimensions of media infrastructures as well as the energy imaginaries that circulate across media, like those found in petroturfing. Central to this analytic orientation are questions of mediation and infrastructure that my invocation of Althusser earlier in this introduction gestures toward. A kernel to my analysis is that there is a mutually informing relationship between fossil and platform capitalism, captured as it is by the concept of platform energetics.[71] Although my analysis leans toward more conventional modes of rhetorical and discursive analysis as it builds an early account of the petroturfing project in these terms, these material energetic and infrastructural relations between the fossil and the platform loom large.

Refining, energy consciousness, and *legitimation through circulation.* This triad of critical terminology I develop allows me to name *what, why,* and *how* the petroturfing project refigures Canadian oil and its infrastructures as progressive forces. Late cultural and literary theorist Lauren Berlant influentially fashioned infrastructure as social form, as that which makes relations possible, and so affect is an important realm through which infrastructures take shape.[72] Geographer and political ecologist Kai Bosworth engages and extends this formation of an affective infrastructure to describe the populist foundations of a coalition of settler landowners, environmentalists, and Indigenous peoples against recent pipeline projects in the United States, particularly the Keystone XL and Dakota Access, both of which have ties to the oil sands materially or financially.[73] Pipeline populism, for Bosworth, describes this broader project of resistance, and affective infrastructure "highlights how emotion emerges from political-economic contexts and material landscapes, nondeterministically conditioning political struggles."[74]

Petroturfing: Refining Canadian Oil through Social Media can be seen as a companion volume of sorts that reveals how similar affects are employed for the maintenance of the fossil economy, not against it. The petroturfing project represents another manifestation of pipeline populism against the one Bosworth theorizes, a kind of subordinate populism to the larger extractive populism that Gunster and others describe. Petroturfing is one component to the affective infrastructure that refines Canadian oil by shaping energy consciousness in favor of Canadian fossil capital and, in Althusserian terms, interpellates subjects of petroculture willing to take to the keyboards and the streets in defense of Canadian oil. Yet, as I pointed out earlier in my engagement with the notion of extractive populism, I hesitate to use populism as a foundation on which to build my account of the petroturfing project. Even though the petroturfing project exhibits characteristics of populism, I want to avoid reifying petroturfing in these terms since a consequence is that populism can become both problem and solution. Populism, in my view, is a compromised political form or genre. "Populism," as media theorist Gholam Khiabany writes, "which at some points used to refer to something specific in Latin America, is now vaguely employed to explain contradictory movements and political leanings."[75] Implicitly in some cases and explicitly in others, "the very concept of populism characterises opposing movements as if they were equally against the established elite and for the people."[76] This tendency appears in North America, and a battle between good pipeline and bad extractive populisms is precisely the kind of conflict my findings caution against.

In the following pages, I tell a story of how culture has become an increasingly visible site in securing a fossil fuel future and disrupting pursuits for a renewable energy transition, just or otherwise. Several thinkers who have examined the pro-oil movement employ Gramscian concepts and frameworks in their analyses of the pro-oil movement to make similar points. Patrick McCurdy, for instance, turns to Gramsci's notion of a war of position, or the ideological battle waged to secure and maintain hegemony, to describe the mediated struggle occurring over energy imaginaries in Canada.[77] Robert Neubauer likewise employs Gramscian concepts of political hegemony supplemented with perspectives from political ecology to examine competing actors, including those I understand as part of the petroturfing project, in the setting of the canceled Northern Gateway Pipeline.[78] My turn to Althusser, specifically his theorization of the role of state and extrastate forces in reproducing the relations of the dominant mode of production, complements these uses of Gramsci rather than challenges them. Althusser enables me to center materialist questions of reproduction and resistance. For Althusser, it is the repressive and ideological state apparatuses (RSAs/ISAs) that serve as sites of reproduction of and resistance to the dominant mode of production. As gestured to earlier, I propose that Althusser provides a theory of mediation between energetic superstructures, including energy imaginaries circulated through media, and infrastructures, including media infrastructures, where repressive and ideological state apparatuses align to maintain and reproduce business as usual. This is visible in how while pipeline projects have been proposed, canceled, or constructed over the past decade, an affective infrastructure in the service of the reproduction of fossil and extractive capitalism has been built, all while the state deploys police to subdue resistance. As *hot* resource wars continue to be waged abroad, the *colder* oil culture wars have broken out at home.

The Flow of *Petroturfing*

This book takes the following as its premise: that alongside the material entanglements between fossil fuels and media, how we collectively *know* energy and infrastructure *matters*.[79] These relations matter for our collective present, and they play a determinant role in our possible collective futures, of which, despite the efforts of petroturfing strategies to convince us otherwise, there are many. If the petroturfing project is ideologically "at home" in the social and cultural milieu of the contemporary mediascape, then it is also equally at home in a material–ecological sense. From the fueling and cooling of data centers to the extractive materials that comprise devices such as computers or smartphones, this mediascape relies on intensifying energetic relations for access and circulation. The chapters that follow are shaped and informed by these cultural, material, and energetic relations, indirectly building on environmental media theorist Jeff M. Diamanti's return to the economic vocabulary of "energy deepening"—the ever-increasing production and consumption of energy under capitalism—as a way of linking postindustrial modes of material and intellectual production.[80] In the petroturfing project, I see an effort to maintain and reproduce the conditions of the fossil economy by mobilizing the form of the present dominant media ecology. Bookended by two historical chapters, the central four chapters more closely map the form and content of the petroturfing project in a mode that resembles ideology critique.

In chapter 1, I provide a historical account of petroturfing that centers on the struggle of signification between "dirty" and "ethical" oil in the oil sands that has played out since 2008. In articulating the political–historical contexts through which petroturfing came into being, I approach petroturfing as a reactionary counterstrategy to Indigenous and environmentalist organizing against the oil sands. This point is not to reify petroturfing but to historicize its emergence by grasping its history on its own terms. That petroturfing is reactionary might seem obvious. But it is important to state the obvious to grasp how petroturfing derives its strategies from the very groups, campaigns, and organizations that it works to undermine. After describing these initial modes of resistance to oil sands expansionism, some of which crystallized in a coalition of Indigenous and environmental groups called the Dirty Oil Sands Network, I perform a close reading of Levant's *Ethical Oil* to draw out key themes that repeat across the petroturfing project. The chapter closes with an overview of the petroturfing mediascape from 2010 onward that ties these efforts to right-wing think tanks and other political contexts while examining the affordances of media forms petroturfing mobilizes to particular ends. As I argue in this chapter and throughout this book, these efforts coalesce to establish a "permanent campaign" for Canadian fossil fuels that culminated in the oil culture wars.

In the four chapters that follow, I turn more directly to the form and content of petroturfing. I take inspiration from Jean-Claude Debeir, Jean-Paul Deléage, and Daniel Hémery's assertion in their expansive cultural and historical study of energy that energy shapes and permeates broader, interdependent economic, social, and environmental spheres.[81] These spheres are interwoven, but I separate them as a means to strategically disarticulate and recontextualize the decontextualized histories and relations that petroturfing relies on and generates in a move that embodies a kind of counterrefining as method. Chapters 2, 3, 4, and 5 critically examine media such as memes, tweets, and op-eds that are anchored to specific episodes in the recent history of Canadian oil infrastructure development, especially pipelines. The chapters also make legible the ideologies of foreclosure that petroturfing expresses in its fortification of barriers to energy transition. Chapter 2 focuses on the economic relations that underwrite the promises of Canada's fossil economy. Extending economic historian Timothy Mitchell's analysis of economentality and the emergence of the economy as an object, the chapter traces Canadian oil's economentality as it takes the form of an oil executive epistemology, a way of comprehending oil that flattens class antagonisms in extractive enterprise.[82] This epistemology takes shape through a resource–economy–nation nexus, speculative cost–benefit forecasts that are circulated as facts, and appeals to balance in energy debates that end up privileging already dominant relations.

In chapter 3, I engage Heather M. Turcotte's theorization of petrosexual politics and Cara New Daggett's theorization of petromasculinity to examine how gender and sexuality are employed in petroturfing.[83] As thinkers such as Sheena Wilson have shown, gender and sexuality have been central to the petroturfing project since the early days of Ethical Oil, leveraging, for instance, formal gender equality in Canada in opposition to racist tropes aimed at major Middle Eastern oil-producing regions, particularly Saudi Arabia and Sudan.[84] Informed by existing work on these fronts, I focus on expressions of masculinity in the figure of Bernard the Roughneck alongside appeals to the 2SLGBTQIA+ community from groups such as Oil Sands Strong to provide a more expansive account of how oil, gender, and sexuality appear in petroturfing, all of which I argue occur in the shadow of petromasculinity. I find that alongside its heteronormative impulses, petroturfing's treatment of gender and sexuality exhibits a refined version of Jasbir K. Puar's influential concept of homonationalism, that is, a homonormative nationalism by which "homosexual subjects . . . gain significant representational currency when situated within the global scene of the war on terror" by promoting a *resource* homonationalism in concert with resource heteronationalism.[85]

In chapter 4, I explore the settler colonial relations of petroturfing as they are expressed in the shadow of Indigenous resistance. Reconciliation and recognition are taken up in the petroturfing project in order to undermine Indigenous resistance in ways that homogenize Indigenous views from the outside in a fundamentally settler colonial gesture. This chapter tracks these gestures through media produced by Canada Action and Oil Sands Strong in the setting of recent industry support for the governmental adoption of a modified version of the United Nations Declaration on the Rights of Indigenous Peoples (UNDRIP). Chapter 5 then turns to the entanglement between petroturfing's technological and environmental imaginaries by focusing on oil sands reclamation and other technologies that mitigate the ecological impacts of extraction. The chapter argues that oil sands reclamation represents a remediation of capital that subsumes scientific knowledge as a force of production that takes place in aesthetic terms, and it shows how such aesthetics underwrite petroturfing as an environmental technology itself. Together, these central chapters track the cultural politics of the petroturfing mediascape by looking to its communicative strategies as a counter-counterdiscourse.

Chapter 6 turns to recent shifts in petroturfing that have played out in the later 2010s. These shifts include a transition from a largely social media–based phenomenon to one that organizes well-publicized, relatively well-attended demonstrations on the ground, as well as the adoption of modes of communication inspired by petroturfing as official state discourse in the province of Alberta. Putting the 2019 United We Roll! convoy demonstration in conversation with then Alberta premier Jason Kenney's establishment of an "energy war room" to "fight misinformation related to oil and gas" alongside its public inquiry into anti-Alberta energy campaigns, I detail the consequences of the petroturfing project's state as a mode of dissent from below *and* official state-backed project from above.[86]

I conclude by reflecting on the amplified stakes of the oil culture wars more than a decade since the petroturfing project's inauguration and describe how fighting in these wars is, and has been, a losing battle for those of us committed to more just energy futures. Taking the impasse produced by the oil culture wars as a point of departure, I close by interrogating the relationship between platform and oil capitalism that petroturfing represents and offer speculative conclusions on how to move beyond this impasse through the generation of alternative energy and infrastructural imaginaries that will aid in the construction of more just energy futures instead of intensifying the oil culture wars. To do so, I advocate for exiting the trenches of the oil culture wars by nurturing relations with oil beyond those dictated by the fossil economy.

1

FROM DIRTY TO ETHICAL
IGNITING THE OIL CULTURE WARS

Speaking in the Canadian House of Commons to the Standing Committee on Natural Resources in 2010, Ezra Levant gave an impassioned speech in defense of Canadian oil. "One day we might discover a fuel source with no environmental side effects that's affordable and practical; but until that day comes, we need oil," he began. Levant carried on to contrast the liberal democratic values of Canada with those of the Organization of the Petroleum Exporting Countries (OPEC), cite low environmental disturbance figures to counter "Greenpeace propaganda pictures," and argue for the moral and economic necessity of constructing a pipeline to Canada's West Coast. "If you don't care about morality, then buy oil from Iran or Sudan. It's just as good as Canadian oil," Levant mused. "But if you believe in making the world a better place, then the moral imperative is to replace unethical OPEC oil with Canadian green oil, conflict-free oil, fair wage oil, human rights oil."[1] Citing his recently published book and offering free copies to everyone in attendance, Levant gave testimony that served as a kind of launch party for *Ethical Oil: The Case for Canada's Oil Sands* that, in many ways, lit the fuse that ignited the oil culture wars.

Over its five-minute duration, Levant's rousing speech performed a series of gestures that have since scaled out to become the foundational rhetorical moves of petroturfing in Canada, punctuated by a raised voice and dramatic body language. First, Levant reminded us that we inhabit a world conditioned by oil's ubiquity. Accordingly, to halt or slow down the extraction, production, and consumption of hydrocarbons is an unrealistic desire. Second, he distinguished Canadian oil from foreign oil by highlighting the discrepancies in the status of human rights between Canada and many other oil-producing regions, arguing that Canadian oil is a more ethical commodity to produce and consume on these terms. Third, he drew attention to the comparatively stringent environmental regulations in Canada to undermine resistance to oil sands expansionism from environmentalist organizations such as Greenpeace, which he directly accused of being beholden to American interests due to its funding ties from the Tides Foundation, an American public charity. Most importantly, he mythologized Canadian oil as a socially and ecologically friendly substance whose extraction, production, and consumption should be increased rather than restrained.

Following the launch of *Ethical Oil,* a larger campaign appeared on the web sometime in 2011. The organization Ethical Oil began with a blog hosted at EthicalOil.org and a presence across popular social media platforms, including Facebook, Twitter, and YouTube. Ethical Oil was first headed by Alykhan Velshi, who was known for his work with the Progressive Conservative Party. Velshi produced and circulated content on these platforms and through publications in news media, including an op-ed featured on the *Huffington Post* blog titled "There Is Such a Thing as 'Ethical Oil.'"[2] Later, Ethical Oil would be headed by Kathryn Marshall, now an employment lawyer who seems to have subdued past associations with the campaign. Marshall was followed Jamie Ellerton, who now works at the helm of Conaptus, a strategic communications and public relations firm based out of Toronto, Ontario. In their roles with Ethical Oil, Marshall and Ellerton also produced and circulated content across traditional and social media that advanced the ethical oil argument, and the career trajectories of these former spokespersons offer a glimpse of the campaign's enmeshment with existing political and professional public relations settings. This larger campaign, whose activity spanned mostly from 2011 to 2014, was a prototype in leveraging the circuit of legitimation through circulation nurtured by the architectures and infrastructures of social media. As I detail in this chapter, in Ethical Oil are the origins of the form and content of petroturfing—a reactionary project that mimics media strategies from environmental nongovernmental organizations (ENGOs) to undermine existing resistance efforts by introducing foundational rhetorical gestures that imbue Canadian oil with socially and ecologically positive characteristics.

Levant's appearance before Parliament came on the heels of an important episode in the history of Canada's fossil economy—a deepening infrastructural inertia that would play out with booms and busts over the 2010s. The date of Levant's contribution reveals the underlying logic of a thinly veiled argument for the building of Enbridge's Northern Gateway Pipeline project. Though the Northern Gateway pipelines had been announced in 2006, it was only in late 2009 that Canada's National Energy Board (NEB) and the Canadian Environmental Assessment Agency (CEAA) moved the project forward to its review stages. In May 2010, Enbridge submitted its formal application to the NEB. Traversing ceded and unceded Indigenous territory along its 731-mile route, the twin pipeline would have carried diluted bitumen westward from Bruderheim, Alberta, to the coastal city of Kitimat, British Columbia, and natural gas condensate eastward to dilute the bitumen so it can travel westward in an intensified trajectory of energy circulation. The project faced immense opposition not only from environmentalists but from Indigenous groups as well, with Wet'suwet'en hereditary chiefs setting up a permanent encampment to resist the networks of proposed pipelines that would form an energy corridor in Canada's northwest. Currently, the pipeline sits in the infrastructural dead zone of cancelation; however, as I point out in the introduction, this does not necessarily mean it cannot be revived in the future. As of at least midway through 2023, the *Toronto Star* still listed the Northern Gateway on the "Pipeline News" section of its website in its header.[3]

The continued expansion of the oil sands in the face of widespread opposition has led critics to view the sands as a site of struggle that has coalesced into the oil culture wars. Since the turn of the new millennium, there has been a dramatic increase in the production of oil in Canada due primarily to increased oil sands activity. This increase follows the aspiration for Canada to become what former prime minister Stephen Harper described in 2006 as an "energy superpower."[4] Sociologist Randolph Haluza-DeLay identifies the struggles that emerged as a set of duels occurring across sites and contexts—dueling websites, dueling videos, dueling media campaigns, dueling science, dueling in court, and dueling ethics.[5] Haluza-DeLay's account is revealing in that he perceives the terrain on which this struggle occurs as one in the domain of culture. "Ultimately," he writes, "the duelling over the oil sands is *cultural* politics."[6] Framing this struggle in terms of culture more precisely brings into view how cultural and material relations function together to reproduce or resist the fossil economy, a distinction I make in order to hone in on the kinds of interventions that petroturfing makes as a cultural technology and that do different work than the material interventions that propel or disrupt the momentum of the fossil economy. These are not, in other words, the material battles waged over the laying of pipelines or the blocking of them. Yet they are entangled with these actions in their capacity to shape energy imaginaries through energy consciousnesses.

In this chapter, I explore how these dueling energy imaginaries took shape to underwrite the petroturfing project through the Ethical Oil campaign. Animating this chapter are three complementary aims: to detail more thoroughly what petroturfing is, how it came to be, and how it functions, which I do in a historical mode that, unlike most of *Petroturfing,* is more an accounting than it is a critique. I begin at sites of resistance by providing a brief account of activist media efforts from the Dirty Oil Sands Network, a campaign spearheaded by a coalition of environmentalist and Indigenous groups that played an important role in framing Canadian oil as "dirty oil." I transition from resistance to reproduction by closely reading Levant's *Ethical Oil,* approaching it first as a reaction to campaigns and organizations such as the Dirty Oil Sands Network and then further examining the foundational gestures of petroturfing that it makes in economic, social, and environmental registers—the very registers that provide the structure for chapters 2 to 5. Finally, I scale out and chart a preliminary political economy of petroturfing, exploring the material and ideological networks that coalesce in a permanent campaign for Canada's fossil economy in the shape of a culture war.

Reactive Energy Imaginaries: Canadian Oil between "Dirty" and "Ethical"

Resistance often follows injustice. The oil sands megaproject—composed of the Athabasca, Cold Lake, and Peace River oil sands deposits—is an exercise in social and ecological injustice and referred to by some activists as the "world's largest industrial project on the planet."[7] Slow ecological violence spurned by more than one trillion liters of toxic tailings ponds leaking into both surface waters and groundwater; vast, irreparable damage to complex ecosystems like wetlands and boreal forests; violation of treaty obligations and persistent undermining of Indigenous sovereignty across ceded and unceded territory: this is an incomplete checklist of consequences of oil sands development that highlights how they function as a vehicle for environmental racism propelled by injustice.[8] Emerging from the U.S. environmental justice movement that brought together civil rights and environmental movements, environmental racism describes the policies, systems, and structures that, among other things, produce a condition in which pollution is disproportionately located in close proximity to racialized communities.[9] The concept has since been taken up to refer more generally to the persistent conditions of unevenly distributed impacts of ecological destruction.

I raise the issue of environmental racism because it partially explains the consequences of Canada's fossil economy and why its expansion is resisted primarily by environmental and Indigenous groups, often together although with sometimes differing motivations. Where ecological relations are disrupted, in other words, so, too, are social ones. And in the throes of upward mobility of the oil sands megaproject in the first decade of the twenty-first century, resistance efforts confronted these socially and ecologically unjust tendencies of Canada's fossil economy and its broader extractive state apparatus, culminating in what climate activists Jesse Fruhwirth and Melanie Jae Martin in 2013 identified as "Blockadia": "a vast but interwoven web of campaigns standing up against the fossil fuel industry and demanding an end to the development of tar sands pipelines."[10] Leading up to this cementing of Blockadia, grassroots organizing and more institutionalized modes of resistance coalesced to challenge oil sands expansionism through direct action, legal mechanisms, and media campaigns that ultimately sought to brand the oil sands as "dirty" by shaping how we consciously perceive our relations to energy in this way—that is, by shaping energy consciousness. Although larger grassroots activist initiatives against oil sands expansionism exceeded the confines of formally organized groups, formal organizations influenced the institutionalization of dirty oil discourse.

Under the banner of the Dirty Oil Sands Network, for instance, a collective effort from Indigenous organizations and ENGOs formed in 2008 to brand the oil sands as inherently destructive through the signifier "dirty." As a signifier, dirty at once refers to the ecological consequences of oil sands extraction and production as well as its social and political impacts, and it is part of a longer history of semantic struggle surrounding the oil sands. The mediated struggle or "duel" between those who decry and those who celebrate Canada's fossil economy through the oil sands is evident in historical public discourse, particularly in terms of the shift from conventionally referring to sands first as tar and then oil sands. For much of its operative history, as I point out in the introduction, "tar sands" was standard nomenclature. But as dirtiness took hold of the collective imagination, backlash ensued and the oil sands became the standard used by industry and government, perceived as a more neutral phrase.

As a result, whenever one writes about or discusses the oil sands, choices in terminology can be perceived as revealing allegiances and biases. Tar sands, once understood as a *descriptive* rather than critical term, became associated with dirty oil positioning. Oil sands, then, became the term for supporters, including industry and government. Literary critic Jon Gordon's "bituminous sands" and communications scholar Geo Takach's "bit-sands" are attempts to side-step the ideological baggage tied to tar and oil.[11] My own use of oil sands stems simply from the fact that, as I write this, communication from official channels uses this phrasing, not from its perceived neutrality or as an attempt to distance myself from critical positions. This is all to say that even before Levant's appearance before Parliament, when he symbolically refined Canadian oil as green and conflict-free in real time, the discursive field was a primary one in which struggles were waged. The efforts from the Dirty Oil Sands Network did not spring up out of nowhere—they responded to a longer history of semantic struggle that recognizes the significance of energy imaginaries in defining relationships to energy sources.

To enter this mediated struggle in direct terms, a now-defunct website, DirtyOilSands.org, was launched to aggregate information surrounding the ecological impacts of the oil sands, highlight activist efforts, and ultimately serve as a hub for the Dirty Oil Sands Network. The network was a consortium of environmental and Indigenous organizations that included the Dogwood Initiative, ForestEthics, Greenpeace, Honor the Earth, and the Sierra Club (see Figure 2). The website hosted an active blog, offered a space for action, and dedicated space to providing visitors "the dirt on oil sands." This dirt provided hyperlinks to a series of "Quick Facts" that highlighted the oil sands as "the fastest growing source of greenhouse gas pollution in Canada," detailed the scale and severity of its pollution of water through tailings pond leakage, described its intensive consumption of liquefied natural gas in the extraction and refining process, and more.[12] The page also contained an embedded five-minute backgrounder video from award-winning Canadian journalist Andrew Nikiforuk, a well-known critic of the oil sands who penned *Tar Sands: Dirty Oil and the Future of a Continent* in 2008.[13]

DirtyOilSands.org was one effort among many in a wider dirty oil sands media ecology that members of the network helped sustain. Greenpeace, for instance, has made campaigning against the oil sands a persistent platform. In 2009, it published a report written by Nikiforuk. *Dirty Oil: How the Tar Sands Are Fueling the Global Climate Crisis* helped set the stage for the broader campaign's interventions by quantitatively

Figure 2. A screenshot of the DirtyOilSands.org "About the Network" page in 2009 via the Wayback Machine.

laying out the scale and intensity of the oil sands' ecological impacts and interpreting these data as evidence of the fading of Canada's global image as an environmental leader. The report echoes arguments from Nikiforuk's *Tar Sands,* but its format lends itself to free circulation and a wider potential readership. In both book and report, Nikiforuk traces the ecological impacts of increased oil sands production by highlighting in particular its high carbon footprint due to the use of natural gas in extractive processes, which Nikiforuk describes as "cannibaliz[ing] Canada's natural gas supply."[14] "Alberta's vast deposits of bitumen, an unconventional hydrocarbon trapped under the Boreal forest," Nikiforuk laments, "is the source of one of the world's most energy- and carbon-intensive fossil fuels."[15] He concludes the report in no uncertain terms: "Canada is now one of the world's leading emitters of GHGs [greenhouse gases], and a global defender of dirty fuels."[16]

A number of documentaries directly and indirectly related to the campaign were released in this same period. Produced by Greenpeace Canada and directed by Peter Mettler, *Petropolis: Aerial Perspectives on the Alberta Tar Sands* (2009) offers a disorienting visual survey of oil sands ecologies. *Petropolis* pairs aerial footage depicting the vast scale of ecological degradation with periodic statistics from Nikiforuk that illustrate how media forms work together to produce or reinforce these particular dirty oil sands imaginaries. The documentary, alongside Edward Burtynsky's well-known photographs in his Oil series, is in part responsible for etching the planetary oil slick imagery of the oil sands into the minds of a broader public. Such imagery expresses what environmental communications scholar Jennifer Peeples describes as the "toxic sublime," that is, "*the tensions that arise from recognizing the toxicity of a place, object or situation, while simultaneously appreciating its mystery, magnificence and ability to inspire awe.*"[17] Representations like Mettler's affectively engage this tension as a mode of critique. A more conventional feature-length documentary film titled *Dirty Oil* was also released in 2009. Directed by Leslie Iwerks, this film serves as a Hollywood counterpart to the highbrow, auteur style of *Petropolis,* and features voice-over narration by Neve Campbell and interviews with Nikiforuk and others. Takach characterizes *Dirty Oil* as a sort of compendium or synthesis of previous ventures in mobilizing the visual economy of the oil sands as a mode of critique. He observes that "the film can be seen as a consolidation of filmic dissent on the bit-sands in late 2009" due in part to its generic conventions set out by previous efforts.[18]

Together, the book, report, and documentaries produced in the shadow of the Dirty Oil Sands Network home page are a time capsule that illustrates a broader discursive shift in how the oil sands were discussed and understood nationally and internationally. As a result of on-the-ground activism and media interventions such as these, the oil sands were, and indeed continue to be, discursively tethered to this "dirtiness." In and around 2008, then, the bituminous oil sands arguably *became* the tar sands as we know them today. This shift in signification was not unintentional or the result of accidental circumstances. Its success is due in no small part to persistent campaigns from ENGOs and other groups that sought precisely this outcome: to imbue the oil sands with signifiers associated with dirtiness, toxicity, and so on. While the Dirty Oil Sands Network has been shelved, campaigns to maintain this signification continue, including as part of Greenpeace and the Sierra Club's platforms as well through an ongoing 2012 campaign from UK-based natural cosmetics company Lush.[19]

In branding the oil sands as "dirty," activists and organizations involved in the larger Dirty Oil campaign participated in the shaping of energy consciousness surrounding the oil sands in a negative register as a means to support disruption of further development. Clearly articulated here is, in itself, a *reactionary* energy imaginary, that is, an energy imaginary that reacts against those dominant energy imaginaries that positively enframe the oil sands by tying its further infrastructural development to, for instance, nation building. These efforts, in other words, operated as counterdiscursive to dominant imaginaries from both industry and government that ideologically and economically support the oil sands. While the laws of physics tell us that all actions are reactions, there remains analytic import in identifying how these larger movements are situated along a spectrum of action and reaction. This process of action and reaction is precisely why Melissa Aronczyk and Graeme Auld develop their analysis of the Ethical Oil project around questions of the coevolution of movements and countermovements.[20] In productive friction with this logic of call and response, what emerges from my account of the Dirty Oil campaign is that it offers the formal ingredients of a circuit for shaping energy consciousness in the twenty-first century that fails to move beyond impasses to the building of a more socially and ecologically just future. Just as the Ethical Oil project produces and circulates a reactionary energy imaginary to the dirty oil imaginary, so is the dirty oil imaginary premised on a reaction to dominant petrocultural imaginaries from industry and government. In pointing out the compromised form of reactive energy imaginaries, however, it is important to make clear that this approach to the Dirty Oil campaign does not necessarily confirm petroturfing's origin story. Certainly, there were and continue to be concentrated and distributed efforts to refigure Canadian oil as dirty, but the power differentials at play here in relation to one of the most powerful industries on the planet calls petroturfing's origin story, which is that Canadian oil needs defending, into question. Blockadia itself, in other words, didn't spring up out of nowhere to target dirty oil—it emerged out of and alongside existing activism against Canadian extractive enterprise in general, like mining or the logging of old-growth forests.

Reading *Ethical Oil*: Energy Realisms and the Foreclosure of Alternative Energy Futures

If injustice continues in the face of resistance, then injustice is reproduced against this friction. Ezra Levant's *Ethical Oil* and the media campaign that followed serve as avenues through which the injustices that underwrite Canada's fossil economy are reproduced in the twenty-first century. Such reproduction is achieved by instigating a direct countermovement to the reach and impact of the Dirty Oil campaign and other resistance efforts. In the opening pages of *Ethical Oil,* Levant builds his case for the ethics of Canadian oil by refuting many of the points that the Dirty Oil campaign was built upon while making clear that his book is a response to these campaigns. "That's what *Ethical Oil* is about," he writes: "trying to separate the propaganda coming from anti-oil sands groups like Greenpeace from the facts, and using those facts to decide which oil is more environmentally clean, more peaceful, more democratic, and more fair."[21] Levant argues that Canadian oil embodies all these progressive economic, social, and ecological characteristics, a claim that hinges upon Canada's place on "the very short list of democracies that sell oil" with formal equality among genders and strict environmental regulations.[22] In broadly invoking environmental regulations as evidence of "environmentally clean" oil, for instance, Levant performs what literary and cultural theorist Mark Simpson describes as the "smoothing" out of "oil's political frictions."[23] This smoothing is done in a way that overlooks the realities of Canada's environmental regulatory apparatus while attempting to saturate the discursive field with positive signifiers attached to Canadian oil. *Ethical Oil,* and petroturfing in general, *smoothens* in order to *saturate.*

Oil cannot be separated from the social relations and political economies to which its production and consumption are bound. In his pathbreaking book *Lifeblood: Oil, Freedom, and the Forces of Capital,* critical geographer Matt Huber argues that oil fueled and continues to fuel neoliberalism, that mutation of capitalism dreamed up by the Mont Pelerin Society in 1947 and materialized in the Global North by figures such as Margaret Thatcher in the United Kingdom and Ronald Reagan in the United States over the 1980s. Huber shows how oil operates as a material means through which neoliberal tenets are propped up, observing that fossil fuels, and oil in particular, "actively shapes political structures of feeling," in turn situating oil "within . . . cherished ideas of private property, freedom, family, and home."[24] Philosopher Mark Fisher argues in *Capitalist Realism: Is There No Alternative?* that neoliberalism's reach and persistence are attributable in part to the ways in which neoliberalism *encloses* possibilities for a future beyond market relations at a subjective level. Captured by the book's subtitle, which is a reference to Thatcher's neoliberal "doctrine that 'there is no alternative'" to global capitalism, Fisher suggests that a powerful ideological mechanism of neoliberalism is in its insistence that there are no viable alternatives to capitalist relations.[25] Capitalist realism, according to Fisher, is a "pervasive *atmosphere*" that acts "as a kind of invisible barrier constraining thought and action."[26] Given the deep, symbiotic relationship between neoliberalism and the dominant petrocultural energy regime, such an atmosphere constrains thought and action against fossil capital as well. *Ethical Oil* demonstrates as much by putting forward a *petro*capitalist realism presented as energy realism that insists explicitly on the necessity of fossil fuels, especially oil, and implicitly on the necessity of capitalism through the commitment to ethical production and consumption. These premises serve as the ideological foundations of petroturfing, all of which aim to foreclose possibilities for imagining an energy transition beyond fossil fuels, let alone pursuing that future. Canadian oil here becomes imbued with these particular social and ecological relations that Levant argues marks its production—that is, progressive social and ecological relations that are voluntarily enacted by oil and gas companies, such as Indigenous employment initiatives, or legislated by the Canadian state, such as formal gender equality.

Equating oil with characteristics that underpin the North American imaginary is a form of naturalization that petroturfing hopes to further cement by actively shaping our collective energy and environmental imaginaries in favor of fossil fuels. These imaginaries, many of which are inflected by nationalist tendencies, will be looked at more closely in the coming chapters, but they most forcefully include a settler colonial frontierism tied to the extraction of natural resources, which political economist Harold Innis canonically identified in his work as part of his "staples thesis." Innis's thesis posits that Canada's economy relies on the extraction and exporting of raw materials such as natural resources in determinant ways that, no doubt, have also shaped what can be perceived as national identity in determinate ways as well, including through the building of the Canadian Pacific Railway, which materially and ideologically established what is now called Canada. Staples thinking conditions petroturfing as it attempts to saturate the social and cultural dimensions of energy systems with oil and other fossil fuels by associating Canadian oil in existing dominant imaginaries, especially national and economic ones that are also conditioned by staples thinking.[27] If, as Huber proposes, "the biggest barrier to energy change is not technical but the cultural and political structures of feeling that have been produced through regimes of energy consumption," then petroturfing, and the petrocapitalist realist worldview upon which it depends, is one way to *deepen* these cultural and political structures of feeling.[28]

As a tendency that aims to generate political subject positions that are one part ethical capitalist and one part oil baron, the petrocapitalist realism of *Ethical Oil* simultaneously naturalizes the production and consumption of fossil fuels alongside neoliberal market relations. Addressing criticisms of the destructive aspects of bitumen extraction in the oil sands, Levant draws a parallel between Indigenous uses of raw bitumen and the widespread industrial exploitation of bitumen deposits in the region:

> It's true, there is oil seeping into the rivers north of Fort McMurray and sometimes the air smells like sulphur and the water is bitter. And that's how it's been for millennia—Aboriginals traditionally used the thick bitumen that bubbled out of the ground to waterproof their canoes. There is so much oil oozing *naturally* into the environment that sometimes the water quality adjacent to an oil sands operation is cleaner than the water upstream, where a seam of bitumen exposed on the riverbank has been leeching into the water for *thousands of years.*[29]

This parallel between Indigenous uses of bitumen as a raw material and industrial production flattens the disparity of scale between these two modes while naturalizing the latter. Temporally and ecologically naturalizing vocabularies functions as the epistemological nomenclature of "natural resources" does—as terminology that in itself signifies what literary and cultural theorist Jennifer Wenzel calls a "resource logic," or "habits of mind that understand nature as other than human, disposed as a resource for human use, and subject to human control."[30] One particularly grievous consequence of this rhetorical move of resource logic anachronism is that it lessens the severe social and ecological consequences of oil sands extraction, particularly Indigenous nations across unceded as well as Treaty 6 and 8 territory most affected by that extraction, which I explore more fully in chapter 4.

Commitments to neoliberalism further shape the economic imaginary of *Ethical Oil* and the larger petroturfing project. Levant tethers his concept of ethical oil to abstractions that exceed neoliberal frameworks, such as freedom and democracy, but these abstractions are materialized in Levant's worldview through consumer choice. The choice that Levant advocates in distinguishing Canadian oil as ethical occurs in the market.[31] Mark Simpson shows this by situating the Ethical Oil project within his concept of "lubricity"—"the texture and mood requisite to the operations of neoliberal petroculture."[32] "The proclaimed ethicalness of 'ethical oil,'" Simpson writes,

> thus converts petrochemical need into petrocultural duty, rendering the specifics of oil use itself interpellative for contemporary capitalism: "the choice we all have to make," as the avowedly "grassroots" organization Ethical Oil memorably insisted to its prospective supporters—an urgent, imperative choice that is no choice at all.[33]

Ethics, then, is an ethics realized through the market; it is this neoliberal framework of market freedom and consumer choice that undergirds petrocapitalist realism. Conversion emerges as a keyword to pinpoint the ways in which petroturfing channels, or *refines,* existing dominant relations and imaginaries in service of the fossil economy.

It is important to keep in mind that this neoliberal imaginary is articulated in terms of both consumption *and* production. Persistent emphasis on the economic benefits of oil sands projects, which always seem to outweigh the social and ecological costs in these accounts, permeate *Ethical Oil* and the petroturfing project. These economic benefits are said to be generated from several avenues: direct and indirect jobs, economic stimulation through taxes and royalties, and increased regional economic activity during infrastructure construction. According to Levant, "the biggest winner in the oil sands boom is the tax collector."[34] "That's an economic story, and it's a story of the success of capitalism, and of the success of science too, which finally solved the puzzle of how to extract the oil in an economically viable manner," he elaborates. "But it's also a story of social justice—the kind of equitable sharing of the wealth that many anti-capitalists talk about."[35] In this view, the extraction, refinement, and combustion of Canadian oil serve as vehicles for economic, social, and ecological justice.

A gendered imaginary plays a forceful role in *Ethical Oil*'s positioning of Canadian oil as a benevolent force for social justice in a way that reinscribes traditional, patriarchal gender relations while claiming progressivism. I explore these aspects of petroturfing more thoroughly in chapter 3, but Levant's framing in *Ethical Oil* sets the stage for the larger petroturfing project. Like the other avenues through which the case for Canada's oil sands is made, Levant's case for how the oil sands promote gender equality relies on comparisons with social and political conditions in OPEC members abroad as well as elaborations on these internal conditions at home to infuse Canadian oil with progressive cultural capital. At home, Levant takes aim at a report produced by Kairos, a consortium of churches across Canada committed to social justice that developed a series of conditions for measuring the morality of the oil sands project and produced a report based on these criteria. The report found—among other things—that gender parity in oil sands employment was nonexistent; employment heavily favored men when compared to other fields at the national level. Levant argues that the report's numbers are misrepresentative because it is unfair to compare sectors of employment in this way. His rhetorical questioning is revealing in its logic and tone: "Is Kairos seriously trying to compare the oil sands—really, a form of mining—with being a clerk at a retail store or a bank?"[36] Levant lays bare his views on the distinction between masculinized and feminized labor—the latter a category that remains undervalued and tied to the often invisibilized labor of social reproduction. For Levant, service work is for women and the blue-collar labor of oil sands work is for men.

Levant raises these issues to fuel claims about how the oil sands promote equality at home through production and abroad through consumption. Returning to the comparative mode, Levant draws upon the fact that at the time he was writing *Ethical Oil,* the mayor of the urban center of the oil sands, Fort McMurray, was a woman named Melissa Blake. He performs a thought experiment—a favored mode of argumentation in the archive of petroturfing and right-wing debate tactics. Placing Blake in Saudi Arabia, Levant then speculates on her treatment there. "If Blake even stepped into the streets in Saudi Arabia without a burka on, and without the supervision of a man who was her relative, she'd be beaten by the mutaween—Saudi's violent religious police," he writes.[37] Direct comparisons between "conflict oil" and "ethical oil" in gendered terms were a central communicative strategy in the early days of the Ethical Oil media campaign, which included billboards and print advertisements alongside its online efforts. Feminist energy humanities scholar Sheena Wilson argues that the "blatantly racist, imperialist, and sexist language" of *Ethical Oil* permeates the campaign more broadly.[38] Following this point, it is apropos that Blake was not asked for consent to use her image on a billboard that placed her in opposition to a generic image of a burka-clad, Iranian woman, which Wilson argues both "situates foreign women in a position of victimization whereby they must be rescued" and puts forth a paradigm wherein "women's liberation from traditional private-sphere roles becomes the only evidence required or necessary to demonstrate the superior status and civilization of Western nations."[39] In an exchange on Twitter that has since been removed, Blake expressed disappointment in how her image was used, despite being a supporter of the oil sands.[40] These ideological expressions are, as Wilson identifies and I take up at length in chapter 3, part of a dynamic

Heather M. Turcotte calls "petrosexual politics" that petroturfing engages to further distinguish Canadian oil's social relations.[41]

Such petrosexual politics are part of a social imaginary that similarly decontextualizes—or *extracts*—racial relations of resource extraction in order to promote extraction, relations inextricably bound to settler colonial ones in the oil sands. Across gendered and racialized spheres, these gestures become particularly egregious given the consequences of building and maintaining extractive infrastructures on Indigenous women in particular, a point that is returned to and expanded upon in chapters 3 and 4. For now, it is worth underscoring that the final report for the National Inquiry into Missing and Murdered Indigenous Women and Girls found that "there is substantial evidence of a serious problem that requires focused attention on the relationship between resource extraction projects and violence against Indigenous women."[42] Ongoing settler colonialism, in other words, shapes oil sands extraction in determinant ways. Sidestepping this crucial context, Levant continues to champion the economic benefits that the oil sands bestow on Indigenous peoples across Northern Alberta. Nowhere in *Ethical Oil* does the word *colonialism* appear, yet claims such as "in Northern Alberta, since the development of the oil sands industry, it's safe to say that Aboriginals have never had it so good" rise to the surface.[43]

These ahistorical, depoliticized gendered and racialized imaginaries are made possible by a politics of recognition that decontextualizes the material realities of gender, sexuality, and race in Canada—an *extractive* relation that parallels the extractivism that motivates Canada's fossil economy. Activist and writer Naomi Klein defines extractivism as "a nonreciprocal, dominance-based relationship with the earth, one purely of taking."[44] In an interview with Klein, Michi Saagiig Nishnaabeg theorist Leanne Betasamosake Simpson extends Klein's definition by speaking of the relationship between resource extraction and acts of settler colonial assimilation:

> The act of extraction removes all of the relationships that give whatever is being extracted meaning. Extracting is taking. Actually, extracting is stealing—it is taking without consent, without thought, care or even knowledge of the impacts that extraction has on the other living things in that environment.[45]

Read back onto the extractive dynamics of *Ethical Oil* that I examined, these uses and abuses of gendered and racialized relations parallel material extraction beyond metaphor precisely due to how these expressions are leveraged to justify the expansion of Canada's fossil economy.

Slogans of the contemporary environmental justice movements announce that another world is possible in which economies and environments are no longer pitted against each other as an inherent, structural tendency of the dominant economies with which we live. In the world of *Ethical Oil,* this future is already here. Employment is an economic thread through which the ecologically destructive forces of Canada's fossil economy are rationalized and lessened. As Levant puts it, "for Aboriginals, for women, for the environment, for Canadians, for migrant workers, for the poor, and for peace, the oil sands represent a more decent way of producing petroleum than any other realistic alternative out there."[46] Embodied in the day-to-day operations of the oil sands, seen by Levant as "green" and "environmentally clean," are relations that brighten the symbolic shade of Canadian oil from black to green. This symbolic transition rests on an environmental imaginary that sits somewhere between a fetishism of technological innovation and the benevolence of extraction. In a world-building thought experiment, Levant waxes poetic on the charity motive of oil and gas companies:

> Only in Alberta's oil sands do companies not only volunteer to dig up naturally occurring petroleum that's bubbling out of the soaked ground and oozing into the rivers, they spend billions of dollars for the privilege of doing it. You might call it the largest cleanup of an oil spill in the history of the world.[47]

Levant's rhetoric here employs a feigned naiveté that seems to recognize its own absurdity. Moments such as these are windows into the mobilization of bad faith reasoning that mark the Ethical Oil campaign through what cultural theorist Imre Szeman describes in his brief analysis of the book's "crude forms of rhetoric" as "high-school debate-club style dismissals," which resemble strategies seen in the contemporary right-wing mediascape through figures such as Ben Shapiro.[48]

But the factual, technological imagination quickly takes over. Armed with a series of statistics surrounding scale and ecological disturbance, Levant directly challenges ENGOs that highlight the destructive aspects of the oil sands megaproject.[49] Knowing that readers are familiar with the kinds of visual economies that the Dirty Oil Sands campaign trades in, Levant offers these figures to lessen the perceived severity of impacts of oil sands production. "Only 20 per cent of the oil sands is mined in those ugly open pits," he writes. "And that 20 per cent takes up just 2 per cent of the oil sands total geography."[50] "The other 80 per cent of the oil, accounting for 98 per cent of the land area, is drilled out of the ground without ripping open photogenic scars," he continues. Innovation in oil sands extraction methods, especially in the transition from open pit mining and hot water separation to horizontal drilling and SAGD that I discussed in the introduction, animates claims of minimal, or at least minimized, ecological impacts. Extending these gestures to the afterlives of extractive landscapes, Levant champions reclamation efforts from oil sands companies, holding up Syncrude's 2008 government-certified reclamation project as a shining example of postextractive mitigation possibilities.[51] Momentum fuels Levant's cheerleading. Now that the first one has been certified, his framing suggests, there will be many more to come, since reclamation is a legally required component to any licensed oil sands project.

Some fifteen years later, Syncrude's reclamation project remains the only certified one. While reclamation plans are contractually required for leases, how reclamation to this scale can be achieved remains uncertain. Taking Levant at his optimistic word, however, reclamation heals the "photogenic scars" so prevalently cited in the visual economy of dirty oil. Or, as in the case of SAGD, these scars are avoided altogether by keeping them underground. In this story of ecological impacts mitigated by technological innovation across extractive and postextractive landscapes are traces of an idealized aesthetic rather than material view of ecological relations, which I take up further in chapter 5.

In these economic, social, and environmental imaginaries found in the pages of *Ethical Oil* are the origins of a larger phenomenon—a growing petroturfing project. Like this emergent project more generally, the impact of Levant's specific interventions, as both Mark Simpson and Szeman suggest, is not necessarily in the validity or truth of the points that he makes but their rhetorical movement.[52] Placed next to the scientific and empirical outputs of the Dirty Oil campaign that offer data on the social and ecological impact of the oil sands, the battle waged by

Levant becomes a duel of competing facts over our collective energy consciousness. Levant's efforts seek to bring the concept of "ethical oil" into being as an equally valid counterpoint to "dirty oil," which can then be, and has been, used by industry and government to justify further expansion of the Canadian fossil economy and deepen environmental injustice. Ultimately, Levant strategically fails to recognize that the fantasy here is *not* that we are capable of a wide-scale transition to renewables but that we *can* continue living under a fossil fuel energy regime without severe consequences.

The "Permanent Campaign" of Petroturfing, or Canadian Oil Meets Social Media

As a former number one national best seller, *Ethical Oil* legitimized a series of positions to shape energy consciousness in favor of Canadian oil. *Ethical Oil* helped establish the *content* of petroturfing. The Ethical Oil campaign, however, offered a *formal* playbook by mirroring the trajectory or circuit of media from grassroots ENGOs such as Greenpeace: books, commissioned reports, larger media campaigns, and on-the-ground demonstrations. Seeking to saturate the mediascape in this way exhibits a circuit of legitimation through circulation that I outlined in the introduction—an ambivalent process made possible by the architectures and infrastructures of social media. Levant admits as much in the tenth chapter of *Ethical Oil,* tellingly titled "Propaganda Wars." He opens the chapter with a critique of Greenpeace for operating as a media organization rather than an activist or lobbying one, as if media production isn't a legitimate tactic. "Groups like Greenpeace aren't scholarly think-tanks or even really political lobby groups targeting politicians," he writes. "They're mass-media campaigners, fighting in the court of public opinion."[53] Despite using mass-media campaigners as a pejorative characteristic, reading between the lines brings into relief the aspirations of the Ethical Oil project as a mass-media campaign entering these so-called propaganda wars to establish the oil culture wars. By design, the claims animating the Ethical Oil project shoehorn into the tense discursive field surrounding Canadian oil as equally legitimate positions to those that recognize the socially and ecologically destructive character of the oil sands megaproject and, most importantly, the increasingly urgent need to transition away from fossil fuels as swiftly as possible. The Ethical Oil project, in other words, served as a kind of prototype of structure and strategy by saturating the conventional mediascape with consistent talking points in the form of op-eds and leveraging the connective characteristics of social media platforms, particularly Facebook, Twitter, and YouTube.

Over the past thirty years or so, *connectivity* and *participation* have emerged as keywords to describe the role of the internet's architectures and infrastructures in mediating everyday life. Theorizations of the shift from the early days of the internet to what communications and media studies scholars see as Web 2.0 often highlight how the contemporary web's architecture and infrastructure have produced an "always-on" condition that garners user participation in unprecedented yet ambivalent ways.[54] This condition shapes the contours of the petroturfing archive and animates its goals. Communications scholars Greg Elmer, Ganaele Langlois, and Fenwick McKelvey's revival of the concept of a "permanent campaign" in relation to political electoral cycles and the functioning of new and social media as a dominant media form in the twenty-first century proves instructive here. The rise of permanent campaigning, they diagnosed in 2012, came from "the exponential rise in political advertising and fund-raising" as well as "networked news cycles."[55] Permanent campaigns, in other words, have become the norm. Elmer, Langlois, and McKelvey's observations show us that "Web 2.0's networked platforms (e.g., blogs, microblogs, online videos, and social networking) . . . have challenged centralized and hierarchical forms of political governance and campaign management."[56] This challenge to centralization through connectivity and participation contextualizes the mediascape of which petroturfing is a part, while also identifying how petroturfing mobilizes the perceived emancipatory characteristics of the contemporary web, especially its participatory apparatus figured through notions of democracy, in the service of oil and other fossil fuels.

As major fossil fuel infrastructure projects gained steam into the 2010s, the petroturfing project began to take shape. Ethical Oil's campaign began in early 2011 and comprised a frequently updated blog, active social media presence, appearances across Canadian media from Levant and the organization's director, a billboard and print campaign, and even a demonstration in front of a Canadian grocery chain in

Edmonton, Alberta, that stocked bananas from a company that allegedly declared a boycott of the oil sands.[57] This model proved influential. In 2013 or so, Canada Action was formed by Cody Battershill, a blogger and realtor from Calgary described in a 2014 article by the *National Post* as "a one-man oil sands advocate" who "hopes to start a national movement."[58] Its iconography is likely the most familiar to Canadians as the producer of designs such as "I ♥ Canadian Pipelines" and "I ♥ Canadian Oil Sands" that circulated in a variety of formats, including free bumper stickers seen on large pickup trucks across Alberta; hoodies worn by politicians, including Alberta premier Jason Kenney; and advertisements under the ice at NHL games in Calgary's Saddledome stadium. In British Columbia, alongside oil sands pipelines such as the Northern Gateway, infrastructural developments related to liquefied natural gas (LNG) pipelines such as TC Energy's Coastal GasLink, proposed in 2012, occasioned the creation of British Columbians for Prosperity (BCP). BCP was formed in 2013 with the goal of bringing balanced perspectives to debates over environment and economy, which it did primarily through a series of YouTube videos. Despite claims of independence, the president of BCP, Bruce Lounds, was a management consultant who has previously worked for the oil and gas industry in a number of capacities.[59]

This momentum continued. In 2015, Oil Sands Strong was started by Fort McMurray resident and media company owner Robbie Picard under the name Canada OilSands Community as a primarily Facebook-based effort that produces and circulates pro-oil memes and, like Canada Action, sells merchandise through an online storefront. Based on early posts to its Facebook page, Oil Sands Strong seems to have started as a Fort McMurray–based outlet for distributing Canada Action merchandise. Some of the first images uploaded in 2015 show Picard with the founder of Canada Action, Cody Battershill, whereas others show Picard setting up Canada Action banners at events in Fort McMurray.[60] A photograph from 2015 also places Picard at dinner with Levant of *Ethical Oil* fame.[61] More recently, Picard was pictured beside Alberta premier Jason Kenney at the podium as Kenney announced $30 million to establish his energy "war room."[62] Finally, Rally 4 Resources formed in 2016 with a more direct focus on organizing on-the-ground events.

Alongside these avowedly grassroots groups and organizations are efforts with explicit relationships to industry or lobbying groups. Oil

Respect, for instance, began in 2016 and is formally tied to what was then called the Canadian Association of Oilwell Drilling Contractors (CAODC), the "oldest oil and gas trade association in Canada."[63] And the "voice of Canada's upstream oil and natural gas industry"—the Canadian Association of Petroleum Producers (CAPP)—has been behind the Canada's Energy Citizens campaign since its launch in 2014.[64] Canada's Energy Citizens has arguably received the most critical attention from scholars to date.[65]

The material and ideological ties shared between many of these groups are difficult to deny. Such connections were made clear when Oil Sands Strong posted a meme in 2017 that pictured logos from Rally 4 Resources, Canada Action, and Oil Sands Strong as well as the logo of Canada's Energy Citizens under text reading "with support from."[66] Moreover, Canada Action and CAPP relied on the same lawyer for their incorporation.[67] All these groups, organizations, and campaigns share degrees of dubious grassroots or citizen-run positioning and formal communicative strategies infused with right-wing, nationalist worldviews and vocabularies that interpellate audiences across platforms to draft them as soldiers for the oil culture wars. Petroturfing operates as an affective infrastructure whose media efforts reach a targeted audience primarily through online modes of participation and engagement. Across social media platforms, content, including memes and videos, is produced and circulated while start-ups such as NationBuilder offer infrastructures of legitimation and authenticity that gather user data. At the level of *content,* petroturfing is antagonistic to ENGOs; at the level of *form,* petroturfing takes lessons from ENGOs. Whereas ENGOs aim to reach a broader audience to garner support for progressive views that, to varying degrees, challenge hegemonic viewpoints surrounding the environment, petroturfing leverages a targeted new media strategy premised on participation as a means to disseminate already dominant ideas surrounding fossil fuels. Through its architectures and infrastructures, social media provides the conditions to oscillate between broad and specific audiences in an effort to gain circulation by recruiting a public of users to participate in the promotion of Canadian oil, while exploiting the close ideological relationship between "democracy" and the internet that theorists such as Jodi Dean have shown is far from the realities of its functioning.[68] Indeed, it is this democratic, participatory aspect of the internet in general and social media in particular that first fueled petroturfing.

Despite these criticisms, viewing the participatory characteristics of the internet as bringing into being a kind of new democratic condition has a long legacy that persists into the social media age. Social media platforms, especially Twitter, have been described as spaces for enacting democracy. In a content analysis of Twitter hashtags related to Canadian politics, for instance, Tamara A. Small argues that the very form of Twitter tends toward democratic modes of communication: "Twitter is a democratic media [*sic*] because it allows for democratic activism."[69] However, as Darin Barney et al. point out in the introduction to *The Participatory Condition in the Digital Age,* online participation is *both* generative and limiting; it is a space both of possibility and constraint.[70]

Petroturfing contributes to constraint by mirroring grassroots engagement through strategies such as campaigns that ask users to sign pledges and petitions as a likely means to gather data. On the Canada's Energy Citizens' home page, for instance, users are compelled to "show [their] interest and support for Canada's oil and natural gas resources" by signing an online declaration of "energy citizenship" and "spread[ing] the word" through other social media platforms (see Figure 3).[71] Much of Canada Action's content is similarly structured around a series of campaigns that involve signing pledges and petitions or showing support (see Figures 4, 5, and 6). In one campaign, users are asked to "Stand up for Canada. Sign Canada Action's pledge to fight back against irresponsible, misinformed, and deliberately harmful celebrity attacks on our country."[72] Canada Action's nationalistic framing here gestures toward the self-construed marginalization of Canadian oil by suggesting that celebrity activism against the oil sands poses a material threat to oil sands production. More important is how Canada Action invokes a distinction between elite celebrities and the masses in a manner that places class boundaries on resistance to the expansion of Canadian extractive developments. Here, Canada Action performs a widespread rhetorical gesture that frames those who advocate for a more just energy future as privileged elites, whereas those who support the oil and gas industry are the kinds of everyday Canadians we can meet on the Canada's Energy Citizens home page. By "taking the pledge," users can become those Canadians as well. Through these actions, these groups ultimately establish associations between the perception of social media as a democratic space for freedom and participation and the perception of oil as a democratic fuel tethered to notions of freedom, precisely those structures of feeling that Huber describes throughout *Lifeblood.* These structures of feeling converge in the collision between oil and social media embodied in petroturfing.

Figure 3. A 2019 screenshot of CAPP's Invitation to Take Action through Social Media widget.

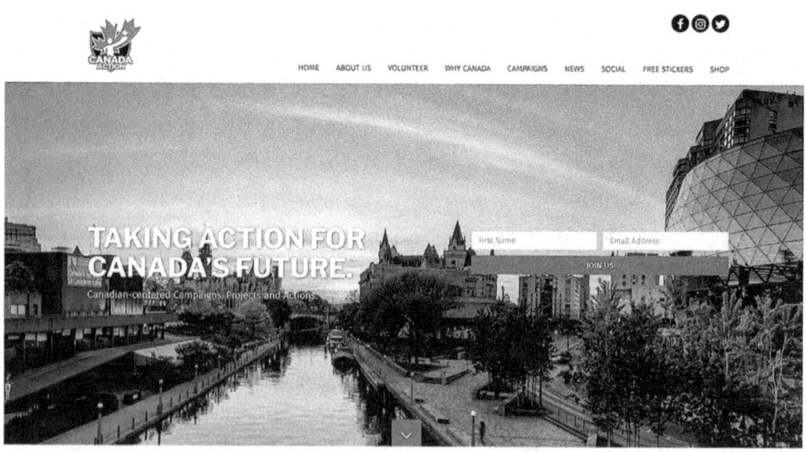

Figure 4. A 2017 screenshot of Canada Action's home page banner.

Each platform mobilized by the petroturfing project offers capacities for legitimation through circulation in differing ways. As described in the introduction, within media studies, these capacities manifest in terms of constraints and possibilities offered by a platform captured in the concept of "affordances." Although the term has been applied differently across fields of study, communications scholars Taina Bucher and Anne Helmond offer a baseline definition: "the concept of affordance is generally used to describe what material artifacts such as media technologies

Figure 5. A 2019 screenshot of Canada Action's Boycott Lush Cosmetics petition button on its website.

Figure 6. A 2019 screenshot of Canada Action's Support Canada's Oil Sands pledge button.

allow people to do."[73] In the context of new and social media, these affordances are shaped by what I have been calling new and social media's architectures, such as the algorithms that determine what kinds of content users will see, on the one hand, and their infrastructures, including the material–energetic relations and impacts of media infrastructures, on the other. This conceptual infrastructure of affordances attunes critical attention to how platforms guide user behavior and experience while shaping the meaning of content in a way that exhibits a softer version of

Marshall McLuhan's well-worn dictum: "the medium is the message."[74] Some affordances of new and social media are virtually universal. These more universal affordances can be found by turning to new and social media buzzwords: participation, networks, connectivity, and so on. Other affordances are platform dependent. Facebook, for instance, encourages engagement to posts through "reacts," buttons meant to capture the affective responses to posts, including "like," "love," "sad," and "angry," all of which influence the reach of a given post. Twitter's affordances encourage brevity in posts called "tweets" and sharing through "retweets." Brevity is embodied in a limited character count that once sat at 140, now 280, a constraint encouraging hot takes that seek retweets. And YouTube's video format is structured around channels run by users in which each video allows for engagement through comments and a "like" or "dislike" button. These three have generally been the most active platforms on which petroturfing took shape over the 2010s and will appear predominantly as the primary media examined throughout this book. Based on my observations, Facebook is the most prominently used by groups like Oil Sands Strong, although more recently efforts on YouTube have increased as the petroturfing project continues to scale up and out.

So far, my account has generally outlined what the petroturfing project has formally and discursively attempted in its early years rather than what it has achieved. If success is measured by social media activity, following, and reach, the degree to which petroturfing has been successful in shaping these structures of feeling was not significant until very recently. Followers of the social media presences in their first years were in the lower thousands across media and, in the case of Twitter, cumulative tweets of around 3,000, confirmed by the limits enforced by Twitter's API when I scraped tweets using Python scripts in 2017. Ethical Oil, for instance, had 2,728 likes on Facebook and 6,137 followers on Twitter in 2018. And before pulling the plug and removing all content from social media in 2017, BCP had 4,542 followers on Twitter. In 2020, Canada Action had 106,339 "likes" on Facebook and its sister page Oil Sands Action had 321,030. Oil Sands Strong had 87,897. Oil Respect had 60,137. And the page for CAPP's Canada's Energy Citizens campaign had 277,337. To put these numbers into perspective, the historically most influential ENGOs such as Greenpeace Canada had

276,514, while Greenpeace International had 3.1 million and the Sierra Club had 1 million.

Petroturfing entered the Canadian mediascape with a whimper, not a bang. But through this entrance a circuit was etched. Perhaps most importantly, this permanent campaign emerged in a political climate and media environment made friendly to these views from already existing efforts from right-wing think tanks, particularly the Fraser Institute, a primarily Western Canadian public policy think tank whose funders have included the Koch brothers.[75] The Fraser Institute has ties to the University of Calgary's political science department and the School of Public Policy, a group of scholars that would come to be known as the Calgary School, a framing that references the intellectual laboratory of neoliberalism, the Chicago School.[76] Levant once worked as a student intern at the Fraser Institute in the 1990s, potentially brought into the fold by senior fellow of the Fraser Institute, Tom Flanagan, a professor at the University of Calgary and Levant's former teacher. In a 2004 profile piece on Flanagan in the Canadian magazine *The Walrus* known for long-form journalism, Levant is quoted as agreeing with characterizations by the *Globe and Mail* that framed Flanagan "as the original godfather of the city's conservative intellectual mafia."[77] An early post that Ethical Oil made on its blog was a summary of a Fraser Institute report arguing that the United States should consume more Canadian oil.[78]

Situating petroturfing within this larger right-wing media ecology brings into focus the project's larger aims, purposes, audiences, and worldviews. As discussed in the introduction, through Levant, the petroturfing project also has ties to Rebel Media, Levant's own far-right news media conglomerate, which produces YouTube videos, blog posts, and other editorials that promote larger ideological views found across the petroturfing project. Most prominently, these views include a naturalization of the free market as well as an obsession with narrowly understood notions of free speech. Notably, the Ethical Oil URL currently redirects to a Rebel News page that announces plans for reviving the project. Rebel Media formed in 2015 and quickly became a key player in far-right discourses of Islamophobia, anti-globalism, white nationalism, and other fascisms that have only increased in spread and legitimacy since Donald Trump's election as U.S. president in 2016 and the rise of the alt-right in the United States and elsewhere, a rise that saw largely online movements stage on-the-ground demonstrations such as the deadly 2017 Unite the Right demonstration in Charlottesville, Virginia.[79] Social media's architectures and infrastructures have nurtured these ideologies.[80] And as the story of petroturfing, from its origins through *Ethical Oil* in 2010 to the 2019 establishment of Alberta's energy "war room," unfolds in this book, the entangled relationship between extractivism, settler colonialism, white supremacy, and the fossil economy surfaces in ways that underscore the role fossil fuels have played in deepening inequalities, fueling what Cara New Daggett, Andreas Malm, and others have come to describe as an emergent "fossil fascism."[81]

Saturating the Mediascape

Just as petroturfing reproduces material–extractive processes of oil sands production and refinement in terms of energy imaginaries, it also takes structural cues from the speculative economy of pipeline proposals. History shows that this speculative economy is fueled by persistence that recognizes while not all proposals land, inertia takes shape. Petroturfing follows the political–economic contours of Canada's fossil economy—the ebbs and flows of boom and bust. The animating goals of this first phase of petroturfing in the first half of the 2010s, which is the phase I primarily focus on in the following four chapters, become clear: to establish a foundation for a more effective permanent campaign at some future conjuncture by fanning the flames of an oil culture war in the present. Simpson's "lubricity" is apt in describing the affective mood of this speculative mode adopted across the petroturfing project or, indeed, its means. Saturation names its end. The more lubricated the condition, the less friction, the more potential for saturation, a condition embodied in the aesthetics of oil's materiality on the one hand and its political economy on the other. From the vantage point of the present, the conjuncture that this saturation anticipated and influenced turned out to be one of a rising "new" right alongside an "old" right whose material and ideological links with fossil fuel interests in Canada have been detailed in work by Kathleen Raso and Robert J. Neubauer.[82]

The formative episodes in the past and present symbolic life of Canadian oil that I recount throughout this chapter are a crucial historical and conceptual backdrop for the closer examination of petroturfing that follows. My examination details how petroturfing refines Canadian oil across economic, social, and ecological spheres as the terms and conditions of the oil culture wars have become more pronounced. Beginning with the Ethical Oil project, petroturfing emerged in order to shape energy imaginaries in the domain of energy consciousness for the benefit of the Canadian oil and gas industry. What follows surfaces this constellation of entangled media efforts that constitute the petroturfing project in order to chart a path toward a future otherwise that begins with moving beyond the deadlock of dueling reactive energy imaginaries across these economic, social, and ecological registers. The economic—an overdetermined relation of fossil capital—and the petrocultural promises that underwrite the future the fossil economy offers are first in line to receive scrutiny.

2

PETROCULTURE'S PROMISE
OIL EXECUTIVE EPISTEMOLOGIES AND THE ECONOMIC IMAGINARY

Canadian prime minister Justin Trudeau delivered a keynote address at an energy conference in Houston, Texas, in 2017. The talk rationalized the ongoing expansion of the oil sands and, accordingly, expressed a strong commitment to the fossil economy now and in the future. "No country would find 173 billion barrels of oil and just leave it in the ground," he told an audience of oil and gas executives in a quip that made headlines. "The resource will be developed. Our job is to ensure this is done responsibly, safely and sustainably." Trudeau's comments were well received. The 1,200 people in attendance gave Trudeau a standing ovation, which, according to CBC reporter Peter Zimonjic's coverage of the event, is an uncommon occurrence at the conference.[1] Trudeau's comments were arguably so well received by the crowd because they sounded a lot like the words of an oil and gas executive. Compare Trudeau's statements to those made by president and CEO of Calgary-based energy transportation company Enbridge, Al Monaco, as he accepted the 2017 Canadian Energy Person of the Year award from the Energy Council of Canada. Monaco closed his speech with an optimistic meditation, musing how "North America has the potential to be an energy export juggernaut," but to realize this future "we need to get beyond the polarized debate" and establish "a vision that acknowledges that energy and the environment can go hand in hand."[2]

Given how deeply oil saturates the contemporary social and political imagination, the resemblance of Trudeau's statements to an oil and gas executive's is hardly surprising. More important to highlight than its expectedness, however, is how his comment subscribes to the very logics underwriting the realism that Ezra Levant deployed in his Parliament speech. Behind Trudeau's comments is a gesture to extractivist impulses as common sense. And this common sense both Levant and Trudeau invoke is one predicated upon the economic promises of prosperity that resource extraction generates.

Trudeau's remarks also express a commonly invoked point of tension that will reappear throughout this book—that between environment and economy. Even as oil and gas executives such as Monaco suggest that "energy and the environment can go hand in hand," opposition between environment and economy remains an ideological front of the oil culture wars. Unlike Trudeau, the previous Stephen Harper administration was characteristically less than interested in expressing how environmental values and economic rationalities can be reconciled. During Harper's reign, the claim that activists are, by any means necessary, attempting to destroy or stifle the employment of everyday Canadians by blocking industrial development became an essential utterance for advocates of fossil fuel production in Canada, including government officials. Recall a frequently cited 2012 statement regarding the accelerated expansion of Canada's energy market made by then minister of natural resources Joe Oliver. "Unfortunately," Oliver writes, "there are environmental and other radical groups that would seek to block this opportunity to diversify our trade." "Their goal," he continues, "is to stop any major project no matter what the cost to Canadian families in lost jobs and economic growth. No forestry. No mining. No oil. No gas. No more hydro-electric dams."[3] Such rhetoric further cements rifts between allegedly idealist, inconsiderate activists and realist, family-oriented working publics—average Canadian citizens that this discourse brings into being, premised, as this discourse is, on concepts such as national belonging and progress. Those who oppose oil sands expansionism, the story goes, oppose the interests of Canada as a nation and its citizenry. Views such as Oliver's have fed Canada's repressive state apparatus as, for instance, the Royal Canadian Mounted Police (RCMP) stated in a leaked 2014 critical infrastructure intelligence assessment that "there is a growing, highly organized and well-financed, anti-Canadian petroleum movement that consists of peaceful activists, militants and violent extremists, who are opposed to society's reliance on fossil fuels."[4]

According to dominant government and industry logics, the only realistic view in the immediate future is something like the following: *the economic benefits outweigh the environmental risks.* Energy realism, in other words, trumps energy idealism. This chapter examines the economic imaginary of the petroturfing project and argues that a crucial aim of petroturfing is to curate what I call *oil executive epistemologies.* Oil executive epistemologies take shape in petroturfing across three interdependent registers, which I turn to after detailing the stakes and consequences of their widespread adoption. Most pertinently, these stakes and consequences are tied to the flattening of class relations that make equivalent the interests of oil and gas workers and everyday Canadians on the one hand with the interests of oil and gas executives on the other. Oil executive epistemologies, I show, are first consolidated through a resource–economy–nation nexus. Throughout petroturfing, a discursive construction of resource nationalism foregrounds the necessity of Canadian ownership of and benefit from resources, yet the vast majority of these projects remain tethered to global finance. Oil executive epistemologies strategically overlook this tension by relying on an internalized logic of economic rationality that lays claim to the future in the name of the fossil economy. Futurity is thus an essential component of the cultural work to which petroturfing aspires, and the second register through which oil executive epistemologies take hold is in the adoption of speculative cost–benefit scenarios as factual, irrefutable modes of discourse. Finally, I explore how oil executive epistemologies are curated through appeals to balance that end up privileging dominant extractive views under the guise of fairness and reasonability.

Thinking Like an Oil Executive

A dominant narrative that travels in the promotional cultures of oil and gas suggests that extraction both produces *and* distributes wealth not only for oil companies, executives, and shareholders but for industry workers, communities, and the regions or nations in which those companies operate. This seductive characteristic of the fossil economy saturates oil sands promotion. Canada, and Alberta in particular, the narrative suggests, is not only a petro*culture*—a society in which everyday patterns of life are primarily centered on and made possible by the consumption of fossil fuels—but a petro*economy* as well. The latter formation describes an economic condition in which the sustained employment of its citizens, the continued operation of its schools and hospitals, and so on is fundamentally made possible by oil extraction. Embedded within this narrative is a teleological insistence on the unavoidability of fossil fuels that we encountered in the previous chapter as petrocapitalist realism. Take, for example, the premise of a series of blog posts by CAPP's magazine *Context: Energy Examined* titled "Petroleum in Real Life." In this series, writers feature an everyday object whose material makeup depends on hydrocarbons. From running shoes to N-95 masks, writers remind us that hydrocarbons, and thus the oil and gas industry, make the materials of a comfortable, healthy life possible.[5] Enbridge's "Life Takes Energy" slogan and advertising campaign similarly universalizes and naturalizes fossil fuels by using the signifier of energy to abstract the historically specific energy sources of oil and gas into forms equivalent with human kinetic energy.[6] Without fossil fuels, life as we know it would not be possible, a tautological truism of sorts that doesn't mean we should carry on that lifestyle.

This insistence on material and financial dependency on oil is strategic. Persistent reminders of this dependency contribute to the atmosphere of foreclosure that I detailed in the previous chapter. Trudeau's rationalization that this chapter opens with is a cynical demonstration of the effectiveness of the ubiquity and dependency narrative, a narrative underwritten by an economic imaginary convinced by the promises of the fossil economy. Promises of jobs, employment, and a vibrant economy are cornerstones to the most convincing reasoning for public support of and consensus for the expansion of oil sands developments in Canada. Promises such as these shaped and continue to shape the discourse regarding the collective benefits of these projects. And this is precisely where their discursive value resides, rhetorically operating as an appeal to the economy. Pausing on the conceptual infrastructure of the notion of a promise proves instructive here. The *Oxford English Dictionary* defines the act: "To make a promise of (something), to give verbal assurance of; to undertake or commit oneself to do or refrain from (a specified thing or act) or to give or bestow (a specified thing)."[7]

Assurance, commitment, and giving: this vocabulary of fossil fuels in Canada lays claims to future relations by shaping energy consciousness. In its efforts to secure the future of Canadian fossil capital, petroturfing employs this vocabulary to curate an economistic understanding of energy built on a depoliticized form of resource nationalism.

Understanding and referencing the economy as a *thing* is a relatively recent discursive condition. Yet the ability to conceptualize the economy in this way has become wholly naturalized in broader political discourse as well as in quotidian, everyday life. This naturalization is evident in Trudeau's extractive impetus as well as Oliver's. Both Trudeau and Oliver place the environment and economy as tangible objects of equal material footing. Political theorist Timothy Mitchell offers a genealogy of the economy's emergence as a tangible, actually existing object. He argues that this emergence brought into being a condition of *economentality* (*pace* Foucault's governmentality), which is "a way to bring the future into government."[8] Mitchell explains that, by 1948, "references to this object in government and newspapers were starting to appear in a routine, repetitive way that made the economy appear for the first time as a matter of fact." Moreover, "it was no longer always necessary to explain what the term meant or to qualify it in some way."[9] This internalization gave way to a conflation of interests between nation and economy on microscopic and macroscopic scales of relation, resulting in a kind of collective consciousness that understands, in the first instance, that what is good for the economy is good for the nation. "The economy," Mitchell writes,

> would embed people's political lives in the future by bringing them to calculate according to its representation. It would locate them in relation to a future formed in a particular way, as a balance, or trade-off, between forces now inscribed as equivalents in the structure of national accounts, with wage earners/consumers on one side and business and banking on the other.[10]

In this way, economentality makes possible the types of metrics that birthed comparative global measures of production as progress such as the gross domestic product (GDP). And through these metrics, economentality inscribes a particular kind of entanglement between economy and nation in public consciousness.

These quantified measures of progress underwritten by the economy as a thing inform the broader promises of petroculture that petroturfing mobilizes. Across the petroturfing project and adjacent promotional discourses, the interests of Canada's fossil economy are made parallel to the interests of the nation and its citizenry by tapping into existing understandings of the economy as a tangible object. Moreover, these promises rely on this conceptual linking of government or nation and economy that Mitchell outlines, all of which is amplified within a neoliberalism that makes claims to a specific vision of the future shaped by speculation regarding the benefits of the production and consumption of Canadian oil.

In the previous chapter, I provided an account of the historical context in which the conflict between dirty and ethical oil emerged. I argued that this conflict ultimately solidified the terms and conditions of the oil culture wars in Canada. Offering further detail on how this war has been waged, political economist Anna Zalik's examination of the neoliberalization of Canada's oil economy links these economic relations and processes with the epistemological struggles that occur alongside them. She describes the fronts on which a prosperous future for the Canadian oil and gas industry has been secured through regulatory capture. In terms of the economic characteristics of regulatory capture, Zalik points to clauses of the North American Free Trade Agreement (NAFTA) "that in part denationalize control over exports to the United States and subject socioenvironmental regulations to the terms of private contracts."[11] A consequence of neoliberalization in post-NAFTA Canada results in a scenario in which

> the western Canadian provinces engaged in oil and gas production—Alberta, British Columbia, and Saskatchewan—are consequently in a race to the bottom, both in terms of revenue policy and environmental protection so as to secure operators to extract and sell their resources largely to external markets, until recently primarily the United States.[12]

Part of this capture, Zalik suggests, also involves subduing what she calls "oppositional knowledges" that resist fossil fuel expansionism. Such subdual has been achieved in part through the generation of conflicting epistemologies that challenge growing resistance to Canada's fossil economy.

Citing the Ethical Oil campaign and lobbying efforts from CAPP as examples, Zalik describes how the future of Canadian oil has been contested through the establishment of "a kind of epistemological battle concerning tar sands expansion."[13] As Zalik puts it in a concluding sentence, "the relations between those resisting the expansion of the frontier in unconventionals and those seeking to promote extractive industry collectively shape energy futures in which powerful business interests, alongside their shareholders, have a stake."[14] The intentional epistemological conflict between resistance and expansion brought the oil culture wars into being in Canada, which shows how and why petroturfing emerged alongside concerted efforts to get Canadian oil to global markets.

Zalik's reading of the encounter between the knowledges of oppositional actors and industry proponents as epistemological battles offers a precise entry point into addressing the conditions under which petroturfing shapes energy consciousness. Although Ethical Oil receives only a passing mention with CAPP, Zalik's vocabulary of capture puts pressure on the epistemological dimensions of Canada's potential hydrocarbon futures. These epistemological battles are the grounds on which the petroturfing project both demarcates and intervenes. But, as I pointed out in the introduction, there is an important distinction to be made between CAPP's efforts and those of Ethical Oil in light of my naming of petroturfing. While both CAPP and Ethical Oil reproduce the same dominant industry narratives surrounding the promises of Canada's fossil economy, they do so with a clearly defined (if questionable) difference with regard to their relation to the oil and gas industry. Whereas CAPP is explicitly tied to the oil and gas industry as a lobbying group, Ethical Oil instead frames itself as a grassroots initiative. In this way, Ethical Oil constructs a political discursive scenario in which it serves as an actor generating modes of oppositional knowledges to what it disingenuously construes as dominant voices of resistance. The more this distanced framing circulates, the more legitimate it appears, which serves as another means to generate wider support for these views because these views are expressed as though they were coming from a source closer in proximity to the petroturfing project's audience.

A crucial dimension of the petroturfing project is to interpellate its audience through a shared subjectivity, which requires a shared epistemological footing. In memes, including those from Canada Action that champion the economic benefits of Energy East and Oil Sand Strong's comparison between the nation-building character of railways and pipelines (see Figures 7 and 8), the expansion of the fossil economy is framed as in the best interest of the nation and its citizenry. Embedded within these memes are, first, a hail in the sense of Althusser's formulation of ideological interpellation, and then a set of expressions that constitute a shared epistemology. But what is this shared epistemology? Patrick McCurdy has shown in his work on CAPP's Canada's Energy Citizens campaign how a kind of petronationalism that fuses patriotism with extraction is manicured through the campaign in form and content.[15]

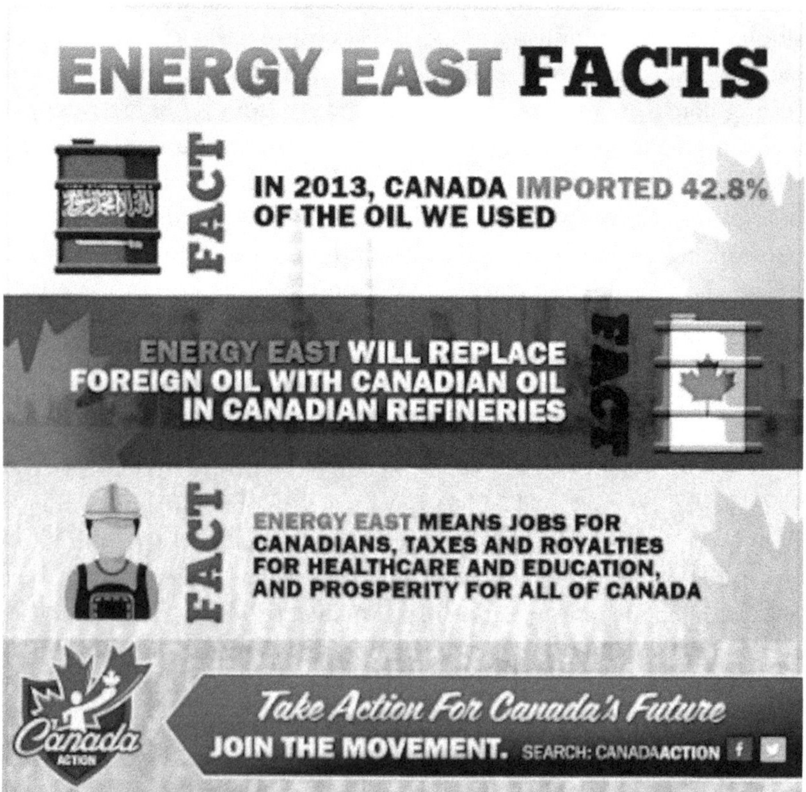

Figure 7. A Facebook meme created in 2014 by Canada Action that highlights Canada's dependence on foreign oil and claims that the Energy East pipeline will create "prosperity for all of Canada."

And Shane Gunster's work on "extractive populism" likewise pivots on the nation as a determinant site through which campaigns such as CAPP's operate as well as how we might challenge these efforts.[16] However, nationalism, as I show in the next section, only plays a select, strategic if overdetermined role in petroturfing's larger energy imaginary.

Gestures to the job-creating powers of oil sands development are as common as invocations of the nation. And these economic promises provide a strong rationale for popular support of the fossil economy. But while the petroturfing project often invokes figures of blue-collar oil sands laborers, known colloquially in the field as "roughnecks," it is neither *through* nor *for* this figure from which these ways of knowing

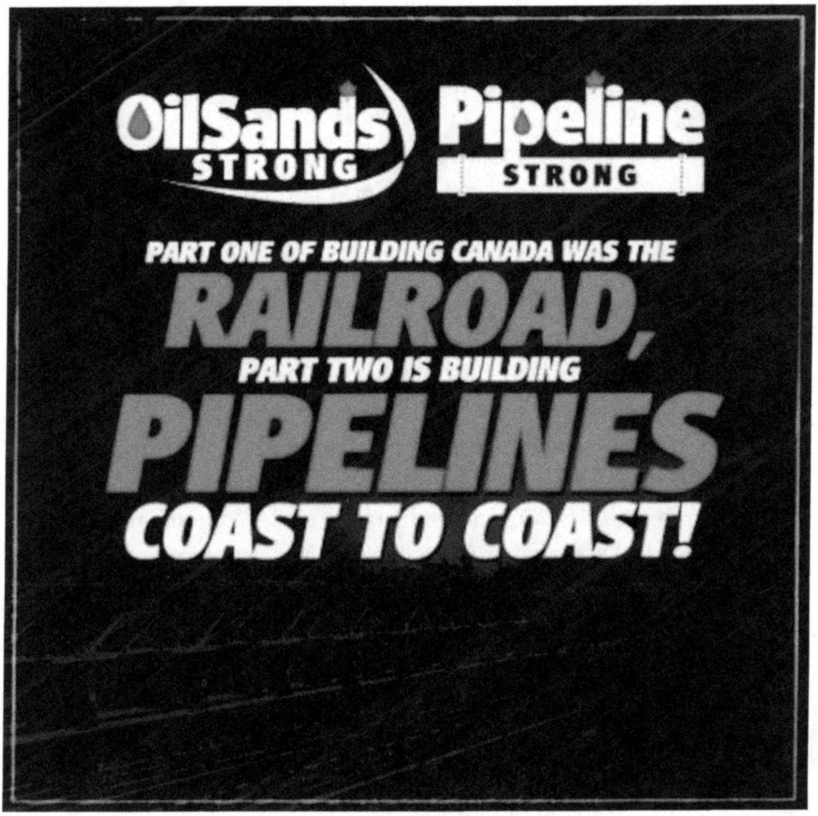

Figure 8. A Facebook meme created in 2017 by Oil Sands Strong that likens the nation-building character of pipeline building with the Canadian Pacific Railway.

emerge. Instead, petroturfing uses the roughneck as an avatar for the macroscopic relations of the fossil economy in order to transform these working-class affects and desires into a worldview that primarily serves the interests of fossil capital rather than the interests of oil workers, which I examine more fully in the next chapter. In these efforts, the two interests are strategically folded into one another to garner support from the working class vis-à-vis petroturfing. Countering the flattening at work here, I call this way of knowing an *oil executive epistemology.*

To think like an oil executive in the context of energy epistemologies is to think in the first instance of the macroeconomic activity that further development generates. Thinking this way internalizes the abstract forces and principles of market and to influence action in the interests of such forces and principles. For oil executives, politicians, agents, and architects of the fossil economy, engaging the world through an oil executive epistemology makes sense. It is simply good business and an act of self-preservation.

But for the everyday Canadian who serves as petroturfing's imagined audience, the assumption that what is good for the fossil economy is good for Canadians is neither a straightforward nor immediately sympathetic position. This position requires careful messaging that channels existing, deeply engrained national mythologies of settler colonial frontierism and resource extraction to establish a unified positioning that frames extraction as both a national and an individual good. And such unification obscures the classed differences and antagonisms between CEOs and roughnecks who occupy the boardroom and the Patch, which is a term locals use to describe the oil sands region. Paralleling the extraction of surplus value that occurs in laboring under capitalism, petroturfing symbolically extracts working-class authenticity from roughnecks to homogenize the interests of labor and capital, as if workers had more in common with their bosses than with a larger public of activists calling for a just energy transition. Scaling out and circulating this oil executive epistemology to become a kind of common sense, then, involves naturalizing the relations of the fossil economy. As a kind of economentality, oil executive epistemologies constrain energy imaginaries to primarily economic ones. Political philosophers Pierre Dardot and Christian Laval theorize how a core characteristic of neoliberalism's affective sway emerges from its insistence on internalizing the principles of the market through the figuration of society as an enterprise.[17] The affective sway of petroturfing is likewise achieved by channeling this mode of market-based subjectivity to favor the oil and gas industry. To naturalize these relations, petroturfing constructs a resource–economy–nation nexus, circulates speculative cost–benefit analyses as facts, and appeals to balance in energy debates that end up privileging already dominant relations.

Resource–Economy–Nation: Oil Imaginaries between Economentality and Petronationalism

When the Calgary-based Canada Action went fully live on the web in 2014, the tagline on its home page offered a future-oriented commitment to the building of a more prosperous nation through the construction of energy infrastructure and general support of the oil and gas industry. The tagline first read "Taking Action for a Better Canada," was then revised to "Taking Action for Canada's Future" sometime in early 2015, and was finally settled on as "Taking action in support of our vital natural resource sector" in 2020.[18] Although these revisions speak to uncertainty in messaging, with each minor tweaking, consistent undercurrents reveal a governing ambition of Canada Action: to articulate a vision of the future in which economic imaginaries are bound to national ones and energy infrastructure projects are understood to be expressions of both economic and resource nationalism. The campaigns launched as part of Canada Action's formation are telling in terms of this resource–economy–nation nexus. Centered primarily on gathering support in the form of petitions for the two most contentious yet most promising pipelines proposed at the time—Enbridge's Northern Gateway and TC Energy's Energy East projects—the campaigns performed the ideological work of national unification through resource nationalism derived from the promises of the fossil economy. In its call for support of the Northern Gateway was the declaration that "Canada deserves full value for our resources."[19] In the call for support of Energy East, Canada Action similarly declared that "Canadian Oil Should Benefit All Canadians," describing the project as "shovel ready" and "set to create 10,000 well-paying jobs for Canadians" that "will generate ten billion dollars in tax revenue and royalties, raising the standard of living for all Canadians by paying for better healthcare, education, or tax cuts for Canadian families."[20] Through the group's social media presence, these calls were reinforced and circulated across broader networks with participation of a wider public. One of Canada Action's first tweets, active before its home page, linked to an opinion piece published in the *National Post* that spelled out the economic benefits of the oil sands. The tweet read: "Ontario to see $63 billion in economic benefits from #oilsands between 2010 to 2035, creating 65,520 jobs."[21]

Highlighting Ontario's benefit from oil sands activity is a significant gesture in the context of resource nationalism. The tweet and op-ed it links invoke a long-standing historical contention between eastern Canadian provinces, particularly in Ontario and Quebec, and western Canadian ones. The experience of this contention from the position of the West is often referred to as Western alienation, which describes the affective expression of a perceived political and economic underrepresentation of the West in national politics. Such experience has recently erupted in calls by right-wing figures for a Brexit-style secession called Wexit, and the formation of a federal party whose aim is secession. A primary motive for Wexit is to accelerate the construction of pipelines and further development of the oil sands, which it sees more eastern provinces such as Ontario and Quebec holding back. In articulating a resource nationalism that framed the bounty of Alberta's oil sands in national rather than regional terms, Canada Action established a unifying discourse around economic benefits of pipeline projects in the face of historical friction between the West and the East. Gestures such as these inflect the project of petroturfing as a foundational impulse that reveals how a particular kind of resource logic bound to relations of economy and nation is construed as the means through which a collectively prosperous future is made.

Questions of nation have shaped Canadian petropolitics and economics from the early days of its oil and gas industry. Initial development of the oil sands in the late 1960s and early 1970s was done in concert with multinational oil company interests. In this way, the "Canadianness" of the oil sands has been, and arguably continues to be, under question. Political economist Larry Pratt's 1976 deep dive into the oil sands' formative years, *The Tar Sands: Syncrude and the Politics of Oil,* reveals, among other things, the rise of a new bourgeoisie in Alberta, and how U.S. and multinational interests shaped the oil sands as an economically viable source of extraction that used public funds to finance its early stages. "It is the handful of multinational companies, holding almost exclusive leasing privileges in the tar sands, that are dictating the conditions for their development," he writes.[22] What Pratt's book exposes is perhaps unsurprising given Canada's historical and, arguably, ongoing status as a staples economy. "Contrary to that comfortable myth [that American corporations are not directly involved in Canada's politics]," Pratt argues, "scrutiny of the politics of Syncrude reveals that the multinational companies which own so much of our economic wealth are also highly purposeful, ruthless institutions engaged in what can only be called a struggle for power in Canada."[23]

Pratt's analysis rings truer almost fifty years later. Rather than being a Canadian venture—as the rhetoric across the petroturfing project and promotional oil sands mediascape suggests—the oil sands are instead a planetary one. The names of multinational oil companies proliferate across active lease maps, superimposed on a cartographic grid of transnational extractivism. While this transnational condition has, to some degree, transformed since the 2015 decline in oil prices with, for example, Royal Dutch Shell effectively ceasing operation and selling off its assets, there remains strong international presence through corporations such as BP and PetroChina.

Despite the planetary character of the oil sands, there continues to be both overt and implicit tendencies of resource nationalism that ascribe regional or national identities to the oil sands. How and when the oil sands appear as Canadian or Albertan is telling on these terms. When proposed pipelines traverse provincial boundaries, regional contention often shapes debates and outcomes. In the promotional saga surrounding the Northern Gateway Pipeline, which would have traveled from Edmonton, Alberta, to British Columbia's west coast, Enbridge's major advertising campaign played on this trope of regionalism through a series of profiles on BC-based employees. These profiles were circulated through print, billboard, television, and web-based video advertisements that emphasized employees' connections to place and, in turn, default concern for local environments.[24] On June 19, 2014, for instance, British Columbians for Prosperity (BCP) retweeted Canada Action, which claimed that the "#NorthernGateway would be B.C.'s biggest private investment" and would generate $1.2 billion in tax revenue.[25] Earlier in

2013, BCP retweeted an infographic made by the Canadian Energy Pipeline Association that showed "how #pipelines benefit Canadians across the country" directly to the official Northern Gateway Twitter account.[26] Here, the networks of mutual legitimation and reinforcement come in to view, illustrating how pipeline projects are simultaneously understood as regional and national ventures.

Selectively framing oil and its infrastructures as distinctly Canadian creates an imagined community that makes equivalent resource, economy, and nation. As Canadian communications theorist Darin Barney points out in his detailed account of the infrastructural apparatuses of Canadian national identity, since the confederation of Canada was achieved through the construction of the Canadian Pacific Railway (CPR), infrastructure has historically served as a material means upon which a coherent Canadian identity rests. Citing historian Benedict Anderson's influential approach to the nation as an "imagined community," Barney instead argues that Canada as a nation is not so much imagined but constituted through nationally binding material infrastructures.[27] This infrastructural undercurrent of national identity travels from the railway of the past to the pipeline of the present. Indeed, nation building was leveraged as a promotional strategy and justification for the CPR and continues to be a consistent talking point for pipeline projects, as Oil Sands Strong's Facebook meme cited earlier in this chapter shows (Figure 8). Yet there is a palpable tension in the distribution of costs and benefits at regional and national levels that shapes the processes of proposal and approval. Tensions between British Columbia and Alberta grew surrounding the construction of the TMX in 2018, for instance, which would eventually erupt into what was described by news media as a trade war.[28] In response to BC's hesitance, Alberta banned the import of British Columbian wine.

Regional conflicts such as these—not to mention modes of Indigenous resistance to extractive projects that are animated by the protection of lands and waters in traditional and ancestral territories—draw attention to the friction generated by the unevenly felt experiences of resource extraction's costs and benefits. One avenue to soften these territorial frictions is to address these unevenly felt experiences through promises of economic benefit that evoke a kind of resource nationalism. Founded on pillars of economentality, a veil of progressive resource nationalism is cast over developments of the oil sands megaproject by petroturfing and adjacent promotional discourses to further naturalize the economic view as the only realistic one. Although I have employed the term throughout this chapter, it is worth defining more thoroughly here. In the vocabularies of political science, resource nationalism "is a strategy where governments use economic nationalist policies to improve local returns from resource industries."[29] There is no single resource nationalism; there are many resource nationalisms. But progressive or radical manifestations are most commonly associated with Latin American postneoliberal governments, particularly those tied to the Pink Tide, a larger left-wing turn in Latin American politics that began with the 1998 elections of Hugo Chávez in Venezuela and Lula da Silva in Brazil.

These particular resource nationalisms, in other words, describe mechanisms not only to "increase local returns" through state control but to do so with principles informed by a mode of redistribution of wealth generated by extraction. Control over resources by the nation-state in these cases was motivated by a pursuit to get a fair deal for resources after years of struggle. Political theorist Thea Riofrancos sees in the radical resource nationalism of the Pink Tide an effort to redistribute wealth without going after the riches of the ruling class. "So long as there was an influx of oil rents," Riofrancos argues, "the income of the poor could be increased without expropriating the wealth of the rich."[30] In the case of Ecuador, Riofrancos details, ongoing extraction has led to conflict between anti-extractivist movements and what she describes as petronationalism. But even if the realities of Latin American resource nationalism are not quite as radical as promised—particularly as it relates to continued impacts of extraction on Indigenous peoples and their exclusion from the decision-making process—the intentions and mechanisms are attempts to address the inequities that often follow in the wake of resource extraction.

Petroturfing taps into these energies of national control and public benefit to circulate oil executive epistemologies. Yet resource governance in Alberta is a far cry from postneoliberal Latin America. First, Alberta has extremely low royalty rates and a scheme that favors industry. This fact was true in the time of Pratt's *Tar Sands* and it remains true in the time of *Petroturfing.* These low rates are a result of attempts to create a friendly environment for exploration and investment by extractive enterprise. Former Alberta leader of the opposition Kevin Taft details how, for instance, companies are obligated to pay 1 percent of gross revenues "until the investors had recovered the full capital cost of their investment, at which point it climbed to 25 per cent of net revenues."[31] "A 1 per cent royalty is virtually a gift to the industry," Taft argues.[32] This royalty structure remained virtually unaltered even after a review from the center-left New Democratic Party (NDP) in 2015, which won that same year in a historically unprecedented election that disrupted Progressive Conservative's reign for the first time in forty-four years. This is to say that the resource–economy–nation nexus privileges the resource–economy aspect of the formation. Nevertheless, the promises of the fossil economy are expressed most concretely in petroturfing's first wave through a factual imagination that leans on figures from speculative future projections as if they were settled facts of the present.

Cost–Benefit Lines of Sight and the Facts of the Future Perfect

Returning to Canada Action's early tweet provides grounds from which to more fully explore the factual imaginaries that underwrite oil executive epistemologies and the circuits of legitimation that petroturfing employs. Recall that the tweet cited two figures from an op-ed regarding benefits the province of Ontario will receive from increased oil sands activity in the coming decades—one figure detailing general economic benefits and one specifying jobs created. Factual imaginaries underwritten by modes of quantification such as these perform two important roles in relation to the process of legitimation through circulation. First, quantification like this expresses certainty about an inherently uncertain future. Second, the circulation of these figures from official, top-down avenues, including government and industry alongside channels from "below" such as petroturfing, performs a dual function of reinforcement. Through circulation, the authority of the quantified figures themselves also reinforces the authority of alternative channels for distributing oil executive epistemologies such as petroturfing.

Speculative reports from which these numbers are extracted are circulated as if they were settled facts. The early tweet from Canada Action illustrates this oft-employed gesture in which numbers are extracted from unspecified sources and cited as certain futures of economic bounty. In the *National Post* op-ed hyperlinked by Canada Action, journalist Jesse Kline vaguely claims that "one study estimated that Ontario see $63-billion in economic benefits from oil sands projects between 2010 and 2035—creating 65,520 jobs in the province."[33] These numbers likely come from a 2011 report produced by the Canadian Energy Research Institute (CERI) titled *Economic Impacts of New Oil Sands Projects in Alberta (2010–2035),* which offers a future scenario generated through a multiregional input/output (I/O) model. This model performs two major steps to arrive at these numbers. First, it takes stock of existing investments using I/O tables provided by StatCan, Canada's national statistics agency, and then it makes a series of forecasts based on predictions of future investments and operations that use these numbers generated in the first step.[34]

Funded primarily by CAPP, the government of Alberta, and Natural Resources Canada, the CERI "is an independent, registered charitable organization" that "actively studies the most relevant energy issues affecting Canadians so that decision-makers can make sound decisions to help move Canada forward." The organization also hosts events, including an annual conference at which delegates can "enjoy golf, networking and an unrivaled technical program."[35] In a 2019–20 annual report, CERI's commitment to objectivity wavers. Calling upon readers for financial support and outlining the impacts of that support, CERI describes its contribution to energy debates. "In a country *weighed down by opposing views* on critical energy issues," the report reads, "CERI research enriches conversations by providing fact-based studies which serve as legitimate, trustworthy sources of information."[36] Here is a sweeping delegitimization of oppositional views toward oil sands developments, which are framed as a national burden, in turn as untrustworthy and divisive. The same page claims that "CERI is not influenced by funding or sponsorship bias."[37] While the tension here between subjectivity and objectivity does not necessarily call in to question the methods of CERI or its figures, it does reveal some of CERI's ideological cards as the organization arguably expresses epistemological alliances with dominant industry perceptions of the oil culture wars, namely that resistance to Canada's fossil economy is unrealistic and unreasonable on the one hand, and not motivated by fact-based understandings of energy relations on the other.

At the corporate level, reports that offer figures such as direct jobs created are produced as part of a mandated process for establishing a larger economic rationale for a given project that, ultimately, hopes to illustrate that the environmental risks and consequences are less than the economic reward. In Canada, official reports that detail environmental and economic impacts are submitted to the National Energy Board (NEB) as part of an application process. The NEB is a body attached to the federal government that has been renamed the Canadian Energy Regulator (CER) as of 2019. For Energy East, for instance, TC Energy claimed that the project would generate ten thousand direct full-time-equivalent (FTE) jobs across the country over its development and construction phases, as well as one thousand sustained full-time jobs over its forty-year operation.[38]

Other independent or think-tank reports add more figures to these potential futures. In the case of the Fraser Institute, these reports often echo existing industry narratives. A report from 2013 directly picks up on Harper's vision of Canada becoming an "energy superpower." The authors note that the term has historically been used to describe those companies and countries that control enough production to influence the price of oil. Opting to use the term *superproducer* instead, the authors detail what such a future would look like for Canada. "Growth in the production of oil sands bitumen alone could be contributing $50 billion per year in royalties by 2033 (current dollars) compared with $4.5 billion in 2011," the authors write.[39] But not all independent reports paint such an economically rosy future for Canada's fossil economy. A report authored by Ian Goodman and Brigid Rowan in collaboration with Simon Fraser University's Centre for Public Policy Research in 2014 calls into question many of the numbers projected by the then-owner of the Trans Mountain pipeline, Kinder Morgan, in their assessment of the impact of the expansion. Goodman and Rowan suggest that projected figures would be roughly half to a third of what Kinder Morgan projects.[40] Differing methodologies produce different figures, and the certainty of the future is called into question as differing scenarios conflict. Yet the cost–benefit imagination becomes the central avenue through which oil executive epistemologies are spread.

Promises such as these are uttered in a future perfect tense, a grammar that figures a future in only one certain, predetermined path. This future perfect tense, anthropologist Kregg Hetherington argues, is the tense of infrastructure in general.[41] In her work on settler late liberalism, a formulation that describes the governmentality of contemporary settler states, cultural anthropologist Elizabeth A. Povinelli critically reads what she calls social tenses as powerful modes of expression and understanding that secure the settler present and its future by relegating Indigenous peoples to the past through a variety of discursive strategies that hinge upon tense.[42] Centering the power of tense in this context reveals how a fossil future—simultaneously settler colonial and extractive capitalist in its orientations—is secured through the petrocapitalist realist prefiguration of a determinate fossil future.

Yet the future is inherently uncertain. And so facts as promises delivered in the future perfect tense are a crucial target of critique in which other facts are introduced as a means to reveal the imperfect undercurrents of this future perfect tense. Literary and cultural theorist Jon Gordon explores these competing discourses of facts at work in the struggle over the signification of Alberta's oil sands in *Unsustainable Oil*. Troubling the rhetorical appeals to facts of the future so prevalent in pro–oil sands discourses, Gordon traces the strategies at work in such appeals. Facts are deployed to bring balance and objectivity to a debate, yet the history of the emergence of facts *as such* shows how appeals to facts in petroturfing are a politically charged endeavor, furthering the kinds of economistic absolutism at the heart of the neoliberal project. Facts are not a universal, objective, or apolitical language, as the competing facts and counterfacts of oil sands discourses that Gordon examines reveal.[43] Cultural historian and literary critic Mary Poovey's work on the genealogy of what she describes as the "modern fact" shows us the economically and politically charged history of the emergence of the contemporary understanding of facts and their now immanent authority. Facts as we understand them today are bound to a particular late nineteenth-century epistemological history that understood numbers as both accurate and precise modes of representation, a kind of hard realism we have seen throughout this book as intentionally drawn upon in petroturfing. "Numbers have come to epitomize the modern fact," Poovey writes, "because they have come to seem preinterpretive or even somehow noninterpretive at the same time that they have become the bedrock of systematic knowledge."[44] In this way, facts qua numbers become a privileged, irrefutable form. By leaning in on the cultural authority that numbers carry, the concentrated example of a single tweet from Canada Action brings the networks of mutual legitimation into clearer view at the levels of form and content. A report, op-ed, and tweet coalesce and offer a lesson in how legitimation through circulation functions on the one hand, and how oil executive epistemologies are spread through the contemporary mediascape on the other hand.

A Balancing Act: Oil Executive Epistemologies as Energy Realisms

The resource–economy–nation nexus and the factual imagination that determine the shape of oil executive epistemologies rely on the formation of a set of mutually intertwined, mutually reinforcing viewpoints. These viewpoints are circulated to become a kind of internalized "common sense" among audiences. As the previous sections in this chapter illustrate, these viewpoints echo more general neoliberal subjectivities saturated by oil, which include making equivalent and individualizing the health of the economy and the nation, which are articulated as facts that underwrite the formation of oil executive epistemologies. In the first wave of petroturfing—from 2010 to 2015 or so—these perspectives were often put forward in the name of balance. This type of framing can also be seen in CERI's emphasis on the weight of oppositional voices on the one hand, and its self-expression of objectivity on the other. Balance is, in many ways, a central rationalization for the oil culture wars—voices in support of industry are perceived as marginalized whereas resistance efforts are perceived as dominant. As Tim Wood's empirical analysis of news coverage of the Keystone XL project in the United States and Canada demonstrates, for instance, media prioritize dissenting activist voices over "corporately funded grassroots campaigns," a concept that internally makes equivalent Indigenous and environmentalist resistance with the voices of the petroturfing project.[45] Balance, then, is a mode through which petroturfing enters into the discursive field that established the oil culture wars and then subsequently carves out further spaces to generate legitimacy through circulation across social media platforms.

Persistent appeals to balance are postpolitical gestures that are effective in depoliticizing debates about energy, infrastructural, and extractive futures. In the context of Ecuador's resource governance, Riofrancos describes how state and industry actors in Ecuador often view levels of support for a given extractive project through a framework of information. In this view, those peoples and communities who resist extractive projects do so out of a lack of access to information or access to misinformation. As a result, state and industry actors "identified what they called 'information' as a panacea for anti-mining protest: it was a means to convince the communities potentially affected by mining projects of the socioeconomic benefits, and minimal environmental impacts, of extraction."[46] Riofrancos's observations travel well beyond the context of Latin American resource governance. Projected economic benefits, for instance, are reified as apolitical, factual representations of a future to come rather than as contested or contingent. And those not employing the dominant economentality as the vector through which to conceptualize the costs and benefits of pipeline and other extractive infrastructure developments simply require better "information." Such technical information transcends economic, social, and ecological domains of extraction and thus depoliticizes extraction. In the petroturfing imagination, this depoliticization is achieved by invocations of balance achieved through the circulation of facts—that is, balancing the books through economic forecasts that offer figures to outweigh environmental risks and balancing the views through oil executive epistemologies.

In media produced and circulated by BCP, information takes the form of a view in which the resource–economy–nation nexus melds with cost–benefit lines of sight to promote oil executive epistemologies. BCP, as discussed in the previous chapter, was established by Bruce Lounds in 2013 under the names British Columbians for Prosperity and British Columbians for International Prosperity, which were used interchangeably, at the arguable peak of active pipeline proposals and liquefied natural gas (LNG) promotion in BC. Despite framing the organization as "an independent group of concerned citizens," Lounds had direct ties to the industry as a management consultant in the heavy oil and tar sands sectors.[47] With no explanation, the group went dark in 2017 by making all its content on YouTube private and announcing on its home page that BCP is closed. My own speculation is that the group was in some manner tied to the right-wing BC Liberal Party, known for aggressive pro-LNG campaigns, which lost power in 2017 to the BC NDP.

BCP's media, primarily blog posts and YouTube videos, employ vocabularies of facts and balance to legitimize oil executive epistemologies on the one hand and delegitimize oppositional views on the other hand. Two short videos produced by BCP serve didactic, pedagogical functions in their dramatization of conversations from characters with oppositional views and oil executive epistemologies. These videos contain the dramatis personae of naive environmentalists and energy realist rationalists. After a minor debate plays out between the two, the videos conclude with an overlay of the BCP logo with text beneath that urges viewers to "check the facts before you decide" and a URL that leads to the BCP home page.

In "The Conversation," a couple who identify as environmentalists have a conversation in which the naive environmentalist is incessantly mocked for his lack of awareness of oil's ubiquity, a move that carries traces of the CAPP and Enbridge campaigns discussed earlier in this chapter. The video opens with establishing shots of Vancouver's shoreline as a young man enthusiastically expresses an interest to his partner in becoming an environmental activist who opposes fossil fuels. Degradation and sarcasm follow as the young man, at her request, imagines ways of being mobile without oil. She contradicts each of his unrealistic musings on potential futures of transportation without oil. Finally, she asks: "By the way, how do you think those out-of-town protesters travel to the rally?" He laughs in response: "I get your point."[48]

In another short, this transformation from oppositional environmentalist to holder of an oil executive epistemology is more pronounced. The video begins with a man watching footage of the *Deepwater Horizon* spill following a prompt to do so by a friend. This friend knew he was undecided on whether new pipelines should be built, and the friend hoped to convince him that they are too risky. After viewing footage of the spill, they video-chat about the oil sands in general and pipeline projects in particular. The friend, surrounded by acoustic guitars in what looks like a minimalist basement suite, is an archetypal naive environmentalist hippie who opposes development, and the young professional pictured in a modern kitchen is offered to viewers as the energy realist rationalist. The hippie's arguments against development are emotional, while the yuppie cites his sources. In a matter-of-fact tone, the yuppie draws attention to a study that vaguely concluded if a spill were to occur from increased oil tanker traffic for the Northern Gateway, "even in the worst-case scenario, the economic benefits outweigh the risks."[49] The environmentalist says he is coming over to settle their feud and the yuppie starts researching. After a montage of intense Googling appears, the yuppie provides his friend with an impromptu defense of pipelines and the oil sands; he even shows his friend a BCP video to seal the deal.

These two videos articulate an acculturation process in which petrocapitalist realism informed by an oil executive epistemology is the only *reasonable* position when faced with the facts. The videos are a kind of how-to manual for viewers in educating naive environmentalist friends while further suggesting that facts exclusively support the industry's claims. Facts, it follows, are for industry, while misinformation is for those who challenge the expansion of the fossil economy. Far from providing a slick conclusion that we need more oil, however, these videos' narratives instead reveal a logic endemic to the kinds of depoliticizing gestures of information-as-panacea that Riofrancos interrogates.

Other short videos produced by BCP forgo the informal, conversational mise-en-scène found in "The Conversation" and "Check the Facts." Instead, they opt for tones of educational, public service announcements by using bright colors and cute animations. "If you're unemployed, nothing feels better than landing a job," a voice-over states in the opening of a short video titled "Can B.C. Afford to Say 'No' to 8000 New Jobs?" The rest of the video emphasizes the number of jobs that will be created from pipeline projects, pointing out that "local businesses will benefit from the sale of goods and services to workers," while closing with the tagline "pipelines benefit people."[50] In a longer video, a teenager walking down a high school hallway looks up and breaks the fourth wall to address the audience. He "thinks it's cool that people want to balance protecting the environment and economic development" but is "tired of all the hot air" and wants "to know the facts." As he opens up a tablet to the BCP home page, the video zooms in to the screen and cuts to an infographic relaying the alleged benefits of pipeline projects in BC. Asking what "the proposed BC pipeline projects mean for British Columbians," the voice-over states that they have "examined the facts."[51] Listing a number of figures citing future job creation as a promotional strategy for touting the economic benefits of pipelines, the video reveals the startling divergence between projected jobs in the short and long term. BCP claims that Enbridge's Northern Gateway pipeline will generate 3,000 temporary jobs during the construction period and 560 long-term ones. Then Kinder Morgan's TMX will generate 4,500 temporary jobs during the construction period and 50 permanent ones. But jobs are not the only economic promises of petrocultures and fossil economies, as the previous sections have detailed. Pipelines and their construction, the video also maintains, are a means for economic stimulus and increased tax revenue, which ultimately result in, according to BCP, more money for healthcare and education.

Like the Ethical Oil project or CAPP's Canada's Energy Citizens campaign, which I discussed in the previous chapter, the motivation for BCP is to provide a counter-counterdiscourse to the kinds of campaigns that have branded the oil sands industry as one that produces dirty oil. The kinds of gestures toward facts seen above and throughout the first wave of petroturfing are centered on a singular conceptualization of balance. Due to the well-funded nature of environmentalist groups, the narrative suggests, petroturfing asserts that the scales have been weighted in favor of environmentalists. In this way, balance has emerged as a constitutive meme within petroturfing. In discussing its core beliefs, BCP states:

> We believe that *balancing* responsible environmental stewardship with accountable, measured development means paying careful attention to *facts rather than rhetoric,* and taking account of technological improvements and regulatory changes that have altered how development impacts the environment.[52]

Petroturfing claims the oil industry and Canadian oil as victims of unfair, foreign-influenced environmentalist ideological sabotage that has tipped the scales in public discourse, despite the realities of the industry's enormous social and political influence. Such a notion of balance is tied to the kinds of liberal preoccupation with centers or middles where accusations of bias arguably fortify business as usual and help carry its relations into the future.

Balance is achieved by carving out a rhetorical and discursive "middle" through appeals to facts, which become privileged modes through which to reproduce dominant petrocultural imaginaries such as oil executive epistemologies against resistance efforts deemed radical. In an analysis of the contemporary ideology of middleness through a critical reading of Gilles Deleuze, cultural theorist Andrew Pendakis provides an account of how particular forms of centrisms emerged as hegemonic in neoliberalism. Such centrisms include a variant of "radical centrism" that describes this dominant contemporary political imaginary that eschews that which is deemed radical, as well as an ontology of "universal middleness" that serves as an "ambience that structures much of what passes for experience in late capitalist societies."[53] "What matters is not whether a center discourse is actually 'of the middle,' but the rhetorical tropes and repetitions it uses to establish itself as such," Pendakis writes.[54] Centrisms on these terms are attempted evacuations of the political (a political gesture in itself), and they mark virtually every instance of petroturfing in its first wave. From the pages of *Ethical Oil* to BCP's commitment to "facts rather than rhetoric," balance serves a dual legitimation function. First, it legitimates petroturfing as an apolitical, nonpartisan project; second, it delegitimates resistance efforts. As a rhetorical device, in other words, balance is a symptom of the kinds of centrisms that Pendakis outlines, and in the context of debates over the expansion of Canada's fossil economy, balance performs specific ideological work for petroturfing that undermines resistance and further legitimates dominant energy imaginaries as if they were simply the most rational, reasonable, or fair ones.

Where such facts used for the ends of balance come from is important. The statistics, projections, and figures that BCP mobilized as facts when discussing the benefits of Enbridge's Northern Gateway Pipeline largely come from a University of British Columbia (UBC) study assessing the risk and impact of tanker spills from increased traffic due to the proposed pipeline. One conclusion BCP draws from this report is that the overall economic benefits of the project outweigh the risks, a conclusion that quantifies ecological disaster in economic terms. The project is slated to generate $628 million while a catastrophic or "high impact spill" would cost between $87 and $308 million to address.[55] What is important to underscore here, as earlier, is that facts in this context are ultimately *projected outcomes,* predicted numbers that lay claim to the future by attempting to restrict its possibilities otherwise in a future-perfect social tense. My aim here is not to suggest that the numbers in the UBC Institute for the Oceans and Fisheries' report are not methodologically sound. Instead, I hope to trouble the certainty established in framing such predictions as facts and to interrogate the cost–benefit frameworks that animate pipeline politics in the first place. It is ultimately more accurate to see the calculus of BCP's pro-pipeline media not as facts but as *promises*—promises that attempt to claim prescience over an uncertain future through the future-perfect social tense.

Tipping the Scales

In challenging the many promises that petroturfing relies on to build a community of supporters who internalize the market forces of the fossil economy and adopt oil executive epistemologies, it is not adequate to simply point out how the fossil economy often fails to deliver on its promises. When a narrowly conceived view of the economic is the privileged site from which to imagine energy futures, the cards remain stacked in favor of the fossil economy. As Gunster writes in a statement that gets to the heart of the stakes of the spread of oil executive epistemologies, "we must vigorously contest the presumption that what's good for Suncor and Imperial Oil and the banks that finance them is good for all of us."[56] Cara New Daggett describes the deadlock produced by the kinds of cost–benefit scenarios that invariably tip the scales to support continued development, as these scenarios are tied to dominant resource and economic logics. "In most energy debates, environmentalists are compelled either to prove that alternative fuels would create more jobs and/or more economic growth than existing fossil fuel systems or, if this is not possible, to prove that the waste associated with fossil fuels outweighs the benefit of fossil fuel jobs," she writes.[57] Daggett's observation reveals the pitfalls inherent in the dominant frameworks mobilized to generate support for or against the fossil economy and, moreover, highlights the necessity of developing and nurturing energy imaginaries beyond those that separate environment and economy or those that produce dirty or ethical oil. This deadlock entrenches already dominant interests and inhibits the realization of a more socially and ecologically just energy future. And such a deadlock is precisely why, in a perhaps unexpected move, I argue in the book's conclusion that in order to exit the trenches of the oil culture wars we mustn't rely on easy fossil fuel abolitionisms but instead must curate and nurture relations to fossil fuels beyond those that the fossil economy offers.

As a cultural technology of sorts, petroturfing instills affects and shapes worldviews in the service of the fossil economy, a process consistent with the emergence of neoliberal subjectivities premised on the internalization of market relations that feed this impasse. In exploring the facets of this petrocultural common sense, this chapter has argued that the oil executive epistemology is a formative expression of petroturfing's economic imaginary that is shaped through an internalization of a resource–economy–nation nexus, the leveraging of a factual imagination derived from economic projections, and persistent appeals to balance. The economy in these terms plays an overdetermined role in petroturfing that hinges upon promises of progress and prosperity, and it serves as an anchor upon which the socially and economically progressive dimensions of Canadian oil are expressed across social media. In the following three chapters, I turn to the gendered, sexed, and sexualized; settler colonial; and ecological imaginaries that petroturfing puts forward in the shadow of its economic imaginary.

3

RESOURCE HETERO- AND HOMONATIONALISM

THE PETROSEXUAL IMAGINARY

Posted to the Oil Sands Strong Facebook page in 2016, the meme in Figure 9 was accompanied by a caption asking if the page's followers "value women's rights."[1] As its key takeaway, the meme invokes the formal equality of women in Canada as a rationale for supporting the production and consumption of Canadian oil by pointing out that "as Canadians we value equality for women!" and "that's why it makes sense to support Canadian oil instead of countries that don't!" Through online sleuthing, it seems as though the original photo comes from a 1960s women's rights demonstration in the United States, placing the energies of demonstrators squarely within the gathering momentum of what is commonly periodized in the West as second-wave feminism. Second-wave feminism was primarily concerned with expanding the gains achieved from winning suffrage to broader equality across social, political, and economic spheres. The feminist revision of the closing imperative of Karl Marx and Friedrich Engels's *Communist Manifesto* written on the banner—"workers of the world unite!" to "women of the world unite!"—declares how such equality will be fought: through solidarity. The scene captures the collective force of solidarity on these terms as demonstrators fill the street. Perhaps more important than the image's origins and expressions, however, is its contemporary online presence. Today, the image circulates across the web as a generic representation of the struggle for women's rights. Tapping into generic emancipatory energies of the image's second-wave feminist setting, Oil Sands Strong extracts these energies in order to refine Canadian oil as an active agent in pursuits for gender equity.

Oil Sands Strong's celebration of Canadian values of gender equity is one example among many more that construes Canadian oil as a vehicle for advancing progressive relations of gender and sexuality. Since the publication of Levant's *Ethical Oil* in 2010 and its adjacent multimedia campaign, gender, sex, and sexuality have inflected the petroturfing project. From Levant's graphic thought experiment about Fort McMurray's then mayor Melissa Blake's fate on a hypothetical trip to Saudi Arabia

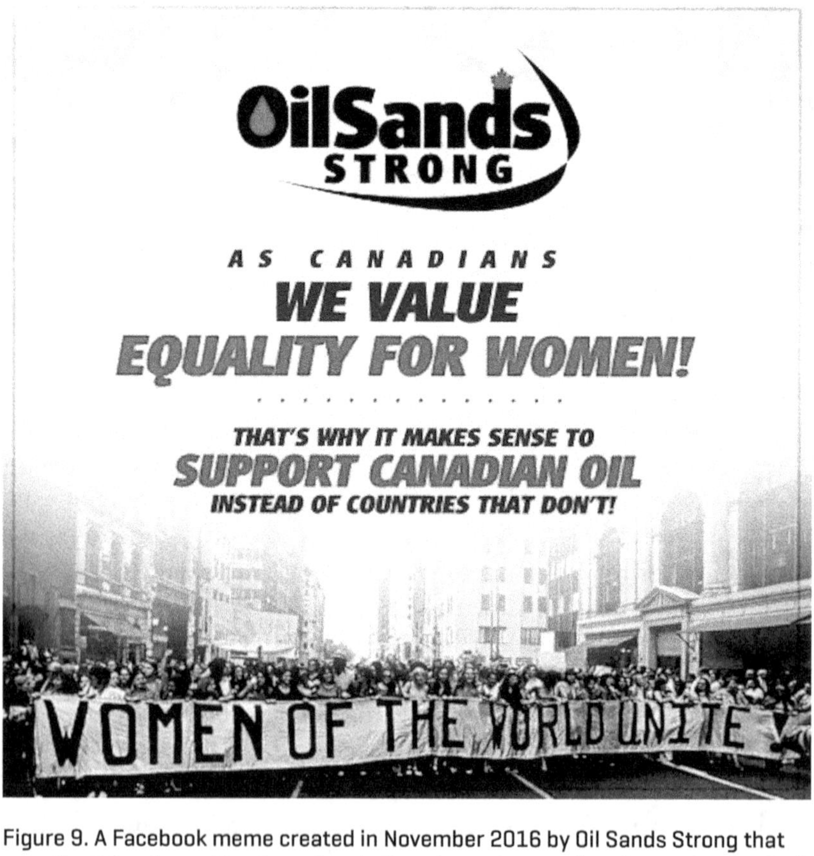

Figure 9. A Facebook meme created in November 2016 by Oil Sands Strong that uses the formal equality of genders in Canada to suggest that the production and consumption of Canadian oil support such equality.

that I examined in chapter 1 to his persistent reference to how "gays" are treated in OPEC nations, gender, sex, and sexuality have been key vectors through which Canadian oil is distinguished from so-called conflict oil.[2] Petroturfing, in other words, has always been a gendered, sexed, and sexualized project in the sense that relations of gender, sex, and sexuality have been leveraged as promotional tools for Canada's fossil economy. In this way, the oil culture wars that derive their gendered and sexualized imaginary against those of Arab oil-producing regions, conditioned by broader Western imaginaries surrounding these regions, are influenced by the War on Terror. Petroturfing employs the very same imaginaries for the oil culture wars as the War on Terror did, particularly those embedded in queer theorist Jasbir K. Puar's influential notion of "homonationalism," or homonormative nationalism. Puar defines homonationalism as a form of "national recognition and inclusion" that constitutes a kind of U.S. exceptionalism in which "homosexual subjects who have limited legal rights within the U.S. civil context gain significant representational currency when situated within the global scene of the war on terror."[3] In petroturfing, homonationalism mixes with oil in an expression of Canadian exceptionalism constituted through resource extraction, taking shape as *resource homonationalism.*

It is certainly no secret that fossil fuels have helped reshape gendered and sexualized relations. Broadly speaking, the persistent formation of the twentieth-century nuclear family owes much to the kinds of freedom—to use Matt Huber's formulation from *Lifeblood*—shaped by oil. Automobility, or the condition of hypermobility naturalized by the ubiquity of the automobile, as a quintessential petrocultural relation also took shape as a kind of gendered freedom informed by the capacities afforded from the commute to work to the family vacation. These conditions speak to how oil has shaped and been shaped by relations of gender and sexuality. Promotional media from industry also often frame the freedoms offered by fossil fuels in gendered ways—less domestic labor for mom, more speed and control for dad. Yet the lived experience of oil's saturation of gender and sexualities from the sites and regions of extraction to those sites of consumption accounted for here are much more complex than the selective, distilled, and refined accounts put forward in the petroturfing project. Feminist energy humanities scholar Sheena Wilson spells this out clearly when she writes that "the age of oil is rife with ironies that have resulted in both feminist advances as well as the reinforcement of long-standing patriarchal conceptualizations of woman as object and as property."[4] These gendered, sexed, and sexualized fossil-fueled relations, in other words, are far from the uncomplicatedly positive visions traded in by petroturfing. Formal equality, for instance, does not necessarily translate one-to-one to social, cultural, political, or economic equality. Canada is no exception to this truism. As Indigenous feminist theorists such as Audra Simpson and Leanne Betasamosake Simpson remind us in their powerful critiques of the intersectional expression of white settler colonial capitalist heteropatriarchy, Canada remains a patriarchal society through and through.[5] The petro-utopic vision of Ethical Oil and Oil Sands Strong is a fantasy that equates abstract, formal equality with concrete, real equality, which obscures the fundamentally uneven conditions through which oil is produced and consumed on the one hand and the gendered character of ongoing settler colonialism that underwrites Canada's fossil economy on the other.

A trove of recent feminist and queer theory that explores the relationship among oil, gender, and sexuality helps surface the tension between petroturfing's oil-soaked idealisms and its material frictions. As the previous chapter, this chapter, and the two that follow show, oil executive epistemologies rely on an idealistic understanding of social, economic, political, and environmental relations that largely evades the material, political, and economic realities of Canada's fossil economy. During petroturfing's emergence over the 2010s, feminist thinkers have refined approaches and vocabularies to address the oil–gender–sex–sexuality nexus outlined in the previous paragraph. In 2011, for instance, Heather M. Turcotte proposed the framework of petrosexual politics to bring "together the moments of violence, within nation-building projects, that intimately link petroleum production, the global circuits of oil and gender–sexual violence."[6] For Turcotte, petrosexual politics "demonstrates that gender violence is not merely an effect of petro-violence, it is the necessary condition for such violence to even take place."[7] Moving from a regional focus on the Global South to the Global North, Sheena Wilson employs Turcotte's framework to approach the Western petrocultural imaginary and "interrogate the relationship between human rights and gender and racial equality and the petro-discourses that are newly oriented around ecology in our contemporary moment"—petro-discourses that include the Ethical Oil campaign.[8] More recently, Cara New Daggett advanced this conversation by theorizing "petro-masculinity," a mode of masculinity that is currently under threat by global warming itself on the one hand and the forms of activism that hope to curb or halt global warming by keeping fossil fuels in the ground on the other hand. One response to this threat, Daggett asserts, is a growing desire among those whose identities are tied to the burning of fossil fuels toward authoritarian modes of political expression to, often violently, secure "petro-patriarchal orders."[9] Though varied in their regional and temporal foci, these critical interventions emerge out of a mutual recognition of how the symbolic and material violence endemic to the fossil economy is expressed through gendered and sexualized avenues.

In this chapter, I engage recent feminist and queer theory on the gendered and sexualized dimensions of the fossil economy, or its *petro-sexual politics,* to examine media and events from across the petroturfing project that express or register gendered, sexed, and sexualized imaginaries. I do so with a motivation to better understand the avenues through which the petroturfing project uses social media to construe Canadian oil as a progressive force. And I argue that it is oil's material, political, and economic tendency to abstract that creates the ripe conditions for this mode of symbolic refinement. Canadian oil is unique in its level of abstraction as a resource-intensive form of heavy oil, and petroturfing extends this condition to further separate the ideal from the material.

To make this argument, I isolate a series of figures and episodes from the first and early second waves of petroturfing. Beginning with Bernard the Roughneck, an out-of-work oil sands laborer who became a right-wing media darling after an interview at a pipeline protest, I examine oil sands masculinities as they are performed through Bernard and his rise to public consciousness. Then, I look at how a politics of recognition informs how gendered labor appears (or doesn't) in oil sands promotional media. From here, I turn to the figure of the oil sands family—a figure often invoked alongside appeals to the economy that I explored in the previous chapter. Focusing on campaigns tied to the Canadian Association of Oilwell Drilling Contractors (CAODC) called Oil Respect, I return to the nuclear family, which is likewise construed as threatened not by the volatile economic forces of the oil economy but by progressive governments and environmentalists. Finally, I look at an early episode in the history of petroturfing to examine representations of women and 2SLGBTQIA+ peoples in the context of rights discourses and employment equity to reveal the friction between traditionalism and progressivism that gets superficially reconciled in the petroturfing project.

Performing Petromasculinity as Bernard the Roughneck Goes to Parliament

At a protest against the TMX in summer 2016, a correspondent for Rebel Media asked a counterprotestor for his thoughts on the demonstration. Outfitted in a camouflage baseball hat and hoodie underneath a bulky jean jacket, which is a sort of unofficial uniform of rural and suburban Canada, the soft-spoken man identified only as Bernard, an oil industry worker, answered. He began by applauding the democratic foundations of Canada that allow for protestors to demonstrate "without retribution." Bernard then expressed his anger with people who protest projects like the TMX yet continue to use fossil fuels in their day-to-day lives. To illustrate the depths of this hypocrisy, Bernard listed a series of everyday products, including eyeglasses and prescription pills, that protestors or, indeed, anyone are likely to use. Prompted by the correspondent to describe how protests such as these affect workers like him, Bernard offered a response lifted straight out of the petroturfing playbook. He explained, for instance, that demonstrating against pipelines only ends up increasing rail transport of bitumen, a method of transport often highlighted by industry and its allies as more dangerous. Then, he described how in "trying to oppose our Canadian oil and gas industry, we're only helping Russia, Saudi Arabia, Algeria, Angola, Venezuela." And, finally, Bernard characterized protestors as "net takers not net contributors" whose actions derail "guys like me who want to go to work for a living and pay taxes and have economic advancement possibly in their future."[10] Bernard's language here is telling. Oil sands workers are "guys" like him whose taxable income supports a dependent population of pipeline protestors, a population that "would never take any of those jobs [created by the TMX] because they like sleeping in and collecting benefits and waking up so they can come to protests like this."[11]

Uploaded to the Rebel News YouTube channel with the title "WATCH: Oil Industry Worker Speaks His Mind at Kinder Morgan Protests!," the video quickly gained traction across social and traditional media as it traveled the circuit of legitimation through circulation. Soon after its release, according to a YouTube user in the video's comments, it was featured on the platform's trending page. To date, it has accumulated more than 600,000 views.[12] In the wake of the video's circulation, Bernard made more appearances with Rebel and soon found himself representing oil sands workers in the Canadian mediascape under the moniker "Bernard the Roughneck."

By fall of the same year, Bernard the Roughneck would be delivering a petition to the federal government in Ottawa asking for the government to do more for the oil and gas industry and its workers in Alberta. The petition was the culmination of efforts from a campaign spearheaded by the Calgary-based industry lobbying organization CAODC called Oil Respect.[13] Oil Respect was created by the president and CEO of CAODC, Mark Scholz, in the wake of the 2015 downturn, which saw crude oil reach some of the lowest prices per barrel since the aftermath of the 2008 financial crisis.[14] Before arriving at the helm of CAODC, Scholz was active in the right-wing provincial political scene, helping establish the precursor to the Wildrose Party, which would eventually dissolve alongside the Progressive Conservatives to re-form as the United Conservative Party, a sort of right-wing coalition party currently in power. According to a profile piece in the now-defunct *Alberta Oil Magazine,* Scholz created Oil Respect "because of the urgency to fight back against a well-funded and well-organized radical and extreme environmental movement."[15] Formally, Oil Respect is virtually indistinguishable from CAPP's Canada's Energy Citizens campaign: it seeks to garner support from a broader public using grassroots modes of signification, yet it is tied to a lobbying group, operating as what Tim Wood generously describes as a "corporately funded grassroots" initiative that aims to establish "subsidized publics."[16] Partnering with Bernard, who Scholz says came to CAODC's attention after his appearances with Rebel, CAODC covered the expenses of Bernard's trip to Ottawa to help deliver the petition.

In the televised speech following the delivery of the Oil Respect petition, Bernard appeared in front of the camera wearing soiled high-visibility overalls and a hard hat with oil carefully painted on his face.

Bernard opened his speech by authenticating his identity as "just an average roughneck." "I'm not a guy from Calgary in a suit. I'm not a guy who's knowledgeable about public policy or processes that go on in buildings like this. I'm a roughneck," he declared. "I'm a guy who has a job in Alberta whose livelihood's been threatened." Bernard carried on by naming those affected by the downturn to frame it as a "Canada-wide issue." He continued his speech, which is worth quoting at length:

> There no longer exists a middle class outside the oil class. Blue collar has turned to bourgeois in this country and Alberta was the last place you could go and—the oil patch, pardon me, Northern British Columbia, Alberta, Saskatchewan—these are places you can go being an average person and if you're willing to work hard and work more than forty hours a week and bust your butt, you can have something and you can have a decent quality of life. I would have never been able to get an education were it not for the oil patch. How was I going to pay off a $40,000 student loan? And these options are being cut off and the people like me who work in the field feel that we don't have a voice because when we talk about these issues here in Ottawa, the only people who have a say in these issues are not the working class, the average Canadian.[17]

These grievances respond to those seen in the previous chapter's examination of petroturfing's economic imaginary, which seeks to transform working-class economic anxieties into an oil executive epistemology. These grievances also anticipate the more intensive expressions of discontent with the federal government's ideological and financial support of the oil and gas industry that I address in chapter 6. By acting as an avatar of a white, male oil sands worker whose livelihood has been disrupted by the bust side of the boom-and-bust calculus, Bernard the Roughneck tapped into tangible economic anxieties that emerge from immanent conditions of the fossil economy in a way that generated sympathy from mainstream media.

But Bernard's call for support embedded in his speech and in the petition that he delivered did not name these ebbs and flows endemic to the fossil economy and capitalist regimes of accumulation in any direct sense. Instead, Bernard put pressure on what he identified as the federal government's failure to support the oil and gas industry on the one hand

and its failure to support the industry workers and communities that rely on those industries on the other hand. The slippage here is a consequence of a flattening of class relations that strategically fails to distinguish between the executive and the roughneck, although Bernard performatively eschewed any association with white-collar labor to legitimize his identity as a roughneck. After all, Bernard is "not a guy from Calgary in a suit." But the calls for action came directly from a guy from Calgary in a suit who formally submitted the petition—Scholz of CAODC, seen behind Bernard during his speech.

The vague language of the petition is telling in its demands when considering these origins. "We, the undersigned, citizens of Canada," the petition declared,

> call upon the Government of Canada to vocally defend the oil and gas industry and the use of pipelines, and to make the building of oil, gas and diluted bitumen pipelines across Canada, to tidewater, and into the United States, a national priority.[18]

There are two demands here. First, the petition called for the federal government to "vocally defend" the industry. In other words, the petition called for the federal government to adopt tenets of petroturfing or, in a more expanded sense, the discourses and rhetorics of the oil and gas industry's promotional culture. Second, the petition called upon the federal government to make pipeline construction a "national priority," a call that was arguably met when the federal government purchased the TMX in 2018. Neither of these calls prioritized the interests of those primarily left behind by the fossil economy that Bernard allegedly represents. But in leveraging Bernard's roughneck image as an avatar for the average oil sands worker, the petition flattened the interests of the workers to those of industry more generally in a maneuver that garnered the support of more than thirty-six thousand signatories.

Economic relations are also social ones, but alongside the complex class relations of oil sands production that Bernard the Roughneck speaks to is a rich context through which to begin exploring the gendered dimensions of Canadian oil, particularly in terms of masculinities that underwrite working-class identity in the oil sands in general and petroturfing as a communicative strategy in particular. Regardless of the degree to which Bernard the Roughneck was an organic formation or a manufactured creation of Rebel News, he remains a character whose performance is a caricature of a white, male oil sands worker. As his image circulated across the Canadian mediascape after his first interview with Rebel News, Bernard the Roughneck took a shape in excess of Bernard Hancock, a graduate of media, communications, history, and political studies at Bishop's University in Quebec, Canada, who would, according to his origin story, end up working in the oil sands to pay off his student debt.

Bernard's character was an embodiment of a stereotypical masculinity found in and constituted by the boomtown imaginary that overdetermines Fort McMurray's place in the national and international imaginary. Bernard's physical presentation as a disheveled, masculine-presenting worker fresh off the jobsite paired with his persistent rhetorical emphasis on the livelihood of middle classes reveals traces of gendered assumptions about who an oil sands worker is in the first place. In drawing attention to the performative, caricatured dimensions of the roughneck persona Bernard expresses, I am not saying that such people do not exist. There is a reason why Bernard, at least in some capacity, briefly captured the hearts and minds of the Canadian public first in his Rebel News appearance and later in his televised speech in Ottawa. But in reading this episode as a performance, it is clear that Bernard's image, complete with bitumen-dusted face, was built on a set of assumptions about who the "average roughneck" actually *is*—white and male.

Of course, the lived realities in the Patch are more complex than caricatures. Indeed, the multiculturalism of Fort McMurray is a point often emphasized when describing the boomtown's socioeconomic makeup. Journalist Chris Turner writes in his study of the myths and realities of Fort McMurray and the oil sands that as much as Fort McMurray is plagued by the common pitfalls of a hypermasculine boomtown, it is simultaneously a family-oriented, suburbanized setting underwritten by a strong sense of multiculturalism akin to the urban centers of Canada.[19] Yet Bernard's presentation is one of a frontier masculinity conditioned by a nostalgia that tethers oil extraction to white masculinity. Empirically speaking, the kinds of jobs that Bernard described in his Ottawa speech seem to be reserved primarily for white men. Drawing on research done by law professor Kathleen Lahey for the progressive think tank the Parkland Institute, Nicole Hill, Angele Alook, and Ian Hussey show "that white men are significantly advantaged in employment in the province, with the highest incomes in nearly every field."[20] Masculinity is, in many ways, a foundational feature of "good jobs" in the oil sands.

Such masculinity that underwrites extraction in these terms is by no means exclusive to the gas and oil industry. Yet, as sociologist Gloria E. Miller points out in her pathbreaking work on masculinity in the oil sands, the oil industry's masculinity permeates social relations in industry life, which is expressed "not only in the historical and contemporary demographic composition of its employees, but in its assumptions, values and everyday practices."[21] Resonating with Miller, in a brief, provocative analysis of the intersections among contemporary class relations in the United States, extractive capitalism, and anti-environmentalism, political theorist John Hultgren details the consequences of the white male worker emerging as a trope that represents the working class in the popular imaginary. As Hultgren points out,

> The now-dominant conception of the working class—tethered to the trope of the white male worker—oversimplifies the actual politics of the white working class, renders invisible the labor of working class women and people of color who bring from the earth (in additional all those who *care for* the earth), and further perpetuates a host of socio-ecological crises.[22]

At the center of Hultgren's observation here is a dominant conception of frontier masculinity that underwrites extractive enterprise and the imaginaries that surround it, all of which has critical purchase beyond the United States as researchers such as Miller show. Frontier masculinity ultimately describes an identity that emerges from symbols surrounding the mythologies of frontierism.

In Canada, such mythologies are historically tied to westward and northward expansion as part of a larger settler colonial project. These mythologies continue to underwrite regional identities in the prairie provinces especially. But, arguably, these mythologies are most pronounced in Alberta, where the cowboy hat, for instance, carries a symbolic weight of homegrown authenticity and the annual Calgary Stampede, a rodeo, exhibition, and festival staged annually since 1923 save for 2020 due to the Covid-19 pandemic, continues to be one of the province's most important public events. Rodeos are such a dominant cultural ritual in Alberta that during the Covid-19 pandemic in fall 2021 Premier Jason Kenney offered them exemptions to the curfew imposed on other alcohol-serving establishments such as pubs.[23] Miller identifies a set of processes through which masculinity is reinforced and reproduced—everyday interactions "characterized by informalism and paternalism based on shared masculine interests that exclude women from power," modes of competition that "reinforce the division of work by gender," and, finally, "gendered interactions and occupations [that] are embedded in a consciousness derived from the powerful *symbols* of the frontier myth and romanticized cowboy hero."[24] Miller's findings came from in-depth interviews conducted with twenty women in white-collar positions in Calgary's oil industry. In addition to these three avenues that reinforce masculinity, Miller also notes that "authoritarian behaviour" was described by interviewees, although these behaviors "were related more to interactions between men, serving to sustain a particular form of masculine hegemony."[25] In other words, patriarchal, settler colonial relations pervade that atmosphere of laboring in the oil sands from the Patch to the office tower. "Masculinity is represented in the field on the exploration rigs, where it is relatively overt and macho," Miller writes, "and at the executive levels where it is much subtler."[26] A picture develops here where, as Miller puts it, masculinity permeates class divisions among blue- and white-collar fields of the oil sands.

But what does the masculine character of the oil sands' working environment have to do with the petroturfing project? Frontloading my analysis as I have done with an account of Bernard the Roughneck's formation as a mascot for petroturfing serves two roles in addressing the gendered and sexed imaginaries of petroturfing. First, Bernard discursively (through speech patterns and direct claims) and affectively (through clothing and body language) presents himself and performs as an idealized image of an average rig worker. His features and mannerisms express his authenticity to a broader public. Second, as an average rig worker, Bernard's masculinity highlights dynamics of gender as they exist in the Patch—his masculinity goes unacknowledged because it is a norm. Bernard is a concentrated expression of white petromasculinity that Daggett puts pressure on in her account of the relationship between fossil fuels, masculinity, and authoritarianism.

The Bernard the Roughneck episode reveals links among economic anxiety, petromasculinity, and the rising right. Bernard was incubated in Rebel News's right-wing media ecology only to briefly enter the mainstream news media circuit through coverage from venues such as CBC News. As Bernard's relative fame waned in the latter half of the 2010s, he ended up entering the Albertan political arena in one of the centers of oil industry labor—Grande Prairie, Alberta—where he unsuccessfully ran for the libertarian Freedom Conservative Party in the 2019 provincial election. The party has since merged with the separatist party Wexit Alberta to form the Wildrose Independence Party of Alberta. Daggett's concluding thoughts on the condition of petromelancholia produced out of lamentation following threats to the status quo track with Bernard's transformation from an industry mascot into a political candidate for a right-wing party. "Taking petro-masculinity seriously means paying attention to the thwarted desires of privileged patriarchies as they lose their fossil fantasies," Daggett writes.[27] These "thwarted desires of privileged patriarchies" are perhaps some of the strongest motivations for the petroturfing project. It is telling that so many figureheads of petroturfing, from its 2010 origins to the present—Cody Battershill of Canada Action, Ezra Levant of Ethical Oil, Bruce Lounds of British Columbians for Prosperity, Robbie Picard of Oil Sands Strong—are all men and mostly white, with the exception, based on publicly accessible information, of Picard, who is Métis like myself. Petroturfing, like the oil and gas industry more generally, is conditioned by petromasculinity, and those relations that flow from and against the fossil economy and the petroculture it underwrites operate in the shadow of petromasculinity.

A Politics of Recognition between Petrofeminism and Petrofemininity

The Ethical Oil campaign's first televised advertisement premiered exclusively on the Canadian Oprah Winfrey Network in 2011 with an afterlife on YouTube. The advertisement primarily focuses on Saudi Arabia's gender politics to introduce the opposition between ethical and conflict oil while closing by soliciting donations from viewers. "The 30-second public information ad," a blog post announcing the launch points out, "highlights Canada's oilsands as an Ethical Oil alternative to Conflict

Oil from regimes like Saudi Arabia that mistreat women."[28] Ethical Oil makes clear through a disclaimer that the paid advertisement "does not reflect the corporate views of the Oprah Winfrey Network."[29] But the cultural and material contexts of this promotional effort crystallize a relation between Ethical Oil, petroturfing, and neoliberal feminism. Oprah Winfrey, whom media scholar and journalist Janice Peck calls in the subtitle of her 2008 book *The Age of Oprah* a "cultural icon for the neoliberal era," is no stranger to this feminist current.[30] Neoliberal feminism refers to a form of feminism that adopts key neoliberal principles—individualism, valorization of free markets, and so on. And neoliberal feminism is bound to what Angela McRobbie identified in 2004 as "postfeminism," understood as "an active process by which feminist gains of the 1970s and 80s come to be undermined."[31] A neoliberal, postfeminist feminist imaginary is a fundamental component of the gendered imagination of the petroturfing project.

As Wilson's reading of the gendered politics of Ethical Oil articulates and to which I have gestured in the opening pages of this chapter, Ethical Oil leverages the legal status of women in the West (formal equality) against what it suggests women's universal experiences are in Middle Eastern oil-producing regions. This associates the production and consumption of Canadian oil with the kinds of liberal, equality-based gender politics of the West. Canadian oil, the narrative suggests, is oil that supports and enables such equality. By emphasizing how women are legally equal with men in ability to participate in society and politics while glossing over the gendered inequities that persist in liberal democracies such as Canada, Ethical Oil extracts the supposed virtue of gender equality by deploying a politics of recognition in an effort to promote Canadian oil. Canadian oil, it follows, is discursively imbued with these characteristics through a symbolic refinement; Canadian oil is refined here as, in the words of Ethical Oil, a form of "social oil."[32] More significantly, perhaps, is that the reproduction of such comfortable and comforting binarisms glosses over a long history of struggle for equality in the West that persists today. In engaging with gender politics solely on a plane of recognition, the agents of petroturfing attempt to construct an ethics that in the first and last instance puts forth an unproductive, ambivalent politics that simply reproduces already dominant relations of patriarchy, capital, and petroculture. In other words, women are used as promotional objects to further the agenda of the petroturfing project.

In more conventional promotional materials from industry and its allied lobbying organizations such as CAPP, this performance of recognition is deepened in relation to gender and employment access. A 2013 campaign from Shell Canada, for instance, circulated profiles of women who work for the company under the headline "Developing the Oil Sands Responsibly: Women behind the Operation." Shell Canada describes the initiative in these words:

> From avid environmentalists, to scuba-diving grandmothers, these women are not only experts in their fields but balance vibrant lives outside of work with their hobbies, families and community involvement. Find out more about the passions that drive their careers and sucesses [*sic*] as they work to sustainably unlock and develop one of the world's most challenging resources.[33]

The write-up reproduces several sexist, patriarchal narratives, including a naturalized concern for environment signified particularly through the vector of motherhood. Profiles include Stephanie Sterling, vice president of business and joint venture management, whose tagline reads, "Fashionista? Farm Girl? Vice President? Stephanie Sterling is all three"; Nicole Stanley, oil sands environment coordinator, whose tagline asks if "someone working in the oil sands" can "be an environmentalist"; and Lorraine Mitchelmore, Shell Canada president and executive vice president of Heavy Oil, whose write-up asks: "Running a company and a family of four—How does she do it?"[34] Wilson's critique of the gendered imaginaries of dominant petronarratives aids in drawing out some important points here. Like Ethical Oil's invocation and recognition of gendered legal equality in Canada, measured by Ethical Oil through such vectors as employment access, Shell Canada draws attention to its women employees' personal lives to demonstrate how the oil sands are being developed responsibly because of the presence of women in influential positions in the company. But in framing its campaign around the responsible development of the oil sands, Shell Canada reproduces an essentialist narrative surrounding women's inherent close proximity with the natural world.

As a media event, Shell Canada's campaign circulated through print advertisements, online social media, and conventional news media outlets. In a 2012 article for the business magazine *Alberta Venture* titled "Why Women Could Save the Oil Sands," journalist Alix Kemp cites the campaign to suggest that more women holding professional, executive positions in oil companies could aid in reinvigorating oil sands production because of the differences between the ways that men and women approach business. Opening with a quotation from University of Alberta professor Karen Hughes in a way that legitimates these essentializing claims surrounding the differences in how men and women think, the article then focuses largely on Shell and the "Developing the Oil Sands Responsibly" campaign.[35] Official traces of this campaign have seemingly been purged from the internet, likely due to Royal Dutch Shell's divestment in the oil sands in 2017.

Shell, of course, is not alone in reproducing these petrosexual imaginaries as efforts to increase gender parity abound in an industry whose formal and informal contours are so determined by the kinds of frontier masculinity that Miller outlines. As the largest oil and gas lobbying organization in Canada, CAPP also mobilizes a politics of recognition when discussing its commitments to gender equality vis-à-vis employment, citing partnerships with Women Building Futures, an initiative that provides resources and training for women to enter industrial construction labor jobs.[36] In offering a critique of these pursuits of industry gender parity in the context of frontier and petromasculinities, my aim is not to suggest that initiatives such as these are not valuable ones, nor is it to suggest that they do not legitimately help women gain employment in traditionally male-dominated industries such as construction. Instead, my critique takes aim at how these initiatives reproduce existing relations with increased gender parity while doing little to challenge the systems and structures that have historically produced the inequities these initiatives are claiming to address in the first place.

Writing in the context of the Bakken oil fields in the United States and Canada, Sean Parson and Emily Ray detail how patriarchy underwrites capital accumulation, first in attempts to increase gender parity in laboring positions despite increased forms of gender violence in man camps and boomtowns, and second in how industry promotion mobilizes women's bodies to promote resource extraction. For Parson and Ray, these expressions reveal a "sexual logic of domination that drives the relationship of the oil industry to labor and land."[37] Industry pursuits of gender parity and efforts to refine Canadian oil as a progressive force for women and the 2SLGBTQIA+ community rest upon a liberal recognition politics that obscures the material conditions of how gender and sexuality function in relation to the fossil economy, while further deepening neoliberal feminism as the dominant expression of feminism in the twenty-first century. Critical theorist Nancy Fraser has influentially argued that feminism's turn from a politics based on equality—that is, a politics based on material demands—to a politics of identity and recognition established the basis for what we can best understand today as neoliberal feminism or postfeminism. "Turning 'from redistribution to recognition,'" Fraser writes, "the movement shifted its attention to cultural politics just as a rising neoliberalism was declaring war on social equality."[38] While Fraser argues that recognition can play an important role in shaping redistributive politics, there is a tension between more just, redistributive politics and the modes of superficial recognition politics of petroturfing that foreclosure such possibilities, as is shown throughout this chapter and the next.

Social Reproduction and Reproductive Futurism in the Patch

At the heart of many calls for support of the oil and gas industry, such as those found in Bernard's speech and the demands of the petition he helped deliver, are implicit and explicit invocations of the family form. The government of Canada's official response to the "e-216 (Oil and gas)" petition, for instance, foregrounds families in its measures to "alleviate the negative impacts of [the oil and gas sector's] recent downturn on Canadians."[39] And one of the animating imperatives of CAODC's Oil Respect campaign is unambiguously tethered to the family form as the tagline that sits below its logo reads: "standing up for Canadian oil and gas families." Appeals such as these often express a latent normative and, consequently, exclusionary vision of what constitutes "family" as such. In concert with this normative vision, the family serves as a stable referent that translates the macroeconomic forces of the fossil economy into a legible social unit complicit in the reproduction of late petrocapitalism—not, say, a larger social unit from which to draw solidarities beyond immediate kin, but the individual "oil and gas" family. And in these normative, patriarchal visions of family are gendered relations that emerge in the shadow of petromasculinity, which in their continued circulation foreclose futures of imagining social relations beyond the nuclear–petrocultural family. The family form as it circulates in the petroturfing project is one site through which fossil fantasies are maintained. As the roughneck is a deeply gendered identity formation, so, too, is the oil and gas family.

Across petroturfing media, the figure of the oil and gas family appears in various guises, the majority of which are vehicles for expressions of traditional, heteropatriarchal relations. As I opened this chapter by pointing out, the nuclear family as we tend to understand it today is a product of petrocultural modernity, and the oil and gas family is a derivative form in these ways. Social reproduction feminists have used the historical emergence of the nuclear family as a point of departure to address the ways in which unwaged, gendered, domestic labor produces the conditions upon which all formal economic relations rely. Under capitalism, the family is a site of capitalist reproduction wherein the burden of reproduction is externalized from capitalism onto caretakers who perform domestic labor and care work, forms of labor and work often un- or undervalued in capitalist schemas of value that historically and in the present continue to be performed disproportionately by women.

In a present whose social relations are increasingly marked by the impacts of climate change, the family form has reemerged as a site through which to address the future in both negative and aspirational registers. The Out of the Woods Collective highlighted this struggle over the family form in a 2015 essay edited and republished in the 2020 collection *Hope against Hope: Writings on Ecological Crisis.* Critiquing an appeal to future generations through children that closes Naomi Klein's bestseller *This Changes Everything: Capitalism vs. the Climate,* the Out of the Woods Collective takes reproductive futurism to task. Reproductive futurism names a worldview that hinges upon a vision for the future that centers (heteronormative, white) children. This vision underwrites conservative appeals to "family values" on the one hand and liberal, progressive narratives of the future on the other hand.[40] Reproductive futurism takes hold because "children are figured as the unit through which private property is passed and through which gendered, racialized, and classed society is reproduced." "What is excluded," the Collective continues, "are the conditions of social reproduction, the multiplicity of forms of kinship, and the immanent possibility of rupture."[41] Since petroturfing aims to secure a fossil-fueled future premised on the dominant relations of the present, reproductive futurism clarifies these efforts by bringing into view the stakes and consequences of appeals to the family as a coherent unit that petroturfing employs. These normative visions of the oil and gas family become an avenue through which oil executive epistemologies are spread. How the gendered work of social reproduction figures into promotional visions of the oil sands through the oil and gas family must be understood through the horizon of reproductive futurism in these ways—whose future, precisely, is being secured by the reproduction and expansion of Canada's fossil economy?

Turning to the Oil Respect campaign offers some answers to this question. Through this campaign, CAODC further cemented the oil and gas family as a key figure through which to perform the work of garnering support for the oil and gas industry. The oil and gas family, in other words, is a main character in the drama constructed and performed by petroturfing. Anchoring the family in these ways follows the same logics that the Out of the Woods Collective detailed in relation to how appeals to children are appeals to particular futures. A vision for the future in these terms is implicitly offered by CAODC, and these futures are construed in terms of threat. The threat is ultimately framed as a dual one, which carries with it the same rhetorical trajectory of Bernard's impassioned appeal to the government of Canada. First, Bernard asserted, the Canadian government has failed to economically support oil and gas families that have been feeling the impacts brought on by the downturn of 2015, whose effects were still felt in 2016 when the petition and speech were delivered. And, second, Bernard suggested that a body of protesters who seek to halt the expansion of the fossil economy have their sights set on workers and their families. Both threats form a foundation on which to construe a threat to reproductive futures in terms of both the oil and gas family in an immediate sense and the fossil economy in a protracted one.

On the Oil Respect home page, stories written by families experiencing hardship from the 2015 downturn are presented that lend further authenticity to the campaign. Done in conjunction with another outfit called Oilfield Dads, the stories came from members of the Oilfield Dads Facebook group and were curated by Oil Respect. The stories are genuine expressions of struggle in an extremely volatile industry. Following the ebbs and flows of a world market overdetermined by the price of oil, the oil economy's infamous cycle of boom and bust crashed toward the latter in 2015 when prices hit below US$40 per barrel.[42] As I have pointed out throughout this book, due to the resources required to upgrade the bitumen found in the oil sands into a useable form of oil, oil prices need to remain relatively high for legacy projects to continue and even higher to bring new ones online, including pipelines. Economists Anthony Heyes, Andrew Leach, and Charles F. Mason estimate that for new projects to be economically viable—what economists call a critical or trigger oil price—oil must be at or above US$84.62 per barrel for open pit mines and $58.06 for in-situ projects.[43] The lived impacts of this downturn are dire. An anonymous couple writes of precarity experienced from sporadic layoffs and rehires over the course of 2015, the impact this uncertainty had on their sleep, and the feeling these conditions produced, which was of being "trapped without a light at the end of the tunnel."[44] Another anonymous contributor writes from the view of decades of experience in the industry that reveal the severity of the 2015 downturn. "Over my years in the Oil and Gas Industry I have seen many ups and downs," they write, "but for the most part there was always a light at the end of the tunnel, but this time, it seems that the light has been shut off."[45] Light appears in both as an image of faded hope, as the power generated by oil that fuels economic relations in Alberta loses its illumination.

The takeaway Oil Respect derives from these personal narratives of loss and hardship is revealing in its didactic tenor. Leading into this collection of stories gathered from members of the Oilfield Dads Facebook page, which visitors to the website can access through a drop-down function, the introductory text points out that although "some people feel 'Big Oil' can handle being taken down a peg or two, the reality is that families are suffering across the country."[46] The family, then, becomes a figure through which the agents, architects, and allies of Canada's fossil economy absolve industry from the larger structural critiques and modes of resistance leveraged against it. For the Oil Respect campaign, the hardship faced by these families is a consequence of those who critique the fossil economy rather than an economic apparatus that has no regard for the lives of those who labor to keep it afloat. The stories "provide a real glimpse into how disrespecting and marginalizing the Canadian energy industry impacts everyday Canadians."[47] Disrespect and marginalization are keywords from which petroturfing derives the terms and conditions of the oil culture wars that occur on the terrain of culture rather than the economic relations to which these impacts can be attributed.

On the campaign's relatively inactive YouTube channel, CEO Mark Scholz is featured in videos that communicate the campaign's mission in these terms, offering takes on contemporary oil and gas issues through the lens of Oil Respect, a lens that posits *respect* of the oil and gas industry as the means through which to resolve the losses faced by oil and gas families. In a set of "weekly updates" that were produced sporadically over 2016, Scholz provides an account of a campaign tour with stops across Canada from Edmonton to Montreal. As Scholz puts it, through the tour, the campaign's message "is being delivered," which is that "this industry matters and oil families matter."[48] Speaking from a bench in a Saskatoon park in April 2016, Scholz says that the goals of the Oil Respect campaign are threefold: first, "to address misinformation and half-truths that are spread by the opponents of the oil and gas industry—and they're the radical environmentalists, the grandstanding politicians, and foreign celebrities"; second, "to give regular people an opportunity to stand up for this industry, to demand respect for this industry"; and, finally, "to remind the media, public, and government that the reason that Canada has some of the highest living standard anywhere else in the world is because we're able to consume affordable energy from oil and gas and develop it responsibly right here in Western Canada."[49] Here the terrain of the oil culture wars is mapped. According to the logics of Oil Respect, oil and gas families should fight for respect rather than, say, more equitable working conditions that would lessen the impacts of downturns. Oil executive epistemologies underwrite an abstract model of industry where "Big Oil" and the oil and gas family are indistinguishable.

As is the case in the context of other boom and bust resource towns, such as those found in the Bakken regions of Canada and the United States, the material realities of work and life and the idealist visions of a good family life offered by the agents, allies, and architects of the fossil economy come into friction in Fort McMurray. Such frictions are particularly pronounced in terms of gender, inseparable from race and class. Sociologist Sara Dorow offers a clear account of the gendered contribution to Fort McMurray. Opening with an account of an advertising campaign by the Regional Municipality of Wood Buffalo that emphasizes Fort McMurray as an ideal place to raise a family, Dorow's essay describes how the "campaign was, in part, a direct response to the negative reputation Fort McMurray had gained as a barely liveable boomtown of raucous single men who allegedly partied away money earned from plentiful work for the short time they were there."[50] Dorow follows this framing to examine the relationship of gender and work in the oil sands through the lens of social reproduction feminism, where work is understood both as paid and reproductive work, such as the care work required to raise a family. Drawing on "dozens of interviews and a survey of more than fifty parents and nannies," Dorow finds that the gendered divisions of labor are often overlooked in the broader boomtown imaginary. For Dorow, these experiences include "how women and visible minorities bear many of the social burdens" heightened in boomtowns, "how both men and women are caught in the gendered structures of the oil economy, and how the oil economy both benefits from and reproduces these unequal configurations."[51] Such dynamics are visible in the Oil Respect campaign's invocation of the oil and gas family.

In their socialist–feminist reading of Alberta's petroeconomy as expressed in promotional media, Alicia Massie and Emma Jackson isolate frontier masculinity and familial ideology, or what Dorow identifies in the context of Fort McMurray as "boomtown familism," as two vectors through which working-class identities are discursively constructed in the oil sands and their promotion by the agents and allies of the fossil economy.[52] Massie and Jackson offer a material–conceptual thread through which petromasculinities on the one hand and the oil and gas family on the other hand are bound together in the broader promotional imagination of the oil sands and in what I have been calling petroturfing. When the family form is denaturalized and historicized, how the oil and gas family is constructed and articulated through petromasculinity becomes clearer. Massie and Jackson's account draws together frameworks of social reproduction with the larger questions of futurity on a warming planet whose warming is disrupting life. The traditional, patriarchal, and heteronormative relations that underwrite petromasculinities equally inform how the family, children, and women are viewed under a gaze conditioned by oil executive epistemologies. The reproductive futurisms on offer by Oil Respect limit what kinds of futures are possible and with whom they can be made. And these limits become more acute when viewed in the setting of ongoing settler colonialism achieved through the necropolitical impetus of Canada's fossil economy, as I detail in the next chapter's account of the settler colonial imaginary of petroturfing. Whose family gets to be part of an oil and gas family, and whose is left out? How does this formation serve as an abstraction mobilized by petroturfing to further refine Canadian oil's symbolic life? When the oil and gas family gets mobilized as a central site through which to generate support, the gendered social and economic relations that fall outside a narrow familism are obscured and thus not included in the calls for support made by campaigns such as Oil Respect.

But in the same breath, Canadian oil is also figured as an agent in securing and promoting the rights of 2SLGBTQIA+ peoples in industry and society. What might be read as a surface-level friction is instead merely part of an idealist worldview shaped by oil executive epistemologies tethered to a substance whose extraction and refinement are endemic to gendered and racialized violence. Alberta, for instance, is home to the highest rates of murdered and missing Indigenous women and girls in the country, a tragic historical and ongoing reality I explore in the following chapter.[53] Returning to Puar's notion of homonationalism clarifies how commitments to the traditional heteronormative, patriarchal family form can coexist; homonationalism provides the conceptual thread that links these appeals as a kind of resource homonationalism is curated and circulated alongside a resource heteronationalism by the agents and architects of the fossil economy as a means to generate further social license for oil sands expansionism as sedimented in the construction of new pipelines.

Against an Oil-Soaked Resource Homonationalism

In the summer of 2016, the precursor to Oil Sands Strong called Canada OilSands Community posted a meme to its Facebook page that questioned why, given the country's treatment of 2SLGBTQIA+ peoples and communities, Canada continued to import oil from Saudi Arabia (Figure 10). The meme depicted two women in a passionate embrace with the following text superimposed from top to bottom: "In Canada lesbians are considered hot! In Saudi Arabia if you're a lesbian YOU DIE! Why are we getting our oil from countries that don't think lesbians are hot?!"[54] Controversy and outrage promptly followed the meme's circulation. And this critical attention brought what was a fringe Facebook page with relatively little following to the national stage as Canadian news media picked up the story. CBC News, for instance, detailed the controversy the post sparked and the apology from its creator, Robbie

Figure 10. A controversial Facebook meme created in July 2016 by Canada OilSands Community, a precursor to Oil Sands Strong.

Picard. In this coverage, Picard's identity was cited to arguably shelter him and the Facebook page from criticisms of sexism, bigotry, and homophobia. The CBC News article opened by describing Picard as both gay and Métis and closed by quoting Picard's since-deleted apology in which he emphasized that it was never his intent to "[demean] women or any people of any sexual orientation."[55] Of course, intent does not always inform impact. To add another layer to the clumsiness of this attempt at humor, the image that serves as the basis of this meme is lifted from what seem to be unwitting contexts. Described by the CBC News columnist as a stock photo, based on its circulation on fan sites and pages, the image instead appears to be a production still from Netflix's *Orange Is the New Black,* a comedy–drama television series that follows the true story of a woman in prison after conviction for money laundering, and whose representation of queer identities has been both celebrated for its representational politics and criticized for its heteronormative voyeuristic form.[56] In both the meme and the television series, homosexuality is repackaged to satisfy the heterosexual male gaze in specific ways.

Parson and Ray turn to this episode as part of their analysis of how women's bodies are used to promote resource extraction. They engage Puar's notion of homonationalism as it has been deployed to justify the War on Terror to articulate the ways that a certain kind of homosexuality (here, white lesbianism) is deemed acceptable in an otherwise often homophobic social milieu. Published in *Theory & Event* in 2020 at a time when the petroturfing project inched closer to the mainstream, the article's treatment of the episode as an isolated incident obscures the significance of the episode as a social media event. For Parson and Ray, the campaign was a corporate endeavor that ended in failure as it "was pulled due to pressure from queer, feminist, and environmental groups."[57] The analysis Parson and Ray put forward as they critique the petromasculine, heteropatriarchal gaze invoked in the meme and put this fetishization into relief with high rates of sexual violence among Indigenous women in extraction zones and the ongoing tragedy of missing and murdered Indigenous women and girls (MMIWG) in these regions is a strong one.[58] But by overlooking the historical setting and media environment in which this episode played out, Parson and Ray understate its impacts. What Parson and Ray identify as a one-off corporate campaign is better understood as a meme made on the edges of industry. From the vantage point afforded by 2020, it is difficult to consider the episode a failure given the presence of Oil Sands Strong today. There is no doubt that Picard's apology covered and circulated by CBC News drew attention to the group in ways that it may otherwise not have received. Legitimation through circulation on social media occurs here in tandem with traditional media circuits even though the meme was largely critiqued. Most importantly, the meme wasn't produced as an industry effort. The meme was made with a curated distance from industry that Picard has maintained since his work began. As a primarily social media–based phenomenon, in petroturfing there remains a leniency in presentation, tone, and tenor quite different from the kinds of standards to which industry or lobbying groups might feel beholden.

Parson and Ray's approach to this episode speaks to the necessity of employing the modes of analysis that I develop throughout this book when grappling with the petroturfing project as a last-ditch effort to maintain the fossil economy that is both parallel with but distinct from conventional advertising and public relations efforts. Although Parson and Ray do briefly move through a series of advertisements while linking these efforts to broader ideological norms within the oil and gas industry in particular and extractive capitalism in general, it is important to historicize this episode within the larger project of petroturfing. After the "lesbians are hot" episode and the transformation from Canada OilSands Community into Oil Sands Strong, memes tapping into this oil-soaked homonationalist spirit did not come to an end. In 2017, for instance, Oil Sands Strong posted a meme background stock photo of a rainbow flag waving in front of blue skies. Posted with the caption "LGBT," the text superimposed above the flag points out, "In Canada we value the rights of our LGBTQ friends! In Saudi Arabia they would die for who they are!" and closes with a familiar question: "Why are we buying oil from countries that kill those that we care about?"[59] Followers of the page responded to this post with mixed reactions. While some defended the spirit of the meme, several comments aggressively dissented. One commenter wrote, "Your [*sic*] gone from my fb [Facebook]" and it was a "big mistake showing this crap." Another simply said, "Goodbye." In this fractured community response, the frictions between the social sensibilities of those drawn to petroturfing rub against each other, which is all the more apparent since comments on Oil Sands Strong's Facebook seem to be rarely moderated. Later, this lack of moderation would turn into what reads as a strategy to elicit strong reactions from followers against activists resisting the maintenance and reproduction of Canada's fossil economy through the building of pipelines. These activists tend to be women and Indigenous peoples, and these posts often garner racist and misogynistic commentary from followers.

As standoffish as they read, the attitudes that register in these comments are not particularly fringe ones in the context of Albertan petromasculinities. Instead, those who made them brought to the surface dominant views in the ongoing heteropatriarchal, queerphobic, and homophobic worldviews that condition the settler colonial resource frontier underwriting Alberta's political economic and social relations. Kimberly A. Williams sets her intersectional feminist sights on the annual Calgary Stampede to explore how gender and sexuality are shaped and expressed in the financial epicenter of the Canadian oil and gas industry. For Williams, the Stampede "is, at its core, a misogynistic, white supremacist institution that is both product and active purveyor of Canada's ongoing settler colonial project."[60] "As part and parcel of this endeavour," Williams continues, "the Stampede is steeped in petrocultures . . . that have been proven time and again to be detrimental to historically marginalized communities as well as non-human animals and the natural environment."[61] The stampede's imbrication with the oil and gas industry runs deeper than mere cultural and ideological resonances. The Calgary Stampede serves as a synecdoche of larger attitudes about resource extraction, gender, and sexuality, which are conditioned by a nostalgia for the Wild West resource frontiers of years past expressed through the frontiers of the present. And these attitudes manifest in more than a cultural politics of nostalgia that valorizes whiteness and heteronormativity; they represent a material threat to the safety of women and queer peoples since, for instance, the stampede is seen by organizations such as the Calgary Sexual Health Centre as promoting and normalizing sexual harassment.[62] Perhaps, then, the subjects of petroturfing are not quite ready for the liberal project of homonationalism, which, as Puar notes in her original formulation of the concept, are in concert with heteronationalism and heteronormativity, not in friction with them.

In the face of these cynical realities of homonationalism, one ultimately wonders about the sincerity of these homonationalist questions of why it is that Canada continues to import oil from Saudi Arabia despite conflicting official views on gender and sexuality, if indeed these questions can be asked sincerely at all. At the level of political economy, the story is straightforward. This answer to this homonationalist question is an economic one more than anything else. Oil is imported from Saudi Arabia, just as it is imported from elsewhere, because that is how the global oil economy operates as a world market.

An episode in recent Canadian pipeline history helps clarify this political–economic reality. Of the major proposed pipeline projects over the 2010s that the petroturfing project took shape around, then TransCanada's Energy East was arguably the most aggressively nationalist in the cultural narratives generated and circulated by the agents, allies, and architects of Canada's fossil economy. To better lubricate the public senses and gain social license for a pipeline project running from the oilfields of Alberta to the shores of the Atlantic in Saint John, New Brunswick, at a refinery to be built by Irving Oil, promises of energy autonomy and sovereignty were sought. From this line of sight, Energy East would carry bitumen eastward and free Eastern Canada from the clutches of foreign oil. But, as journalist Jacques Poitras recounts, despite calls from, for instance, Alberta Wildrose member of the legislative authority Prasad Panda to ban "foreign dictator oil," Irving Oil president Ian Whitcomb made it clear that Irving would continue to import oil from Saudi Arabia even after Energy East.[63] Speaking to the *Financial Post,* Whitcomb didn't mince words: "We will add Western Canadian crude to our portfolio as the economics dictate, but probably not at the expense of our Saudi barrels."[64] This is all to say an obvious point, but one worth making in the context of petroturfing's homonationalism: the oil economy does not care where or how oil is produced; neither do the agents and architects of the fossil economy. To ask the oil economy otherwise is to ask for nothing short of a fundamental shift in business as usual, perhaps even revolution. But the goal of petroturfing is not to overhaul the fossil economy and reform it into some more equitable mode of extraction, refinement, and distribution akin to Latin American resource nationalisms. The goal of petroturfing is to aid in the increase of the presence of Canadian oil on the global market by shaping national and international energy consciousness in favor of Canadian oil.

Beyond the Oil Executive Epistemology's Petrosexual Politics of Recognition

From Bernard the Roughneck's performance of petromasculinity to oil-soaked resource homonationalism, the petrosexual politics of petroturfing rely on recognition politics that strategically overlook the material realities of the fossil economy's intersectional harms. All these treatments of gender, sex, and sexuality reveal an internal limit to a politics of recognition in achieving material change as they play out in the context of late capitalism or neoliberalism. A politics built solely on recognition does not challenge the fossil economy, and this is precisely why petroturfing and other promotional efforts from the agents, allies, and architects of Canada's fossil economy employ recognition politics in support of the maintenance and reproduction of the Canadian fossil economy, achieved in no small part due to an appearance of progressivism in concern over the treatment of women and 2SLGBTQIA+ peoples that reproduces business as usual both materially and ideologically.

This alliance between neoliberal postfeminism, homonationalism, and extractivism as embodied in petroturfing's politics of recognition shares structural and ideological characteristics with how Indigenous peoples are engaged with in the petroturfing project. In my view, such engagement reveals petroturfing to be a socially and culturally extractive enterprise that mirrors the material practices it supports as it symbolically refines Canadian oil as both traditional and progressive, heteronationalist and homonationalist. These petrosexual politics of recognition are inseparable from its settler colonial politics of recognition. Alongside the appeals to the economy that deploy a depoliticized resource nationalism, these gendered and racialized imaginaries deploy a politics of recognition to spread oil executive epistemologies among a wider audience and draft soldiers to fight in the oil culture wars.

4

RECONCILING EXTRACTION
THE SETTLER COLONIAL IMAGINARY

> We might say that energy infrastructures constitute the contemporary spine of the settler colonial nation.
>
> —Winona LaDuke and Deborah Cowen, "Beyond Wiindigo Infrastructure"

PIPELINES ARE TERRITORIAL CREATURES. If the four pipeline projects this book views as the material inspiration for petroturfing were to be built, more than six thousand miles of steel coated with what engineers call a sacrificial metal for weatherproofing would bisect vast swaths of ceded and unceded Indigenous territory across North America. Enbridge's Northern Gateway alone would affect the traditional territories of at least forty-one First Nations along its path from Bruderheim, Alberta, to Kitimat, British Columbia, as it travels 731 miles between Treaty 6 and the unceded territory of the Haisla people of Kitamaat Village. The Northern Gateway, as mentioned previously, would send bitumen from Alberta to the British Columbia coast and liquefied natural gas (LNG) from BC to Alberta.[1] In their construction and their everyday operation, these lines would negatively affect soil composition as well as surface water and groundwater, increase emissions, disrupt wildlife migration patterns, and more.[2] In their nearly guaranteed failure, impacts would be amplified. If a pipeline failed during its operation, for instance, spills would exacerbate and concentrate these persistent conditions, resulting in potentially irreversible contamination of ecosystems and death of wildlife. In other words, the pipelines that are talismans of the oil culture wars threaten the lands and waters of these territories. Both the continued operation of these pipelines and their potential failure are destructive scenarios. And from points of production to circulation, these processes unevenly distribute the costs and benefits of the fossil economy while offloading risks to peoples and ecosystems.

Through these threats, pipelines today undermine Indigenous sovereignty and prospects for self-determination. Such threat to these prospects has inspired a plethora of Indigenous-led movements of resistance to oil and gas expansionism and Canada's extractive state apparatus writ large. For people whose livelihood rests upon a strong, generative, and reciprocal relationship to the lands and waters that support them, the deleterious and unevenly distributed consequences of extractivism are as much social and cultural impacts as they are ecological ones. This point is not an attempt to homogenize the distinct practices, relations, and worldviews among the diverse First Nations, Inuit, and Métis peoples in what is now called Canada, of which there are more than six hundred distinct First Nations.[3] Yet an Indigenous internationalism within and beyond the borders of Canada has continued to forcefully take shape over the past several decades. From Idle No More, a 2012 movement that spurned a bill proposed by Harper's conservatives that sought to revise and erode existing environmental protections that could affect treaty rights, to the broader Indigenous resurgence that has emerged alongside and in concert with the international movement of Blockadia, powerful coalitions underwritten by shared commitments to a more equitable, decolonial future beyond the fossil economy abound.

As conflict over the futures of these pipelines took hold over the national imagination and the oil culture wars ignited in the early 2010s, an entangled, overlapping struggle surrounding questions of Indigenous sovereignty and self-determination followed to challenge the ongoing legacies of settler colonialism in Canada. On the heels of Harper's official apology for residential schools in 2008 and Prime Minister Justin Trudeau's 2015 declaration during a speech at an annual Assembly of First Nations gathering that "it is time for a renewed, nation-to-nation relationship with First Nations peoples," a commitment to reconciliation has been set as a priority.[4] These official government visions of reconciliation were pursued through the formation of a Truth and Reconciliation

Commission (TRC), whose aim was "to contribute to truth, healing and reconciliation," primarily regarding the ongoing legacy of the residential school system on Indigenous peoples.[5] Taking place from 2008 to 2015, the commission concluded with a series of ninety-four calls to action for governments and institutions to promote reconciliation. Here, a link is made between violent settler colonial practices of assimilation as expressed in initiatives such as residential schools as well as practices of dispossession embodied in the encroachment of the fossil economy. In what can more broadly be understood as the struggle over the securing of material self-determination, the TRC calls to action include demands for the adoption of the United Nations Declaration on the Rights of Indigenous Peoples (UNDRIP) by all levels of government as well as by the corporate sector.[6] Among the provisions of UNDRIP are a set of positions that affirm rights to self-determination. These conditions include Article 19, which calls on states to obtain "Free, Prior, and Informed Consent" (FPIC) of Indigenous peoples "before adopting and implementing legislative or administrative measures that may affect them," an article that has informed demands relating to territory and title in the shadow of Canadian extractivism.[7] UNDRIP was put to vote in 2007 and, tellingly, the only four votes against its adoption were Australia, Canada, New Zealand, and the United States—all nations with settler colonial foundations whose legacies are ongoing.[8] Although these nations eventually reversed their positions, their initial refusal speaks volumes in terms of how settler states maintain their internal power in the global arena.

In the long shadow of demands for a material overhaul of the relations among Indigenous nations, communities, and peoples and the settler state of Canada, recognition arguably remains the primary framework through which Indigenous peoples, nations, and communities are engaged with by both government and industry. Against and beyond recognition, many recent Indigenous movements of resistance to the settler, extractive state apparatus gather under the collective demand of *land back,* which effectively and unambiguously centers the material goals of resistance. A framework of recognition, conversely, creates ripe conditions through which powerful actors imbricated in settler colonialism such as the fossil fuel industry can leverage recognition to absolve or obscure their historical and ongoing perpetuation of settler colonial relations. In the lines of sight and ways of acting in the world generated from the kinds of oil executive epistemologies I detailed in the previous chapters, corporate social responsibility (CSR) discourse is a bedrock from which material social, economic, and ecological grievances are reduced to an affirmative identity politics that hinges upon notions of recognition to absolve these tensions. Recognition, after all, is a discursive or cultural process that need not be premised upon material commitments to or expressions of equity and justice. Implementations of UNDRIP to date in Canada expose the limitations of recognition politics in affecting material change when considering, for instance, that, in 2019, British Columbia became the first jurisdiction in the world to pass UNDRIP while invoking principles of FPIC.[9] Yet the province carries on with controversial infrastructural development on ceded and unceded Indigenous territory such as BC Hydro's Site C megadam or the TMX itself. As UNDRIP is set to become enshrined in law at a federal level through Bill C-15, which was passed by the Senate, how reconciliation shapes future social and ecological relations beyond discursive modes of recognition carries urgency.[10]

Engaging with these histories that expose the settler colonial form of extractive capitalism in Canada alongside prominent voices from Indigenous resurgence, this chapter examines the settler colonial imaginary of petroturfing by turning to media that represent and engage Indigenous peoples in the context of oil sands extractivism. My approach oscillates between an accounting of petroturfing's settler colonial imagination and a critique of this imagination grounded in perspectives from theorists of Indigenous resurgence. I argue that petroturfing attempts to *reconcile* extraction through a politics of recognition that reproduces a settler colonial imagination in its employment of corporate social responsibility discourse on the one hand and its critique of Indigenous land and water defenders on the other hand, a move that sees petroturfing as a predominantly settler enterprise that lays claim to what it construes as authentic Indigenous positions in the oil culture wars.

Recognition and Reconciliation in the Fossil Economy

In the previous chapter's interrogation of petroturfing's petrosexual politics, recognition emerged as a foundational rhetorical move from which to cast the production and consumption of Canadian oil as beneficial in myriad ways. First, Canadian oil appears as a force for maintaining traditional gendered relations tied to petromasculinity and the nuclear family; then it appears as a force that supports 2SLGBTQIA+ peoples more broadly. Such expressions are made through a surface-level, individuated identity politics. In the case of petroturfing's settler colonial imagination, these individuated identity politics underwrite expressions of recognition, an avenue through which the settler colonial dimensions of resource extraction are reconciled by asserting the economic benefits of extraction for Indigenous communities and peoples. When government and industry promote the benefits of extraction in these ways, they contribute to the formation of a paradox of the present where, as Kyle Conway and Manjulika E. Robertson have detailed, the extractive pursuits of the fossil economy are offered up as a solution to the problems produced by such pursuits in what they call the "petromodern paradox."[11] More oil, as Conway and Robertson point out, is framed as the antidote to the social and ecological consequences of oil.[12] In the context of this chapter's examination of the settler colonial imaginary of petroturfing, Conway and Robertson's petromodern paradox wears a decolonial veil as oil sands extractivism is promoted as a force for reconciliation and a panacea to ongoing dispossession.

Official government visions of reconciliation, as pointed out in the opening pages of this chapter, are premised upon a politics of recognition. By politics of recognition, I mean a relational politics that hinges upon a demand for a dominant group to recognize a marginal or, indeed, marginalized group in ways tied to questions of representation. Philosopher Charles Taylor classically defines politics of recognition in terms of demands for recognition from "minority or 'subaltern' groups, in some forms of feminism and in what is today called the politics of 'multiculturalism.'"[13] While the origins of this political project are relatively recent, its structural impetus has a deeper philosophical origin in Hegelian dialectics embodied most famously in the master–slave dialectic, a relation that has received extensive criticism from anti- and decolonial thinkers such as Frantz Fanon. More recently, Yellowknives Dene theorist Glen Sean Coulthard's 2014 book *Red Skin, White Masks: Rejecting the Colonial Politics of Recognition* shows how the Canadian state engages Indigenous peoples through a politics of recognition, which establishes the contours of Indigenous identities as always already defined in a bounded relation to the Canadian state, not as autonomous from it.[14]

But whether or not recognition should serve as a primary mode of political activism is not a unanimously held position. The degree to which a politics of recognition advances the broader political project of Indigenous self-determination continues to be debated, and this debate is conditioned by broader debates on the efficacy of identity politics in achieving material gains for marginalized peoples or groups. Coulthard forcefully critiques recognition as a determinant site through which emancipatory aims can be realized. This critique suggests that the limit a politics of recognition hits is done so swiftly in terms of how it can offer the foundation for a truly emancipatory politics. An explanation for this limit to recognition is that it operates more as a discursive relation than a material one; recognition can be *said* in service of reconciliation, but it need not be *done.*

Materiality is, then, a condition of praxis that links these more abstract interrogations of the politics of recognition to the more concrete relations at the center of pipeline politics and territorial dispossession. While offering a critique of what he describes as the colonial politics of recognition, Coulthard employs a historical materialist method of analysis that revisits David Harvey's influential concept of "accumulation by dispossession" to detail how Indigenous peoples in Canada have faced a kind of double alienation in the shadow of primitive accumulation.[15] Primitive accumulation describes the process by which noncapitalist relations to land and environment are made into capitalist ones. Marx, for instance, famously cites England's enclosure of the commons as an example of primitive accumulation.[16] Some orthodox readings of this process relegate primitive accumulation to these originary moments of capitalism's emergence as the dominant mode of production, whereas Indigenous thinkers such as Coulthard challenge these narrow readings by positing primitive accumulation as a continuous process, evidenced through the ongoing dispossession of land experienced by Indigenous peoples into the present. In this way, for Coulthard, dispossession "has structured the political relationship between Indigenous peoples and the state to a greater extent than" proletarianization, the two primary characteristics of primitive accumulation in Coulthard's view.[17] This dispossession historically materialized in, for instance, the creation of so-called

Crown land and today in the continued expropriation and destruction of lands and waters across both ceded and unceded territory for the benefit of extractive capital. And though dispossession may determine Indigenous peoples' relationship with the settler state and capitalism in a more determinant manner than proletarianization, the latter is often put forward to reconcile or absolve dispossession, especially in the promotional cultures of the extractive state apparatus. This dual alienation of sorts—a condition that emerges from the continued theft of land on the one hand and the theft of labor on the other hand—continues into the present and offers an analytic entry point for making sense of how petroturfing refines Canadian oil as a decolonizing force.

Seen in the relief of this historical context, the spectral promise of hydrocarbon proletarianization, that is, of access to wage-labor employment in the oil and gas industry and, accordingly, a spot in capitalist modes and relations of production, is a veil for the settler colonial impetus of extractive capital. A friction emerges whereby an appearance of reconciliation is nurtured by this promise of employment, while the material conditions of the fossil economy propelled by extractive capitalism and settler colonialism are obscured. The powerful story told by the forces of extractive capital is a partial one that eschews its agency in ongoing settler colonialism—it offers up wage-labor employment as a desirable condition, and a marker of progress, to rationalize extractive capitalism.

As a totalizing system, extractive capitalism makes, unmakes, and remakes relations between human and nonhuman worlds. In this remaking, a new economic system is installed that is at odds with Indigenous economies premised upon deep, reciprocal relations with lands and waters. Without essentializing these relations, it is important to underscore the gendered aspects of the kinds of extractivist settler colonial violence that affects communities and disrupts their means of social reproduction. It is no coincidence that Indigenous women are often on the front lines of experiencing and resisting the encroachment and consequences of extractivism.[18] Michi Saagiig Nishnaabeg theorist Leanne Betasamosake Simpson puts it clearly when she writes that "dispossession is gendered" and "settler colonialism is gendered."[19] Kahnawake Mohawk theorist Audra Simpson also details the consequences of the gendered character of settler colonialism, declaring frankly that in its continued process of settler colonization, the Canadian state "is killing Native women in order to [continue settling] and has historically done this to do so."[20]

These intersectional characteristics and consequences of settler colonialism inform the politics of recognition that theorists such as Coulthard take to task. Leanne Betasamosake Simpson's extended critique of dominant neoliberal modes of political engagement helps further explain the limits of a politics of recognition that paves the way for a depoliticized, ahistorical cultural resurgence. This mode of cultural resurgence forms the bedrock of how the oil and gas industry and its allies promote what it often calls Indigenous or, using the official government terminology, Aboriginal relations. "In the context of settler colonialism and neoliberalism," Leanne Simpson writes, "the term *cultural* resurgence, as opposed to *political* resurgence, which refers to a resurgence of story, song, dance, art, language, and culture, is compatible with the reconciliation discourse, the healing industry, or other depoliticized recovery-based narratives."[21] When the cultural and the political are separated in this way, a depoliticized version of reconciliation is made possible without any genuine modification to material practices and relations that might shape more equitable relations and challenge ongoing settler colonialism in the present and future. "Cultural resurgence can take place within the current settler colonial structure of Canada because it is not concerned with dispossession," Simpson argues, "whereas political resurgence is seen as a direct threat to settler sovereignty."[22] Under this rubric of cultural resurgence, Canada's fossil economy turns to its employment of Indigenous peoples and its mutual-benefit agreements with Indigenous communities to participate in its own version of reconciliation discourse rooted in the very conditions that made such reconciliation necessary in the first place.

Such promises of employment and community benefit through economic stimulus are familiar tropes in the *longue durée* of Canadian pipeline politics. In the 1970s, for instance, the unbuilt Mackenzie Valley natural gas pipeline set a precedent of sorts for how Indigenous peoples enter into settler energy and infrastructural relations on these terms. The case *for* the construction of the Mackenzie Valley Pipeline, detailed in a report titled *Communities of the Mackenzie: Effects of the Hydrocarbon Industry,* rested in part on developing a convincing argument that the project would be socially and economically beneficial for existing, largely

Indigenous communities along the path of the pipeline without detrimental impacts to the possibilities for these communities to continue to live subsistence-based lifestyles. *Communities of the Mackenzie* is direct in its claims surrounding the positive economic impact the pipeline would generate. "It is difficult to locate any other economic generator that might prove to be a substitute for the employment-creating capacity of the hydrocarbon industry," the report states, "even if measured only in terms of sustaining current levels of economic activity."[23] Further, the report promotes the wage-labor economy that the pipeline would usher in as a means for escaping what the authors, an architecture, planning, and design firm called Van Ginkel Associates Ltd., describe as "persistent poverty":

> the stimulation of economic activity could be bent to the furthering of desirable programs for northern residents; it could broaden an individual's choice of employment and lifestyle and permit decisions by an individual as to whether or not to participate in the wage economy: unemployment and persistent poverty permit no such options.[24]

The stakes of this proposed pipeline project were high, especially in terms of the deleterious effects it would have on the complex, biodiverse ecosystem of the North on the one hand and on Indigenous communities and their ways of life on the other hand. If built, the pipeline would have been historically unique. It would be the longest pipeline of its time to be built in an environment that posed numerous socioeconomic and environmental challenges. And, as Coulthard points out in a chapter of *Red Skin, White Masks* that details the role that struggles surrounding the Mackenzie Valley Pipeline played in establishing a context for politicizing and advancing arguments for self-determination in his home community, the pipeline would be "the largest private sector development project in the history of Canada, and quite possibly the world."[25]

In this capacity, the pipeline would establish an energy corridor, bringing with it a momentum-turned-inertia that would drastically alter the existing political economy, a mixed one tied to land-based practices. The first proposals faced a series of delays after the government of Canada commissioned an inquiry to examine the social, environmental, and economic impacts of the pipeline. Led by Justice Thomas Berger and known colloquially as the Berger Inquiry, the commission recommended that the pipeline be delayed for ten years in order to resolve outstanding Indigenous land claims and establish conservation areas that would necessitate rerouting the path to mitigate its impact on sensitive ecosystems in the Northern Yukon in particular. This initial ten-year delay conditioned its unbuilt status in the present; it cast over the pipeline project a perpetual uncertainty that future proposals couldn't shed.

In light of this history marked by a persistent unequal distribution of the costs and benefits of oil and gas expansionism in Canada, it is difficult to shake the creeping feeling of déjà vu that takes hold when reading the lines of promotion in *Communities of the Mackenzie* and those of critique by Berger in his final report, published in book form as *Northern Frontier, Northern Homeland.* Even if the ideal vision of an extractive capitalist utopia offered by *Communities of the Mackenzie* were realized, as Berger points out, "except during the construction phase of a project, the petroleum industry is capital- rather than labour-intensive."[26] This point remains true today. Indigenous employment statistics mobilized as evidence of the reconciliatory powers of Canadian oil—such as those that appear in media produced and circulated online and through social media by Canada Action or Oil Sands Strong that I will examine in this chapter—obscure the historical conditions of dispossession that made wage-labor employment necessary for survival in the first place and foreclose possibilities for imagining futures beyond the fossil economy.

Many theorists working in the energy humanities have argued that the promises of the fossil economy more generally tell a story of what literary and cultural theorist Lauren Berlant has influentially termed "cruel optimism."[27] For Berlant, cruel optimism is a condition that "exists when something you desire is actually an obstacle to your flourishing."[28] Shaped by the dual character of alienation from land and labor mediated by the extractive state apparatus of extractive capitalism's theft of land and territory as dispossession and the theft of labor as proletarianization, the obstacles that the settler colonial petromodern paradox conceals are tied primarily to the socially and ecologically deleterious consequences of oil sands extractivism. Such consequences are particularly acute for Indigenous peoples and communities whose ways of being in the world are premised upon good relations with the land, relations threatened and disturbed by resource extraction.

Corporate Indigenous Washing after Reconciliation

As petroturfing symbolically refines Canadian oil, it does so in specific registers that separate and then depoliticize economic, social, and ecological relations. Through these modes of refinement, Canadian oil is refigured as a force for good across these relations, and the authenticity and legitimacy of such refinement are supported by the architectures and infrastructures of social media. Promises of proletarianization are central to the promotional trajectory of petroturfing, particularly in terms of how it negotiates impacts on Indigenous peoples and communities. Here, the dual alienation described earlier comes into view as these promises of extractive capitalism rewrite loss as benefit. In rewriting loss as benefit, these efforts exhibit a kind of Indigenous washing of extractive processes that is repeated across the oil sands promotional mediascape, where Indigenous washing is understood following Sara L. Crosby and Anna J. Willow's formulation as "narratives [that] make a show of engaging with Indigenous perspectives but only as a feint designed superficially to incorporate—even while actually undercutting—any substantive Native perspectives or politics."[29] For Crosby and Willow, Indigenous washing is an extension of settler colonial erasure; they mobilize this framework to examine how "genre fictions inspired by the North American oil boom of the 2000s" express modes of Indigenous washing.[30] But as Crosby and Willow highlight when introducing the concept, Indigenous washing is in the first instance a promotional discourse adjacent to tactics such as greenwashing where a politically sanitized environmentalism is leveraged to promote the consumption of particular commodities. Recognizing this promotional impetus of Indigenous washing, I first look to dominant corporate invocations of reconciliation discourse and then apply this framework to the fictions of petroturfing to interrogate its settler colonial imagination.

Like petroturfing's economic and gendered imaginaries, promises of employment and community support underwrite its settler colonial imagination as it selectively elevates Indigenous perspectives on and relations to extraction. These promises, however, are not unique to petroturfing—they are a constitutive characteristic of broader CSR discourse that seeks to draw attention to the ways that extraction benefits Indigenous peoples and communities. Canada's largest energy company, Suncor, for instance, gathers its discourse on Indigenous peoples on its home page under the header of sustainability. On a page dedicated to "Aboriginal relations," Suncor details the principles that inform these relations—respect, communication, benefits, and environment—while promoting initiatives such as "partnering with Indigenous youth" as well as "improving Indigenous workforce development."[31] Suncor also provides public access to its internal "Aboriginal awareness web-based training," a platform that hosts a series of videos that visitors can navigate. The videos offer a grade-school history of Canada's colonial history, with Indigenous elders, community leaders, and employees invited to reflect on a series of topics in an interview format. Covering topics ranging from land treaties to residential schools, the historical narrative is one that recognizes the traumas inherited in the present but relegates settler colonial events to the past, while offering a narrative of hope for the future by emphasizing that things are changing. Gestures to the legacy effects of colonization in these ways obscure the presently bound relations of settler colonialism and extractive capitalism, which produces an amnesia that relegates instances of settler colonialism to a past far removed, even if the training explicitly recognizes the impacts of settler colonialism on Indigenous peoples in the present. These amnesiac moves repackage the fossil economy as a force for reconciliation.

Another of the major oil sands producers, Syncrude, echoes this depoliticizing tendency. Throughout the web page that hosts its discussion of what it calls Indigenous relations, Syncrude employs vague, conditional phrasing to describe the extent of its commitments and the implementation of commitments. Syncrude points out, for instance, that "since our earliest days [we] have worked to accommodate [local Indigenous peoples'] interests *wherever possible*" and, in terms of consultation, it "strive[s] for early engagement *wherever possible*."[32] In its detailing of how Syncrude achieves its vision, the page underscores efforts that center primarily on environmental stewardship for postextractive landscapes and reclamation projects that incorporate traditional knowledge alongside statistics surrounding economic relationships with Indigenous-led businesses and levels of Indigenous employment. Perhaps more surprisingly, Syncrude also details support for the implementation of UNDRIP "in a manner consistent with the Canadian Constitution and law."[33] However, as my earlier engagement with UNDRIP's fraught Canadian history shows, it is precisely in the terms and conditions of implementation where the concrete, material impacts of UNDRIP take shape, and the oil and gas industry is invested in influencing what these terms and conditions look like.

Endorsing the implementation of a yet-to-be determined version of UNDRIP has become a default position among the agents and architects of Canada's fossil economy and, more generally, the Canadian extractive state apparatus. Known for setting the benchmark for dominant pro-oil narratives in Canada through strategic communications, CAPP has been active in influencing the contours of industry support for UNDRIP and in shaping what its implementation might look like. In 2016, on the heels of British Columbia's adoption of UNDRIP, CAPP released a discussion paper that recognizes industry impacts on Indigenous peoples, while clarifying the position of the association and its members. "Within this process [of reconciliation]," the paper reads, "we acknowledge our activities have impacted Indigenous communities."[34] The report contains headers that respond to key articles of UNDRIP, including "Preservation of Human Rights," "Recognition of Culture and Education," "Right to Self Determination," "Free Prior and Informed Consent," and "Economic and Social Sustainability."[35] Under these headers, CAPP expresses commitments to these principles with repeated refrains that implementation should be consistent with existing Aboriginal and Treaty rights in the Canadian Constitution and that the brunt of the responsibility for reconciliation efforts falls squarely on the shoulders of government. "While we acknowledge that the resource extraction industries, including ours, have an important role in contributing to the economic and social sustainability of Indigenous Peoples in Canada," the paper states, "government has the primary responsibility." The paper carries on in this tenor:

> It is important for government to fulfill its duty in reconciliation and not pass this responsibility or cost on to industry. Our industry should play its role by engaging meaningfully with Indigenous Peoples about its projects and the associated economic benefits. Government must also play its role.[36]

This is similar to language that Syncrude employs in its discussion of UNDRIP. Here UNDRIP becomes a vehicle to refine Canadian oil in ways that satisfy industry's autonomy while promoting a narrative that, rather than impeding reconciliation, intensified oil and gas extraction is an avenue toward achieving it.

Taken together, this brief accounting of industry approaches to Indigenous relations in the age of reconciliation reveals a disjuncture between the histories and materials of the fossil economy's imbrication in settler colonialism as smoothed out by recognition politics. Recognition trumps action; culture trumps politics. And questions of land seem to factor into the equation most directly *after* extraction in visions for reclamation, which I discuss in the next chapter. This account is not merely a cynical dismissal of each instance of corporate engagement with Indigenous peoples as an instrument of the fossil economy—as if mutually beneficial agreements do not or cannot exist. This type of dismissal rests on a simplistic argument that does not adequately account for the complexity of the current conjuncture marked by ongoing settler colonialism, out of which there are many paths to a more equitable future. Moreover, it is not my, nor anyone's, *individual* place to determine precisely what equitable relations now and in the future look like; this is a *collective* endeavor. Yet what is certain is that the rhetorical and discursive strategies employed in ways consistent with Indigenous washing obfuscate the degree to which corporate commitments beyond the letter of the law are not binding agreements and even the letter of the law is influenced by the agents and architects of the fossil economy.

The scenario industry fears most, and that arguably conditions its engagement with and formation of recognition and reconciliation discourse in recent years as a response to the TRC calls to action, is the possibility of Indigenous nations and communities holding veto power over extractive developments. This power would arguably be an opening for realizing the very kinds of material–political action that motivates Indigenous resurgence movements and land back demands. The forms of Indigenous washing performed by industry through CSR avenues, which elevate the most basic economic acts such as employment initiatives or privileging Indigenous-owned businesses for service contracts to a form of reconciliation, are made possible precisely by the separations between the cultural and the political that Leanne Betasamosake Simpson critiques in *As We Have Always Done.* And in the frameworks of recognition employed by the agents and architects of Canada's fossil economy, oil and gas companies become mediators of Indigenous knowledge and experience in ways that require little, if any, material commitment that would alter or slow extractive practices. Voluntary cultural and economic initiatives are held up as avenues for reconciliation that obscure the historical conditions that disrupted existing vibrant Indigenous economies and relations, while offering up oil sands extractivism as an antidote to issues it in part created. Petroturfing, as I will show in the rest of this chapter, infuses these default positions with a populist flavor to further refine Canadian oil and reconcile extraction.

The Politics of Voice at the Impasse of the Settler Colonial Petromodern Paradox

Petroturfing recasts dominant CSR rhetorical strategies as if they were not institutionalized discourses. Here, petroturfing's attempts to operate as a counter-counterdiscourse come into clearer view, and the aim of *saturating* the discursive field is in full force. The most aggressive efforts to construe the oil sands megaproject as one that is socially and ecologically beneficial for Indigenous peoples and communities come from Oil Sands Strong and Canada Action. Using decontextualized quotations from chiefs and more general statements about the benefits of oil sands development for Indigenous peoples and communities, these efforts sidestep the extremely complex histories and presents, such as those detailed by Indigenous theorists, including Coulthard and Leanne Betasamosake Simpson, who have unearthed the collective amnesia surrounding dispossession and the persistence of settler colonialism. While state-sponsored initiatives such as the TRC as well as grassroots modes of activism that comprise Indigenous resurgence have made strides in fighting this collective amnesia, the amnesiac condition runs deep as Indigenous washing emerges as a way to claim Canadian oil as a force for reconciliation, and in this gesture individuals stand in for collectives, especially business-friendly Indigenous leaders who subscribe to what Tsimshian (Kitselas/Kitsumkalum) and Nuu-chah-nulth (Ahousaht) scholar Clifford Atleo calls "Aboriginal capitalism" or what defense lawyer and legal scholar Christopher Nowlin calls "Indigenous capitalism," which are positions that emerged out of neoliberal conditions.[37]

Across the petroturfing mediascape, Chief Jim Boucher appears frequently as an authoritative, representative Indigenous voice in support of Canada's fossil economy. Boucher is a former elected chief of the Fort McKay First Nation who is known for his amicable relationship with the agents of Canada's fossil economy to the degree that he has been publicly described as a "pro-pipeline chief."[38] On its Facebook page, Oil Sands Strong has produced and circulated several memes that include an image of Boucher with a quotation overlaid that reads: "If it weren't for oil my people would be in poverty." This quotation is attributed to "Chief Jim Boucher of the First Nations." Boucher's statement was notably made at a 2016 Assembly of First Nations gathering where he described the positive impacts that oil sands development has had for Fort McKay First Nation, including a nonexistent unemployment rate at the time.[39] Ultimately, Boucher's position informing this statement is that revenue from extraction is a means to pursue self-determination through economic autonomy, and he is deeply critical of the environmental movement due to the role environmentalists played in decreasing demands for fur, a major source of revenue for communities like Fort McKay First Nation.[40] Despite Boucher's clear support for oil and gas extraction, Oil Sands Strong's 2018 posting of the meme elicited hateful, racist commentary that remains on the post today, including one commenter who wrote that "the most useless people are First Nations god [*sic*] for nothing to live for free on taxpayers [*sic*] money."[41]

Boucher's record of statements and public presence, however, is not the one of unwavering support for development his appearances in the petroturfing mediascape might suggest. An article written in 2018 by freelance journalist James Wilt for *The Narwhal* details the complicated relationship that Fort McKay First Nation has had with government and industry in relation to the Rigel Oil Sands Project, a proposed ten-thousand-barrel-per-day project that would threaten the Moose Lake region, which is considered sacred among Fort McKay and neighboring nations.[42] Boucher makes the stakes and prospects of his demand for the preservation of the Moose Lake region clear by situating the demand within a larger legacy of dispossession:

> We've lost 70 per cent of our land to the oilsands developers so far. We'd like to maintain a little piece of land so our people can

> continue to hunt, trap and fish and exercise our treaty rights on the lands we have available to us.[43]

Lost. Little piece of land. Treaty rights. This language is revealing, particularly when put into relief with Boucher's statements in support of Canada's fossil economy. Here, Boucher makes explicit how oil sands development has required land dispossession. Moreover, he draws attention to the ways in which existing modes of extraction have the capacity to threaten treaty rights by dictating where and when Fort McKay First Nation and others across Treaty 8 territory can practice crucial aspects of land-based living enshrined in the treaty, such as hunting, trapping, or fishing. Put next to the kinds of commentary that bequeathed Boucher the title of "pro-pipeline chief," the complex realities of how Indigenous self-determination confronts the inertia of resource extraction rise to the surface, as do the limitations of existing models of FPIC.

Positions like Boucher's point to existing frictions within Indigenous individuals, nations, and communities surrounding questions of the costs and benefits of resource extraction as these costs and benefits impact the possibilities for exercising treaty rights. As in the case of any peoples or communities, Indigenous peoples are not homogenous in their views. Nor does a recognition of the difficult situation that Indigenous peoples have been collectively put in translate into a commitment to the machinations of fossil and extractive capital. Indigenous self-determination's contours are by definition not determined by settlers, progressive or otherwise. Such a complex and nuanced condition is often flattened by petroturfing.

Petroturfing is by and large a settler enterprise; its treatment of and engagements with Indigenous peoples and perspectives both in support of Canada's fossil economy and against it must be understood in light of this fact. From its inception in the pages of *Ethical Oil,* which, as I show in chapter 1, expends great efforts to distinguish Canadian oil as a kind of fair-trade alternative to OPEC oil, to the torch bearers that followed, including Canada Action and Oil Sands Strong, petroturfing has and continues to draw attention to Indigenous employment figures as evidence of the unique power that Canadian oil and its infrastructures wield. Recall Levant's lofty words: "it's safe to say that Aboriginals have never had it so good."[44] In the wake of reconciliation discourse taking hold as conventional industry views, Oil Sands Strong pushed this sentiment to its zenith by circulating a meme on its Facebook page offering followers a hypothetical scenario to choose between: "Middle Eastern conflict oil" or "Canadian Aboriginal produced peace oil."[45]

To further legitimate this view through circulation, there have been concerted attempts across petroturfing to represent environmentalist organizations as tokenizing Indigenous peoples, as if there were not a plethora of Indigenous-led groups and efforts to resist the expansion of Canada's fossil economy and promote environmental justice that prioritizes decolonization. In 2017, Cody Battershill of Canada Action, for instance, took to traditional news media to spread the word that "First Nations actually want resource development—if paid activists would just get out of their way."[46] Published as an opinion piece on the website of the *Financial Post,* a newspaper that is part of the Postmedia Network known for amplifying pro-oil voices, the essay charges activist organizations such as Greenpeace with speaking for Indigenous peoples and co-opting Indigenous voices.[47] "It's outrageous that paid activists drown out the hopes and aspirations of so many First Nations people," Battershill writes with bravado.[48] In a gesture that further crystallizes my earlier point about the circulation of Boucher across petroturfing media, Battershill cites Boucher's statement on the poverty-relieving characteristics of Canadian oil as the sole piece of evidence that the default Indigenous opinion is in support of extractive development. Battershill pivots from Boucher to encourage readers to consult with First Nations leaders and gather their own information, not to receive a more nuanced perspective on the complexities of the costs and benefits of resource extraction for communities facing ongoing settler colonialism, however. Rather, Battershill encourages this mode of consultation because "First Nations leaders across the country will tell you that the large majority of First Nations are open-minded about pipeline and petroleum development." And it is through that engagement with a predetermined outcome defined by Battershill that "you'll realize that support for fair-trade energy from Canada is the best choice toward peace, progress and prosperity, not only for First Nations peoples, but for all Canadians."[49]

In these more conventional, legacy media settings, the agents of petroturfing often put on a diplomatic front, even in the second wave of petroturfing, that is distinguished by its firm stances opposed to earlier gestures to balance. Battershill does so here to suggest that it is the progressive environmentalists who have been co-opting Indigenous voices, not the oil and gas industry. Certainly, there is a tense history between Indigenous activism and environmentalism, as I discussed in chapter 1, but Battershill's critique is in bad faith as he uses Boucher as a stand-in for all Indigenous perspectives. Placing this opinion piece next to Boucher's own statements of criticism centered on questions of land dispossession and treaty rights that would come after Battershill's *Financial Times* op-ed troubles the ease through which Battershill scales out in these ways.

Divisional tactics inform Canada Action's broader media strategy when it comes to its engagement with Indigenous perspectives on and relations to resource extraction. Such tactics became most visible in early 2020 during the eruption of support for the Wet'suwet'en, who have been occupying their unceded traditional territory since 2009 to block a series of pipeline projects. Materializing as the Unist'ot'en Camp, the reoccupation effort culminated in the construction of infrastructures of resistance—a log cabin, pit house, healing center, and more. Formed in solidarity with the camp, the Gidimt'en Access Point controls access to Wet'suwet'en territory in accordance with UNDRIP and Wet'suwet'en law.[50] In the first half of the 2010s, the camp's highest-profile target of resistance was Enbridge's now-canceled Northern Gateway. More recently, these efforts have been primarily leveraged against TC Energy's Coastal GasLink LNG pipeline, which is currently under construction and will travel 420 miles inland from Dawson Creek to the BC coast in Kitimat in order to access Asian markets. Leveraging Aboriginal title rights, which were affirmed by a landmark Supreme Court case in 1997, this occupation of traditional, unceded territory is an assertion of jurisdiction. Against these assertions of jurisdiction, the RCMP raided the camp by violently enforcing court injunctions in 2019, 2020, and 2021. Documents accessed by *The Guardian* showed that during the 2019 raid, officers were prepared to use lethal force.[51] After the 2020 raid, demonstrations of solidarity were executed under the banner "Shut Down Canada" across the nation, including rail blockades on Tyendinaga Mohawk Territory.

At the height of these actions of solidarity in 2020, a post authored by Canada Action argued that "the media isn't even close to reporting a balanced view of the situation."[52] To provide this balanced view, Canada Action took to its blog and Twitter in a coordinated effort. In a blog post titled "Wet'suwet'en Member Says Her People Are Being Misinformed on Gas Pipeline," Canada Action covers a pro-pipeline and LNG rally at the Civic Centre in downtown Prince George, BC, the nearest major municipality where many of the court cases related to the Northern Gateway and Coastal GasLink have taken place. Prince George is also my hometown and where I attended rallies against the Northern Gateway in and around 2012. In a video tweet embedded in the post, Wet'suwet'en Nation member Bonnie George makes the case that there would be more support if there was less misinformation, a position that echoes the kinds of information-as-panacea that Riofrancos describes in *Resource Radicals,* which I discussed in chapter 2. In another video posted on Twitter, Hereditary Chief Helen Michelle of Skin Tyee Nation, Wet'suwet'en, alleges that many of the protesters participating in the blockade are "not even Wet'suwet'en."[53] The tweet received 4,759 likes and 2,738 retweets. In response, the official Gidimt'en Checkpoint account pointed out that Michelle "is speaking on behalf on [*sic*] the Skin Tyee First Nation whose reserve is nowhere near the pipeline route."[54] Issues surrounding voice, representation, proximity, and scale, however, reappear. Canada Action has gone through great lengths across its social media presence—particularly by using Twitter's paid promotional posts function—to articulate what it circulates as definitive Indigenous views on resource extraction, performing a strategy that one critical response tweet aptly described as "divide and conquer."[55]

In what reads as a direct response to the questionable optics of settler voices such as Battershill's providing exclusive commentary on Indigenous perspectives on resource extraction in mainstream media venues and on Canada Action's home page, Canada Action recruited an Indigenous oil sands worker to write content. Since 2020, Cowessess First Nation heavy equipment operator and member of the Indigenous Resource Network (IRN) Estella Petersen has contributed a series of blog posts that primarily detail the benefits of resource extraction for Indigenous peoples and communities in terms of employment and tertiary economic benefits. The IRN is an Indigenous-led business advocacy organization whose values include "having a positive and nonpartisan message" and "avoid[ing] polarization and focus[ing] on balanced perspectives and solutions for moving forward."[56] With these echoes of the kinds of commitments to balance as a means to promote Canada's fossil economy discussed in chapter 2, the organization describes its animating imperative: "To provide a platform for Indigenous voices that are supportive of Indigenous participation in resource development."[57] Petersen's own story is a moving one of overcoming generational poverty that ongoing settler colonialism often ensures. In an op-ed published in a nationally syndicated newspaper, the *Globe and Mail*, Petersen tells her story. She describes the racism she has experienced throughout her life and in the Patch: "I've heard all the epithets and slurs: 'lazy Indian,' 'welfare bum,' and accusations that I was only hired because I'm Indigenous. The oil sands are certainly not immune to such thinking."[58] We will encounter these stereotypes again soon. Petersen notes, however, that this is changing, and she spends the rest of the piece refuting the kinds of critiques I explored earlier, including the relationship between resource extraction and violence against Indigenous women, while ultimately articulating the impetus for the article encapsulated in its title: "I'm an Indigenous woman who works in Alberta's oil sands—and I can speak for myself." Petersen concludes by confirming how employment in the oil and gas industry has helped her as she pleas for oil sands jobs to be supported in the future. "For me," she writes, "Canada's resource sector was a great choice, as it's a great place to create opportunities, and I don't want to see these jobs taken away from Indigenous people, or any Canadians."[59]

The positions expressed in this op-ed are echoed throughout Petersen's posts on the Canada Action home page. In "Indigenous Peoples in Canada Can Speak for Themselves," Petersen describes the desires of Indigenous peoples to have access to "clean drinking water and safe housing," and she views resource extraction as an avenue to achieve these aims. She writes:

> What do many Indigenous People in Canada want? We'd like to have clean drinking water and safe housing. We'd like our treaty rights and promises upheld. We want the right to earn a good livelihood, since living off the land is not enough to survive. We also know that many of our reservations are rich in natural resources including but not limited to to [*sic*] forestry, fishing, oil and gas and minerals.[60]

With memes produced by Canada Action embedded throughout that detail, for example, the economic impacts for Indigenous-owned businesses generated by the TMX ("$1.4 billion in Indigenous contracts as of Dec. 31st, 2020"), the post addresses the question of who speaks for whom, which culminates in a vague critique of organizations that speak for Indigenous communities and an articulation of the ways in which resource extraction can fuel self-determination. In another post, Petersen criticizes Bill C-15 and the looming implementation of UNDRIP as federal law from a number of standpoints, particularly as it relates to clarity of terminology such as self-determination. She also questions what role an international organization such as the UN should play in shaping Indigenous relations in Canada since, in her view, it "doesn't fully understand the majority of Indigenous communities in Canada."[61] An ahistoricism enshrouds this view, given that there is a long history of UN advocacy when settler nations such as Canada fail to respect sovereignty and, moreover, that the terms and conditions of UNDRIP were drafted over two decades with "extraordinary participation of indigenous peoples from around the world."[62] And as Petersen urges readers to learn more about the bill and UNDRIP from a video produced by the IRN, a closed loop of information forms that privileges opposition to Bill C-15 as a default Indigenous position.

In the wake of a cultural politics of recognition permeating extractive industry, there are high stakes in building consensus on the reconciliatory possibilities of oil sands extractivism. Yet, as industry and its allies perform this ideological work in support of Canada's fossil economy, tensions persist at the sites of conflict in the oil culture wars. Where Petersen highlights individual choices as the avenue for economically escaping the legacies of ongoing settler colonialism, the choice of continued and intensified resource extraction arguably comes at a cost. Lubicon Cree energy and environmental justice activist Melina Laboucan-Massimo has described the conjuncture that requires Indigenous participation in resource extraction for economic stability as a kind of economic hostage scenario.[63] This position is echoed by the story of Marvin L'Hommecourt, a Dene oil sands worker who appears as a central figure in Chris Turner's *The Patch*. L'Hommecourt's story draws attention to the tensions inherent in living off wages from extractive labor and living off the land, which is told throughout a section of chapter 7 titled "The Site and the

Trapline."[64] As Turner writes, "he lives it [the tension] every day up at Kearl, where he drives big bulldozers and maintains a traditional trapline just outside the site's perimeter."[65] The trapline, Turner details through L'Hommecourt's story, is no longer what it once was, as it has been affected by the impacts of ongoing resource extraction—there are ultimately fewer animals each year as land is disturbed by cut lines and increased human activity primarily due to traffic around an airport built in support of extractive industry. Neither Turner nor L'Hommecourt offer solutions to this impasse, but the story is instructive in its articulation of how choice is a fraught concept given the contours of the present defined by a settler colonial petromodern paradox.

From Indigenous Washing to Petro Trolling

Alongside celebrations of increased representation of Indigenous peoples in extractive employment and persistent appeals to the ways in which oil sands extractivism benefits Indigenous peoples and communities, tensions over who represents a majority of Indigenous voices are another site through which petroturfing extracts legitimacy for its project in particular and for the Canadian fossil economy in general. In many ways, these articulations of the economic benefits of oil sands extraction for Indigenous peoples construct a discursive gateway for calling into question the legitimacy of Indigenous resistance efforts to then undermine this resistance.

Against Indigenous activists, the most aggressive attempts to undermine Indigenous movements of resistance come from accusations of hypocrisy. Here, Indigenous activists are accused of selling out for partnering with global environmentalist organizations such as Greenpeace or even by simply consuming fossil fuels. Such rhetorical attacks are exhibited in the trolling behavior by Oil Sands Strong that often sets its sights on Indigenous women, a telling point when considering Sisseton Wahpeton Oyate feminist theorist Kim TallBear's powerful expression of the crucial role Indigenous women play in resistance movements.[66] Some readers may have noticed that I have yet to use the vocabulary of trolling to describe petroturfing, which is because the first phase of petroturfing mobilized balance and appeals to reason as a legitimating strategy more than it did by, say, bullying. In the case of efforts to undermine

Indigenous activists in recent years, however, trolling aptly describes the strategy that animates groups such as Oil Sands Strong and Rally 4 Resources. For communications scholar Jason Hannan, trolling has crept out of the dark recesses of the internet to become a mainstream communicative and political strategy—a condition of the contemporary political atmosphere that runs deep in the age of social media because it is nurtured by social media's architectures and infrastructures. "With the rise of social media," Hannan writes, "we are witnessing the birth of a new political language game, in which one of the primary moves is the speech act of trolling."[67] As an emergent form of online bullying, trolling encompasses the kinds of aggression that are now a default setting for petroturfing.

Taking aim at Indigenous activists, Oil Sands Strong flexes its trolling muscles. With the caption "Strike a pose! Jet setter Melina Is at it again! How many air miles do [*sic*] she have?," Oil Sands Strong posted a meme to Facebook in 2019 criticizing Laboucan-Massimo for traveling to New York for a promotional photo shoot for the Indigenous-led collective Seeding Sovereignty. The meme includes a screen capture of Laboucan-Massimo's own Facebook post describing the event with overlaid, boldface, all-caps text that reads:

> Melina Laboucan Massimo who has taken 13 trips to Europe and countless others, is in New York City "Fighting Climate Change" with a photographer of Game of Thrones! She also hosted Jane Fonda in Fort McMurray. Share this post if you're sick and tired of these so-called environmentalist pretenders![68]

Laboucan-Massimo currently operates Sacred Earth Solar, which installs solar energy infrastructure in Indigenous communities, organizes with Indigenous Climate Action, and has worked with the David Suzuki Foundation and Greenpeace. She is a fierce critic of the oil sands who speaks and writes often about the deleterious social and ecological impacts that oil sands extraction has had on her home community of Little Buffalo, Alberta, and across traditional Lubicon Cree territory, which spans more than six thousand square miles. As Laboucan-Massimo details in a short documentary produced by Greenpeace, Little Buffalo experienced a massive oil spill of more than one million gallons in 2011 from a ruptured pipeline. The handling of the spill by government and industry was abysmal, with the community left in the dark about what exactly had occurred and to what degree until days after the disaster, which contaminated a sensitive muskeg ecosystem that is connected to larger water systems and integral to the health of the region's ecosystem. Laboucan-Massimo draws political inspiration from this event and her community more broadly. "This type of development doesn't have to happen," she argues.[69]

Though the meme does not directly charge her with hypocrisy, allegations of hypocrisy loom behind most posts by Oil Sands Strong that engage or represent Indigenous activists. And it is effective, since a host of people who follow the page on Facebook seem to be excited by the prospects of an Indigenous woman betraying her cause or acting inauthentically. The invitation to share this meme shows a recognition of how legitimation through circulation performs a crucial function for making such narratives take hold. The post itself received more attention than was common for the page at the time with 234 reactions, 67 comments, and 237 shares. Many of the comments focus on hypocrisy, rendering that which was first implicit explicit. One commenter, for instance, calls Laboucan-Massimo a "fake environmentalist," while another calls her "a pathetic hypocrite."[70]

Elsewhere, Oil Sands Strong directly addresses the content of Laboucan-Massimo's activism, which hones in on the symbiotic relations among settler colonialism, extractivism, sexual violence, and patriarchy. Throughout her activism and writing, Laboucan-Massimo elegantly links the consequences of resource extraction on Indigenous peoples across Canada as tied to extractivism underwritten by patriarchal relations and the kinds of frontier masculinities discussed in the previous chapter. With the caption "This has to stop she has gone too far," Oil Sands Strong posted a meme of Laboucan-Massimo in 2018 with the following text: "stop implying that Canadian oil workers are rapists! Grow up, you have a pretty sweet life being able to travel to Europe 13 times!"[71] The meme is a response to Laboucan-Massimo's article written for the David Suzuki Foundation's blog, which was shared on Facebook by Oil Sands Strong before the meme was posted. The article pointedly argues that "violence against the land begets violence against women" and details the heightened risks that Indigenous women face when living near extractive sites, citing research compiled by Honor the Earth that "found that the number of reported rapes increased as man camps more than doubled the region's population" during the 2010–13 Bakken oil boom in North Dakota.[72]

In a similar tenor, Oil Sands Strong also targeted the Tiny House Warriors and one of the main activists behind the movement, Kanahus Manuel, a daughter of the late Secwepemc leader Arthur Manuel. The Tiny House Warriors are a Secwepemc-led movement who have been building tiny mobile houses along the route of the TMX since 2015 as a means of resistance. These mobile tiny houses can be strategically positioned to blockade ongoing development and are a material and symbolic counterinfrastructure to the TMX and ongoing settler colonial encroachment that seeks, in the movement's own words, "to assert Secwepemc Law and jurisdiction and block access to this pipeline."[73] As Manuel details in a short documentary on the Tiny House Warriors, half of the pipeline runs through traditional Secwepemc territory. Along with her late father, Manuel has effectively targeted the economic lifelines of the TMX, sharing with international funders and insurers to underscore the risk and uncertainty involved in moving forward with the project without the prior and informed consent of the Secwepemc peoples.[74] Taking a jab at a funding call that Kanahus Manuel posted to Facebook, Oil Sands Strong produced a meme with a screenshot of the call and an image of Kanahus Manuel; in the page's signature boldface, all-caps text, the meme beckons: "Hey Kanahus! I have some great fundraising advice for you! Get a job!"[75] In another meme, Oil Sands Strong sarcastically demeans Manuel's activism. "Congratulations on being arrested," the meme declares. "Maybe your husband could bail you out if he wasn't already in prison. It's OK, you're a business-woman and you own a gas station."[76] The gas station referenced here was started by Arthur Manuel; as detailed in a chapter of *Unsettling Canada* appropriately titled "Don't Let Them Bully You," it sits on reserve lands that the Trans-Canada Highway travels through and was an effort on Arthur's behalf to generate revenue for his community that required little oversight to establish. "On a community level," Manuel writes, "it would allow me to create some jobs for young people, and on a personal level, it would give me a way to support my children in a way that my father, with his unrelenting commitment to the struggle, hadn't been able to."[77] Decontextualization or, perhaps more appropriately, extraction such as this is a modus operandi of petroturfing that gathers the raw materials from which to symbolically refine Canadian oil.

A plan of attack on these terms becomes visible that exhibits a toxic mixture of misogyny infused with a racism that either deploys conventionally held stereotypes of Indigenous peoples or declares inauthenticity in ways that tap into longer-held settler colonial views. Where Oil Sands Strong may leave the most egregious unsaid, as with Boucher's appearance on the page, the comments often fill in the gaps to perform and enact the very kinds of racism that Petersen recounts in her *Globe and Mail* op-ed—that Indigenous peoples are lazy and opportunistic. Fast forward to 2021, however, and Oil Sands Strong has leaned on its Indigenous-owned status to quell accusations of white supremacy, which came in the form of a tweet from the Carleton Federal Liberals Association (CFLA). In the since-deleted tweet, the CFLA shared a picture of the Ontario-based Conservative Member of Parliament and prime minister hopeful Pierre Poilievre wearing an Oil Sands Strong hoodie, alleging that its white clenched-fist logo is a white supremacist symbol. Robbie Picard made a number of posts to the Oil Sands Strong Facebook page on the heels of this controversy, including by sharing the coverage of the media event by the *Post-Millennial,* an online news magazine based in Montreal whose editor-at-large is the far-right journalist Andy Ngo.[78] When asked in an interview with Travis Beauregard of the *Buffalo Tribune* what his thoughts on the incident were, Picard responded by invoking his identity: "As a gay Metis man in the energy sector, I've experienced different forms of abuse and microaggressions but I tend not to let it bother me." "However," he continues, "we do need to stop these disastrous misinformed attacks on our energy sector."[79]

Picard has mobilized his Indigenous identity to create space for and to deflect accusations of racism. Like his public assertion of his gay identity when faced with criticism that memes he produced were sexist and bigoted against lesbians, Picard's Indigenous identity primarily appears as a reaction when pressed on the content he produces rather than as a positive or generative foundation through which his project explicitly takes shape. Occupying a marginalized identity category, whether gendered, sexualized, or racialized, does not absolve oneself from the possibility of reproducing dominant tendencies or worldviews. And while Oil Sands Strong may not express unabashedly white supremacist visions in its unwavering support for extractive capitalism and Canada's fossil economy, the content produced surrounding Indigenous peoples often reproduces settler colonial worldviews.

For Reconciliation without Qualifiers

When tethered to recognition politics, the shape and meaning of reconciliation are ambivalent, opening the floodgates for the agents, architects, and allies of the fossil economy to refine Canadian oil in the ways I have outlined and interrogated throughout this chapter. And such modes of reconciliation rely on and reproduce divides between the cultural and political in ways that leave dominant settler interests and institutions unscathed as they redefine the meaning of reconciliation. In late 2017, Oil Sands Strong took to Facebook to post a meme that refigured the ongoing development of Canada's oil sands as "economic reconciliation" for Indigenous peoples.[80] In 2020, the page followed up with a meme using similar language that served a dual purpose—first to further legitimate the concept of economic reconciliation and then to undermine Indigenous resistance through a personal attack on Kanahus Manuel. Posted with the caption "people like Kanahus Manuel are roadblocks to economic reconciliation that the oil sands are providing," the meme declares that "the oil sands, Canada's energy industry, provides economic reconciliation for Canada's First Nation [*sic*]" and calls on users to "please share this post."[81] On a page dedicated to "Indigenous & Natural Resources," Canada Action employs similar language, pointedly declaring that "for Indigenous Peoples, there can be no political self-determination without economic self-determination."[82] Where voices from industry rely on a form of Indigenous washing that promotes a version of UNDRIP whose terms and conditions it hopes to define, the field of dubiously grassroots groups, campaigns, and organizations I call petroturfing repackage this messaging as if it were not a dominant position. Through lobbying organizations like CAPP, industry promotes this view to government in private consultation; petroturfing instead lobbies the broader public with the same content in a different form. The consequences of a wholesale refining of Canadian oil as a force or vehicle of reconciliation are immense as reconciliation gets redefined in narrowly economic terms by the agents of Canada's fossil economy—that is, a reconciliation made palatable to oil executive epistemologies.

In petroturfing, the refining of Canadian oil into a force for reconciliation is achieved through an extractive tendency that uses ahistoricization and depoliticization as conceptual weapons in the oil culture wars. Through memes, videos, blog posts, and op-eds, petroturfing deploys long-standing racial stereotypes of Indigenous peoples to undermine Indigenous resistance efforts and call into question the legitimacy of these efforts. Petroturfing's settler colonial imagination exposes the limits of politics of recognition and the official project of reconciliation in nurturing material conditions for Indigenous self-determination that foregrounds questions of land dispossession. Where petroturfing extracts and decontextualizes in order to nurture an ahistorical and depoliticized worldview in support of Canada's fossil economy, I have strategically *re*contextualized these efforts in light of ongoing legacies of settler colonialism. Recontextualization as a method counters petroturfing's extractive character and reveals why recent expressions of Indigenous resurgence against extractive capitalism that have focused on *building* infrastructures of resistance to the infrastructures of extractive capitalism are such powerful expressions of self-determination.[83] Along the TMX with the Tiny House Warriors or on Wet'suwet'en territory at the Unist'ot'en Camp, these material assertions of jurisdiction are some of the most promising avenues to achieve reconciliation without qualifiers.

5

SUSTAINING PETROCULTURES
EXTRACTIVE LANDSCAPES, FORCES OF PRODUCTION, AND THE POST-ENVIRONMENTALIST IMAGINARY

> Many of the human-altered landscapes of the present appear to be landscapes beyond resurrection.
>
> —**Alberto Toscano, "The World Is Already without Us"**

> We will ensure the land disturbed by our operation is returned to a stable, safe condition that is capable of supporting biologically self-sustaining communities of plants and animals.
>
> —**Syncrude Canada, *2011 Environmental Sustainability Report***

A MAN IN A HARD HAT, high-visibility safety vest, and sunglasses strolls through a lush green landscape in a short 2011 promotional video produced by the Canadian Association of Petroleum Producers (CAPP). Uplifting piano music plays in the background. He opens his hands to gesture widely to the landscape that surrounds him. "This is an active mining operation in the Canadian oil sands," he says. "It's not a pretty sight when you open up the earth in order to extract the oil," he elaborates, "but after this operation is finished, it will be reclaimed." "Where there was once an oil sands mining operation, you now have a beautiful biodiverse landscape again, where you'd never know there'd been a mine there in the first place," he concludes. A white screen with black text fades in that declares, "New ideas are making a difference."[1] The landscape featured here is a reclamation project in the oil sands, a greenspace nested within a wider landscape of active mines, ongoing deforestation, and widespread ecological disturbance: a now-pretty sight amid some not-so-pretty ones. Featured in this short is Patrick Moore, a cofounder of Greenpeace and self-described sensible environmentalist who made a name for himself in 2015 by telling an interviewer with the French television network Canal Plus in a video that went viral that the glyphosate-based herbicide Roundup was safe to drink. Moore refused to drink a glass when offered one.[2] Moore's endorsement of the project deploys his environmentalist cultural capital to imbue reclamation, and bitumen production in general, with a green, renewable flavor. Since his comments about Roundup went viral, however, the video all but disappeared from the internet except for a post left on CAPP's Facebook page.

Like the process of drilling or mining and refining bitumen that necessitates such reclamation in the first place, the reclamation process is incredibly resource intensive and has been historically developed in a way that lags behind innovation in production methods. Speculation, of course, is a constitutive condition of the oil sands megaproject. And this condition continues to place faith in a future in which the ecological contradictions of the present are resolved through innovation. On a research trip I took to the oil sands in 2015 with a group of mostly engineering undergrads from the University of Alberta, I witnessed the results of the uneven distribution of resources for developing scientific knowledge for the refinement of extractive processes on the one hand and those for the mitigation of ecological impacts on the other hand. During a bus tour of the first commercial oil sands production site, the Suncor guide played a promotional video on the screens above the seats. The video highlighted the innovative measures Suncor spearheaded to mitigate the ecological impact of its extractive endeavors, including through its reclamation practices. We were told of the ten-year effort to solve a critical problem. Sapling trees were frequently dying off once winter hit, unable to mature to a point where they could stand on their own throughout the changing seasons. Over the course of ten years, reclamation scientists determined that an annual crop could be used to shield the saplings. The tour ended at a site undergoing reclamation in its later stages, which brought to mind a post-clearcut tree-planting plot, an extractive landscape familiar to me as a child of a Northern BC forestry town. Reminders that we were on private property through imperatives to keep off were never far from view.

The temporality with which I was confronted during this visit was a startling one, shedding some light on why so few exhausted landscapes have been fully reclaimed. All land leased by oil companies in Alberta must be reclaimed at some end point of a given development project. This agreement is built into the terms and conditions of the lease in the first place. And that reclamation clause specifies that the land is returned in what regulators describe as "an equivalent land capability."[3] "If an area meets stringent requirements for reclamation," the government of Alberta states while describing the process of reclamation, "regulators will issue final certification and the land is returned to the Crown as public land. To date, one area called Gateway Hill is certified reclaimed."[4] Gateway Hill spans 104 hectares, nestled in 89,592 hectares of all land affected by oil sands mining.[5] There is little compelling historical and material evidence that landscapes disturbed by oil sands extraction can be fully reclaimed in the sense of undoing damages in their entirety. Although there is a legal requirement for companies operating in the oil sands to commit to this process, what counts as equivalent remains an open prospect, defined by the lessee to be later judged by regulators.

Yet an air of certainty and confidence is palpable in a future-perfect refrain repeated by the architects, agents, and allies of Canada's fossil economy. As Natural Resources Canada (NRCan), the federal department under which oil sands activities fall, puts it, "100 percent of land *must* be reclaimed." NRCan, however, admits that reclamation of both tailings ponds and disturbed land is "just beginning, and will take many years."[6] The temporalities at work in these processes destabilize the rhetorically firm foundation upon which reclamation imaginaries are built, an uncertain future cast in the future-perfect tense through tenuous proofs of concept. Official figures point out that the life span of a given oil sands project is between forty and eighty years. This timescale means that the possibilities for reclamation cannot be evaluated in good faith even well into the twenty-first century, further underscoring how industry controls the terms and conditions of reclamation in what can still, almost sixty years after the establishment of the first commercial oil sands production sites, be considered the early stages of reclamation.

I open this chapter on petroturfing's ecological imaginary with an extended meditation on reclamation because sedimented within this speculative practice are traces of the broader characteristics of this imaginary. Alongside persistent gestures to Canada's strict environmental regulations—a petroturfing mantra—reclamation efforts, successful or otherwise, are a crucial promotional vector through which the oil sands are positively figured, particularly in terms of lasting ecological impacts. And like more generalized promotional material from the agents and architects of Canada's fossil economy such as CAPP, petroturfing echoes these sentiments as allies, using the legitimation-through-circulation feedback loop to disseminate the oil sands econarrative.

Reclamation projects like Gateway Hill or the one Moore surveyed sit in stark relief to the ever-compounding problem of tailings ponds in the oil sands, which are a representative case study in what Rob Nixon has famously described as "slow violence."[7] Tailings are the waste byproducts of extractive processes. In the case of the oil sands megaproject, these tailings have yet to be effectively treated. As early as 1973, less than a decade after the first commercial oil sands facility went online, the government of Alberta found that oil sands tailings were unique in their material makeup and, ultimately, unable to be treated to a degree in which they could be returned to the flow of the Athabasca without severe ecological consequences.[8] But a solution was not found in those early days when the Great Canadian Oil Sands Corporation plant went online; one hasn't been found yet, and extraction has carried on while tailings ponds accumulate across the Northern Alberta landscape, primarily Treaty 8 territory. Fast forward to the third decade of the twenty-first century and we have evidence that the now more than 1.3 trillion liters of tailings ponds have broken containment methods and are leaking into groundwater. Called "seepage" by industry, the ponds leak 11 million liters per day, or 4 billion liters annually.[9] And, it seems, they have been leaking for a while.

If tailings ponds are a material and symbolic site that spurns activism against oil sands extraction, reclamation and environmental technologies that mitigate the ecological impacts of extraction should be understood as a material analogue to petroturfing. As an Ethical Oil blog post explains, reclamation projects "are just one of the things that make Canadian oil sands ethical."[10] Both petroturfing and reclamation, in other words, are a means to sustain Canada's fossil economy; they maintain and reproduce the fossil economy in terms of aesthetics, culture, and ideology to curate a green petroculture. While refining refers to the material process that produces economic value from oil sands by workers, I have employed this term throughout this book to describe the parallel symbolic process of refining the cultural narratives that define Canadian oil through petroturfing. So, too, do the environmental technologies developed and deployed in extractive practice serve as mechanisms of refinement in these ways. This chapter turns to reclamation as it appears in the petroturfing mediascape, showing how reclamation and other modes of innovation are mobilized as a promotional–ideological layer through which to figure Canadian oil as a socially and ecologically benevolent force. It does so in the same way that petroturfing leverages a politics of recognition, that is, to refine Canadian oil as, in the words of an op-ed by Canada Action's founder Cody Battershill, "fair trade."[11]

In this chapter, I chart and interrogate petroturfing's ecological imaginary and, in turn, the ecological imaginary of oil sands production in general, all while putting pressure on how petroturfing operates as an environmental technology and promotional device for the fossil economy. To contextualize reclamation and other oil sands environmental technologies and draw out their relationship with petroturfing in general, this chapter begins with a theoretical account of the politics and aesthetics of reclamation as a capital- and resource-intensive, technoscientific process that maintains and reproduces the fossil economy rather than resolves its contradictions. In this way, reclamation embodies the partnering of science and fossil capitalism–made material but in a manner that, among other things, privileges human experiences of the aesthetic over a nature for itself, in turn continuing the extractive legacies that produce the conditions necessary for reclamation in the first place rather than moving beyond these legacies.

Following this account, I employ the Marxist conceptual vocabulary of forces of production to show how extractive capitalism subsumes Western modes of scientific knowledge for the means and ends of maintaining and reproducing extractive capitalist relations. As part of this process, petroturfing uses advancement in scientific knowledge in these terms as a promotional device. Just as the oil sands apparatus subsumes Western modes of scientific knowledge production for its maintenance and reproduction, so too does it subsume Indigenous knowledges and relations. Examining how bison figure into petroturfing's ecological imaginary, I zero my analysis in on a population of bison managed and stewarded by Fort McKay First Nation on a former oil sands site. I question how Indigenous knowledges and relations as forces of production are subsumed by the fossil economy and how that subsumption serves as promotional raw material. Finally, I close by turning to a multimedia campaign by CAPP that registers and expresses the tension at the center of this chapter's focus—a tension between the limitations of the present forces of production and their speculative futures that are used as rationale for intensified extraction today.

What emerges from my account is that petroturfing's ecological imaginary is informed by a fundamentally post-environmentalist position that superficially reconciles ecological damage with an environmentalist outlook through a constructivist and neoliberal environmental perspective that suggests all human impact can be mitigated through technological development. By post-environmentalism, I mean an environmentalism that has been fundamentally depoliticized through strategically and selectively adopting tenets of environmentalism that on the surface reconcile extractivism and environmentalism. This strategy aims to legitimate, while in turn creating the conditions of possibility for, the claim that Canadian oil is no longer *dirty,* as now-conventional wisdom tells us, but *green.*

The Post-environmentalist Politics and Aesthetics of Reclamation

Reclamation is often used by the agents, architects, and allies of Canada's fossil economy as a trump card against criticisms of the ecological impacts of the oil sands. On its Twitter account in 2016, for instance, Canada Action played this card when sharing a tweet that was a response to criticisms made on a thread started by its sister account, Oilsands Action, celebrating the industry-wide reduction in carbon emissions per barrel produced that has occurred since 1990.[12] Linking to a 2009 *National Geographic* exposé on the social and ecological impacts of the oil sands, the criticisms drew attention to the fact that emissions aren't the only ecological impact of oil sands production; so is loss of habitat.[13] Seizing the opportunity to spread the good word of reclamation, one follower of Oilsands Action replied with a dismissive imperative: "maybe you should go have a look around at the reclaimed land around Alberta," which Canada Action retweeted.[14] In 2017, Canada Action made a similar move by retweeting a comment from the president of the Ukrainian Canadian Congress in Calgary, who called out activist Tzeporah Berman, writing: "While @Tzeporah, was on her hate rallies, Syncrude reclaimed Mildred Lake oil sands mine."[15] Throughout the petroturfing mediascape, the single certified reclamation project is invoked and then scaled out to absolve the ecological consequences of past and present extraction by signaling future capacities and capabilities—which remain a speculative science fiction. Of course, as history has taught us, speculative science fictions can indeed become realities, but these fictions have yet to become entirely realized, if they ever can be, despite being baked into policy as if this were possible since at least 1993, when the language of equivalent land capability was enshrined.

At the center of reclamation's claims about the possibility of returning a damaged landscape to equivalent land capability are questions of use value and exchange value on the one hand, and nature and production on the other hand. For Karl Marx, the concept of nature is deeply rooted in his understanding of production and the creation of value (use value in particular), which can be captured in the following formula: labor plus nature equals production. A tempting impulse emerges here to critique Marx's calculus as a perpetuation and reproduction of a kind of binaristic, Enlightenment view of the oppositional relationship between the human and the nonhuman, and society and nature, where the former subsumes the latter. But for Marx this is not so straightforward, as a chorus of ecosocialist thinkers has addressed over the past several decades. As Alfred Schmidt, an early theorist of Marx's ecological thought who studied at the Frankfurt School, notes, "Marx considered nature to be 'the primary source of all instruments and objects of labour,' i.e. he saw nature from the beginning in relation to human activity."[16] Schmidt summarizes: "nature was for Marx both an element of human practice and the totality of everything that exists."[17] Use and instrumentalization, notions tied to a productivist imaginary, are complicated here in the way that Marx views nature as an aspect of "human practice" as well as a totality under which everyone and everything exists.

Less an attempt to perceive and characterize nature as a space for extraction, that is, for purely human use, Marx's view of nature arguably opens up several ways of accounting for the complex relationships and exchanges between human and nonhuman nature.

This dynamic is embodied in Marx's development of the notion of the rift, a concept that ecosocialist thinkers such as John Bellamy Foster, Brett Clark, and Richard York influentially reevaluate in relation to contemporary ecological relations under capitalism.[18] Such a "metabolic rift" names the deepening rift between humans and nature under capitalism, part of what Foster calls Marx's "mature analysis of the alienation of nature," that is, "a systemic critique of capitalist 'exploitation' (in the sense of robbery, that is, failing to maintain the means of reproduction) of the soil."[19] Cultural and media theorist McKenzie Wark describes the metabolic rift in terms of exchanges and flows that are nonreciprocal: "Labor pounds and wheedles rocks and soil, plants and animals, extracting the molecular flows out of which our shared life is made and remade. But those molecular flows do not return from whence they came."[20] As crystallized in the concept of the metabolic rift, Marx's understandings of nature and its relation to production is an important starting point when theorizing reclamation and interrogating its epistemologies of equivalence between extractive and postextractive landscapes. The epistemological basis of reclamation relies on a hubristic disavowal of metabolic rifts, promoting instead the perception that we as a species can carry on large-scale extractive processes without any serious, irreparable, or long-term damage to landscapes and ecosystems because of human ingenuity.

Within reclamation's terms and conditions is an anthropocentric and, indeed, capitalocentric productivism that conditions what counts as equivalent land capability. Literary and cultural theorist Jon Gordon elaborates on the implications of this anthropo-capitalocentric productivism as it manifests in the reclamation imagination:

> This discourse of productivity asserts that the land will be more humanly useful, more profitable, because its productivity will be oriented to marketable ends. . . . The amount of profit land can generate determines its value rather the diversity of life it supports, even if the latter must be sacrificed for the former.[21]

Oil sands reclamation, then, understands ecological relations primarily as a relation to capital and in this sense is consistent with its own logic conditioned by visions of equivalent land capability. But such a narrow view of ecology that hinges entirely upon a landscape's profitability reaches its limit when considering the material complexities of natural landscapes and ecosystems that reclamation, at least in spirit, hopes to mimic.

If part of reclamation's limits lay in its artificiality as a landscape stripped of its use value and then rebuilt in the image of an idealized form, part of its problematic is aesthetic. Environmental philosopher Timothy Morton's earlier work on environmental aesthetics helps develop this point further. Morton establishes a conceptual apparatus—what they call a "device" by tapping into literary traditions—from which to critique dominant Romantic notions of nature as they work in the genre of nature writing and artistic cultural production in general. They do so by developing the notion of "ecomimesis." Ecomimesis, Morton explains, is an environmental literary aesthetic that seeks to privilege, reflect, and embody nature—including nature's ambience and atmosphere—in its poetics. In its weak form, ecomimesis often reproduces the very same troublesome power relations between humans and the natural world that it hopes to erode or erase.[22]

But what does a largely literary aesthetic have to do with reclamation or notions of innovation and progress? To view reclamation, and indeed the contemporary energyscape more broadly, as somehow outside the realm of aesthetics is to overlook its core imperative, especially in relation to the purpose of reclaiming natural, postextractive landscapes, which is in the first instance to reconstruct an environment based on a pernicious mixture of aesthetic and anthropocentric productivity measured by exchange value. Despite the fact that there are a number of potential or imagined end uses, including recreation sites, that guide reclamation, there remains a primary emphasis on the aesthetic characteristics of postextractive landscapes.[23] Such an emphasis is arguably due to the relative ease with which an aesthetically pleasing landscape can be re-created and maintained with current technologies when compared to a self-sustaining one. "Equivalent land capability" in a self-sustaining, auto-productive manner (i.e., as an autonomous environment) has yet to be achieved, if it is at all even possible. This is why Moore's evaluation of reclamation's success hinges on "pretty sights," an anthropocentric way of experiencing nature that underscores reclamation's aspirations to aesthetically mimic that which has been internalized as "nature" in the cultural imaginary. In their privileging of the idyllic aesthetics of nature that can be traced to the types of Romantic conceptions of nature that Morton elaborates upon and critiques, reclamation projects reinscribe the problematic dynamics of nature versus culture that privilege the latter over the former. Whereas Morton's antidote is to call for an ecology without nature—an ecology that is not built upon the same problematic concept of nature that marginalizes it in the first place—reclamation projects invert this relationship in their mimicry of nature, producing a (capital N) Nature without an ecology of any dynamism or vitality beyond the pristine.

The entangled relationship among ecology, Romantic aesthetics, and technoscientific pursuits in the service of the fossil economy crystallized in reclamation reveals its roots as an artificial landscape embedded in a colonial epistemological framework. In a dialectical fashion, Geo Takach argues in his reading of the Albertan imaginary of nature—as expressed through, for instance, tourism promotion of the Rocky Mountains—that the gazes underpinning Romantic views of nature, such as those that likewise shape approaches to reclamation projects, are wedded to the extractive views they initially seem to oppose because both are based on consumption. Visions such as these, Takach writes, "may be more a part of a tradition dating back to Romantic landscape painting that views nature as unspoiled, separate from humanity and, as rhetoricians argue, thus open for human conquest."[24] Takach accordingly concludes that Romantic and "extractive" gazes "are both consumptive and so two sides of the same coin."[25] It serves us better critically, then, to view landscapes like Gateway Hill as always already human altered, an extension of extractivism rather than a rupture from its logics. A fundamentally post-environmentalist logic is at work in these visions, which condition the oil sands environmental imagination more generally and petroturfing's in particular. Building on the concept of postfeminism brought to bear on the petrosexual politics of petroturfing in chapter 3, which describes how feminist achievements of the twentieth century were undermined through a depoliticization of feminism in consumer society lubricated by the neoliberal condition, post-environmentalism signals a similar process at work for environmentalism akin to what is understood in the popular parlance as greenwashing.

Post-environmentalism and the Greening of Canada's Fossil Economy in the Shadow of Tailings

Reclamation is only one aspect of petroturfing's ecological imaginary, but the rhetorics that underpin petroturfing's engagement with it are a site from which to glean the larger ecological imaginaries at work in the oil sands during and after the extraction process. These imaginaries are often deployed to posit environmental technologies as a panacea for resolving the ecological contradictions of petroculture. As became clear in chapter 2, the environment more generally figures into petroturfing and other oil sands promotional discourses, such as those from politicians, in relation to the economy. The two are often invoked together to gesture toward the tensions between economy and environment that, as the narrative claims, environmentalists take as an organizing principle. Ethical Oil's 2014 tweet sharing a *Huffington Post* blog post written by Janet Holder, the former project lead of Enbridge's Northern Gateway Pipeline, summarizes a common refrain repeated by the agents, architects, and allies of Canada's fossil economy in its title: "Northern Gateway Will Create Jobs while Protecting the Environment."[26] There is, however, a pervading sense that while it may be unfair to suggest that environmental well-being is not considered at all in oil sands production, it remains an afterthought—something to be considered after economy if it cannot be folded into the economic apparatus entirely. Much of the promotional material surrounding reclamation confirms this, as discourses of innovation are mobilized to reconcile material environmental contradictions and tensions of oil sands production. These discourses of innovation are also often mobilized through a strong nationalist rhetoric that manifests in gestures to Canada's strict environmental regulations.

In this way, the nation is a constitutive vector through which petroturfing's ecological imaginary is expressed. Canada's image as an environmentally friendly nation is used to promote Canadian oil. Canada Action, for instance, equates an increase in production of energy from Canada with a positive, planetary ecological impact in a 2017 Facebook post. "Canada is beautiful and our natural resources are a blessing," the post begins. "Oil, natural gas, uranium and hydro-electricity that's made in Canada," it continues, "is a tremendous opportunity for our families while also being a positive for the global environment."[27] Attached to a photograph of a pristine lake and the Rocky Mountains on the horizon with a woman in the foreground wearing iconic Canada Action swag, an "I ♥ Oil Sands" sweatshirt, the captioned text calls on users with a patriotic bravado to "be proud" and "be vocal." By placing the subject of the photo in this line of sight and pairing it with these imperatives, the meme textually and visually suggests that appreciating nature and supporting Canadian oil are complementary tendencies, a kind of celebratory affirmation of Takach's romantic/extractive gaze. Petroturfing and other promotional oil sands media view the negative impacts of production and consumption not as material consequences inherent to the fossil economy but primarily as a problem of discursive framing.

In a CBC News opinion piece, business columnist Don Pittis makes a frank case for the greenwashing of Canadian oil to increase its international appeal and, in turn, increase its production. Echoing the ethical capitalist discourses of fair trade leveraged by petroturfing figureheads such as Ezra Levant of Ethical Oil and Cody Battershill of Canada Action, Pittis writes that branding Canadian oil as green "could also mean that environmentally minded consumers around the world might be willing to buy more Canadian oil—a prestige product at a premium price—increasing sales overall while displacing less environmentally produced crude from the marketplace."[28] Pittis's article is telling: fossil capital is so entrenched in the political economy of Canada that the distinction between branding and doing is muddled. Pittis recognizes the potentials of contradiction by invoking greenwashing and speaking to the limits of branding rather than acting: "branding alone—like BP's attempt at greenwashing—is not enough."[29] Yet, in speculating on strategies to "green" Canadian oil—including increasing transparency on behalf of industry for independent investigations akin to fisheries supervised by the Marine Stewardship Council—Pittis suggests that market-based interventions, such as Alberta's carbon tax, indicate that Canada is well on its way to establishing the preconditions for greening its oil. These interventions take place within the confines of the market, reproducing neoliberal tenets, and, like the post-environmentalist imaginary at the roots of reclamation, Pittis's proposals are a form of mitigation strategy primarily for fossil capital, not environment.

Petroturfing's ecological imaginary mirrors the oil and gas industry's ecological imaginary. Instrumentalized understandings of nature form the basis through which environment is figured and, in turn, technologies that mitigate the vast negative ecological impacts of the production and consumption of oil are valorized, celebrated, and promoted as viable solutions to the ongoing, intensifying climate crisis. How these technological solutions are traded in conventional news media articles, which are circulated across the petroturfing mediascape, further reveals how promises for the future are leveraged as solutions for the issues of the present. In November 2013, Ethical Oil tweeted a *Financial Post* article examining the formation of Canada's Oil Sands Innovation Alliance (COSIA), which the article's author, Claudia Cattaneo, identifies as "the biggest effort of environmental self-improvement on the planet."[30] Cattaneo here refines Tzeporah Berman's designation of the oil sands as "the single largest and most destructive industrial project on earth" into a green promise. As its title—"COSIA: Some Progress Made in Environmental Innovation, but Breakthroughs Will Come Later"—suggests, the article contains a critical edge, pointing out that the coalition's "aspirations are lofty."[31] COSIA aims

> to produce oil with lower greenhouse gas emissions than other oil sources, to transform tailings from waste into a resource that speeds land and water reclamation, to produce energy with no adverse impact on water, and to restore land disturbed by development and preserve biodiversity of plants and animals.[32]

Cattaneo, for instance, points out that, at the time of writing the article some two years after COSIA began operations, "anyone expecting major breakthroughs—or even hard targets—will have to wait a little longer."[33] Yet these criticisms are conditioned by a certainty of breakthrough. A 2014 tweet from Ethical Oil links to a more favorable assessment, a *Wall Street Journal* article by Chester Dawson.[34] Dawson describes COSIA as a "technology-sharing partnership" between research and development departments of fourteen energy producers brought together "in an effort to reduce the environmental impact of oil sands production."[35] The article's drophead makes clear the extent of the level of innovation being celebrated: "Cosia Commits to Reducing Fresh-Water Use at Some Operations." In the face of modest achievements, promises in the future-perfect tense are what COSIA trades in.

While Dawson celebrates this initiative, he is, like Cattaneo, careful to include some criticisms. In writing that "Cosia's toughest issue by far is dealing with highly controversial wastes known as tailings, a byproduct of surface mining when bitumen, or heavy oil, is separated from clay, sand and silt," Dawson does not overlook the scale and severity of the oil sands' damaged landscapes. "Toxic waste ponds have become a magnet for critics," he elaborates, "who say they are an eyesore and dangerous to migratory wildlife."[36] Tailings ponds once again enter as a foil to the celebrated environmental mitigation technologies being developed. And this is for good reason since as of this writing no tailings pond has been certified reclaimed or looks to be designated as such in the near or far-off future. But Dawson's rhetoric undermines the scale, severity, and uncertainty surrounding the persistent, growing problem of tailings ponds. By suggesting that the *aesthetics* of tailings ponds are of equal concern to critics as impacts on wildlife and casting doubt toward critics by underscoring that they merely "say" tailings pond are a risk in the ways they factually are, the article casts aside scientific consensus. More work, in any case, is needed to understand the full impacts of tailings ponds on the surrounding ecosystems and waterways, but many of their impacts are well known and well documented since they have been one of the core ecological problems of the oil sands since their commercial inception.

Energy Tomorrow or Energy Today?

Who, and what, do the environmental technologies developed and deployed at the oil sands serve? Following Marx, philosopher Isabelle Stengers identifies those who serve capital and, simultaneously, the destruction of the planet by deploying their knowledge—including financiers, scientists, politicians, and so on—as our "guardians."[37] There is a productive overlap between Stengers's idea of guardians and Marx's notion of general intellect, a term from the *Grundrisse* that describes the ways in which knowledge is deployed as a force to reproduce capital, operating as a kind of immaterial productive force. Through general intellect, Marx predicted the hegemonic role of knowledge in the maintenance and reproduction of capitalism.[38] In the case of reclamation projects, the knowledge deployed by our "guardians" establishes the perceived possibility for a reconciliation of the contradictions of the fossil economy. In other words, we can sustain our current fossil-fueled energy culture by leveraging science as general intellect to superficially eradicate the metabolic rift. We need no longer worry, the story goes, about the destruction of landscapes, about anthropogenic climate change, and so on, when our petrocultural guardians can mitigate these mere symptoms with "new ideas."

The role of science in oil sands reclamation and in the maintenance, expansion, and reproduction of the fossil economy and its cultural expression of petrocultures reveals how science and fossil capital can function symbiotically. Stengers's guardians name a pervasive and problematic relationship between benefactors of capitalism and its supporters (including, consciously or not, some scientists) by collapsing seemingly heterogeneous factions of capital into a homogenous group based on a single, shared, and constitutive effect: the self-justified furthering of the interests of capital, of extractivism, and of ecological destruction well into the twenty-first century and beyond.

Consider the land reclamation program, offered as a major of bachelor of science in environmental & conservation sciences through the University of Alberta's Faculty of Agricultural, Life & Environmental Sciences. The University of Alberta, located in Edmonton some 310 miles south of the oil sands and where I earned my PhD, has a close historical relationship with the emergence of the oil sands as a viable site of (profitable) extraction, having introduced many of the technologies currently in use in the oil sands through scientists like the oil sands' godfather Karl Clark. According to the University of Alberta's website, a potential career for graduates of the land reclamation major is "reclamation specialist."[39] ECO Canada, a professional resource whose aim is "to build the world's leading environmental workforce," offers a glimpse of the career goals of a reclamation specialist.[40] Its website features a profile of a "role model" who points out that "a reclamation specialist's role is 'to create a win-win-win scenario, where industry, the environment, and landowners all win.'"[41] But, as I have argued in this chapter, such a "win-win-win" scenario remains uncertain if not unfeasible, especially in the case of natural landscapes returned to Crown land after successful reclamation. Such a process forms the dialectic of bitumen extraction: exhausting a landscape's resources on one end while superficially reconstructing them on the other, providing the appearance of a reconciliation of the metabolic rift. It is a category error, then, to view reclamation projects like Gateway Hill as a kind of postextractive procedure that absolves us of ecological responsibility. Rather, these projects carry on extractive relations into what is deemed productive at the level of political economy as a postextractive landscape, while serving as rationalization for further extraction.

At work in this employment of scientific knowledge in the sustenance of the fossil economy is a form of subsumption, which describes how capitalism absorbs noncapitalist relations and process into its productive apparatuses or generates new ones. Generally referred to in political economy in terms of the subsumption of labor (real or formal), subsumption also applies to other modes of absorption and integration into the capitalist mode of production. In the case of scientific knowledge such as those developed in and applied to the reclamation process, these forces of production are subsumed to maintain and reproduce extractive capitalism. Political economist Nicolas Graham revisits Marx's understanding of forces of production; as Graham details, the concept has historically been understood within Marxist political economy in narrow terms, often referring to technology as such. But in Graham's reinterpretation, forces of production are more expansively conceptualized as "the practices, objects, techniques and knowledges through which we are purposefully linked to and transform the rest of nature."[42] To frame forces of production in this way "clearly situates human beings as a part of nature, while drawing attention to the various means and mediations by which our metabolic interchange with extra-human nature takes place."[43] Forces of production in these terms are sites of reproduction and resistance, of maintenance and transformation.

Scientific practices against and beyond capitalism, in other words, are necessary to nurture in transition to a more equitable social and ecological future. But in the context of reclamation and other environmental technological developments in the oil sands, forces of production are subsumed to carry on extractive relations into postextractive landscapes. In my collaborative work with literary and cultural theorist Jacob Goessling, we have described this process as extractive reclamation.[44]

Against subsumption like this, forces of production must be nurtured and generated from below rather than above, as geographer and environmental social scientist Holly Jean Buck and media and design theorist Benjamin Bratton have argued.[45] Yet the realities of actually existing reclamation make such aspirations seem distant.

Reclamation is a complex process in both a material and a cultural sense. As an extractive discursive practice, petroturfing decontextualizes reclamation from these broader political, economic, cultural, and material processes that shape reclamation and the ecological imaginary of the oil sands in general to champion industry efforts, however modest they may be. More recent petroturfing efforts uncritically gesture to the process of reclamation in a way that suggests reclamation technologies are at an adequate stage to reclaim all disturbed land.

This emphasis on reclamation has always been a fundamental mobilizing point for petroturfing since the publication of *Ethical Oil* and the launch of its campaign. In *Ethical Oil,* Levant reassures readers that land disturbed from mining "will be reclaimed once the oil is pumped out" since "it's the law in Alberta."[46] An Ethical Oil blog post makes a similar gesture as it cites and celebrates how much Syncrude has invested in reclamation. "Syncrude, for instance," the blog post reads, "has spent billions of dollars 'reclaiming' over 1,000 hectares of mined land since 2005," which equates dollars spent to land restored as if this were a seamless conversion.[47] It is arguably unsurprising that industry and the petroturfing project celebrate the process of reclamation technologies as leases themselves and figure reclamation as an already possible venture throughout the entirety of disturbed areas. Yet the limits to current and future technologies haunt these celebratory impulses.

Subsumption of scientific knowledge for the maintenance and reproduction of the fossil economy, then, becomes a promotional device from which to curate energy consciousness in favor of the oil sands megaproject. CAPP's 2017 Energy Tomorrow campaign does just this as it pushes this technoscientific mitigation logic to its limits as a means to sustain further extraction while deflecting criticisms by suggesting that environmentally friendly oil is within the industry's reach. Like its Energy Citizens campaign, which I discussed in chapter 2, CAPP's now offline Energy Tomorrow website was structured with individual profiles of scientists and others who were "changing the future of Canadian energy," such as Jessica, who was "building forests and wetlands to reclaim mined lands"; Anne, who was "capturing and storing carbon to keep it out of our atmosphere"; or Neal, who was "using light oil and steam to reduce greenhouse gases."[48] Images of each "innovator" sitting on a couch next to their spouse or parent were displayed on the front page, which linked to an interview hosted on YouTube. Each interview began with spouses or parents being asked to describe what the innovator did for a living, which they had a comically difficult time doing. Alongside these videos were detailed descriptions of each of the innovators' particular technology that emphasized how these technologies addressed ecological issues faced during and after extraction. Jessica's profile, for instance, discussed the ongoing Sandhill Fen reclamation project, a fen wetland being constructed on top of reclaimed tailings.[49] Anne's profile described efforts to perfect carbon capture and storage technologies wherein carbon dioxide is captured before reaching the atmosphere and injected two kilometers underground to be stored. The write-up naturalized the process by equating it with naturally geological processes, stating that "the carbon dioxide is trapped in a porous layer beneath multiple layers of rock and salt, just like oil, gas and CO2 have been naturally trapped in geological formations for millions of years."[50] Neal's profile described Solvent-Assisted Steam-Assisted Gravity Drainage (SA-SAGD), an extraction process that adds a solvent containing light oil to the conventional SAGD process developed in the 1970s for accessing deposits too far underground to reach through mining. SA-SAGD "can help make oil extraction more energy efficient, use less water and reduce greenhouse gas emissions."[51]

Processes such as these not only solve efficiency problems; they also open up a new frontier to extract deposits located deeper than existing methods might be able to access. This frontier further cements the future of the fossil economy as one constituted by what literary and cultural theorist Stephanie LeMenager details in the opening pages of *Living Oil* when she engages activist and scholar Michael T. Klare's diagnosis of the present as a "Tough Oil World."[52] As technologies are refined to better access this Tough Oil, what counts as a recoverable deposit expands. No longer is the scarcity of oil as expressed in the concept of Peak Oil an anxiety of the future. Instead, anxiety stems from Tough Oil's abundance, making calls to keep oil in the ground all the more urgent.

These profiles and the technologies they describe serve two key purposes that form the foundational aims of the Energy Tomorrow campaign. First, the profile format anthropomorphizes the technologies and, in turn, companies, by establishing a vibrant relationship between the technologies in development and the human "innovators" involved in their development. Visitors to the campaign website and viewers of the YouTube interviews are compelled to associate an individual scientist and family member with what, in some cases, may seem like dispassionate, sterile scientific work, culminating in what can be seen as case studies in science communication 101. Second, the profiles emphasize the necessity of developing these technologies by reminding users of the central role that oil plays now and pointing out that "fossil fuels [are] expected to supply the majority of the world's energy needs in the coming decades," in the future.[53] From this campaign emerges another variant of the kinds of petrocapitalist realism that inform petroturfing writ large: premised on a particular vision of our energy future that encloses possibility, persistently reminding us of how we will remain reliant on fossil fuels now and in the future.

From tailings reclamation to carbon capture and storage, there is a breadth of technologies in development highlighted in the campaign. Yet virtually every initiative not only takes for granted an increase in fossil fuel production and consumption in the future but is helping realize this future by materially refining extractive processes on the one hand and serving as promotional for shaping energy consciousness in the service of Canadian oil on the other hand. Energy Tomorrow, then, is not much different from energy today, save for monitoring and mitigation technologies working behind the scenes during the life and afterlife of extraction.

While these technologies serve as material means through which to sustain and reproduce the fossil economy in a time when the deleterious effects of the production and consumption of fossil fuels are increasingly clear, the promotional efforts from petroturfing and other entities such as CAPP serve as symbolic means to do the same. Alongside citations of Canada's strict environmental laws, discourses of innovation are used to reframe Canadian oil as technologically advanced and environmentally friendly. In framing Canadian oil this techno-utopian way, petroturfing refines bitumen from its origins as an ugly, heavy, tar-like substance into a fuel suitable for the future. The environment thus serves as a site through which to reconfigure Canadian oil not as the dirty oil it was once considered to be but rather the green oil that Pittis and others suggest Canadian oil can be.

Bison Imaginaries, or the Subsumption of Indigenous Knowledges by Fossil Capital

"This is what reclamation looks like!" So declares a Facebook meme posted by Oil Sands Strong in 2018.[54] The meme pictures bison roaming on a grassy plain landscape. Superimposed on the bottom left of the meme is a smaller image—a selfie of a man standing in front of a fence in which the bison are contained. A similar declaration was made in a 2019 tweet by Oil Sands Action linking to a Canada Action page hosting twenty-six photos of reclaimed oil sands landscapes. Stating "This is what #Oilsands reclamation looks like," the thumbnail preview of the post shows a bison photoshopped on top of wetlands.[55] Revising the chant often heard on the street during demonstrations—"this is what democracy looks like"—these declarations channel the energies of protest to promote oil sands reclamation on the one hand, while employing bison as a signifier of a thriving ecosystem on the other hand.

One of the most pervasive signifiers of the material, cultural, and, ultimately, scientific possibilities for successful oil sands reclamation is the figure of the wood bison. In Syncrude's successful, certified reclamation project, wood bison, and particularly their continued survival surrounding reclaimed landscapes, have played an instrumental role in demonstrating the ecological viability of reclamation, of (re)building a landscape to its former capabilities. The continued survival of bison, imported from Elk Island Provincial Park in the 1990s and studied over several years in partnership with Fort McKay First Nation, serves as a vibrant testament to the success of reclamation techniques.[56] Images of bison roaming in what is now called the Beaver Creek Wood Bison Ranch can be found in news articles, promotional materials, corporate websites, and petroturfing. Like reclamation in general, however, peeking behind the promotional curtain reveals bison to be a reminder of the fundamentally constructed nature of these landscapes and, indeed, their inhabitants. In attempts to establish "equivalent land capability" through a re-creation of wilderness vis-à-vis the application of scientific knowledges and technologies, efforts to reclaim damaged landscapes require significant, continuous human inputs while carrying on the extractive legacy of enclosure into its postextractive state. Writing for the *CIM Bulletin* in 1999 in the wake of the five-year study on the viability of bison survival in Syncrude's reclamation project, R. W. Pauls underscores the ways in which the bison are managed as captive animals. "Because the project area is in the heart of a large industrial operation and within range of diseased bison straying from Wood Buffalo National Park," he writes, "the herd has been managed as a captive, ranched herd."[57] Like the managed flora in re-created landscapes that culminate in "pretty sights," the fauna sustain themselves only through human intervention and management, which is why the McMurray Métis understand these bison as "urban buffalo."[58]

It is within this context that cultural and political theorist Nicole Shukin theorizes wood bison "as Syncrude's unofficial corporate mascot" in her dissertation on what she terms animal capital, or how animals are materially and symbolically rendered to maintain and reproduce capitalism.[59] Through this "mascotry," Shukin argues, Syncrude enables itself "to naturalize the denatured nature and racialized labour of neo-colonial capitalism."[60] I would, however, like to push Shukin's observations further and suggest that while Syncrude's corporate iconography is deeply attached to both the bison and reclamation in general, as the image circulated on Facebook by Oil Sands Strong demonstrates, restricting the discursive power of the image of the wood bison to Syncrude alone overlooks how reclamation projects serve the aim of positively framing the oil sands in general. In the long shadow of former prime minster Stephen Harper's national agenda to establish Canada as an energy superpower, whose call we first confronted in chapter 1, it is clear that the oil sands operate as an ideological totality beyond the sum of its individual corporate parts. After all, as political economists such as Graham remind us, Marx identified cooperation, not just competition, as integral to capitalist expansionism.[61] Petroturfing, which sees no allegiance to a particular company but instead to Canada's oil and gas industry as an abstract economic formation, is evidence of this understanding.

Tours of the oil sands like the one I undertook in 2015 reinforce the ideological significance of wood bison. In this space, the Romantic touristic gaze conditioned by Western aesthetics of landscape collides with its extractive mirror image. Describing her experiences during a tour of Syncrude's Wood Bison Viewpoint, Shannon Walsh quotes a Newfoundlander guide: "as long as the buffalo can live here, anything can live here."[62] Walsh's aim in the article is to offer a political–economic and political–ecological overview of the oil sands megaproject for unfamiliar readers. But by beginning at a reclamation site, Walsh puts immediate pressure on the unrealized promises of Canada's fossil economy and the complex symbolic economy at work. Shukin confirms this role of the bison when discussing her own tour, pointing out that "the promise of environmental reclamation will be mediated at both the first and last stop on the tour by a charged animal sign: endangered wood bison."[63] Promise underwrites the lives and afterlives of extractive processes.

Although certified reclaimed land, of which Gateway Hill is our only example to date, is officially returned to the state as Crown land as the final and constitutive part of that certification process, its continued maintenance does not rest entirely on the state. This makes immediate logistical sense, considering that reclaimed land now and in the future will be embedded in landscapes alongside active oil sands operations. Yet the power relations at work in the management of the landscape and the bison that live on it rely on the very same kinds of paternalisms found in discourse surrounding industry relations with Indigenous peoples in general, as I discussed in the previous chapter, wherein extractivist projects are made legitimate through superficial acts of inclusion. Shukin describes the semiotic dynamics at work when using the bison as a master signifier of the ecological dimensions of the oil sands. "Communicating with the public via an endangered animal sign popularly perceived as synonymous with Aboriginal life," she writes, "Syncrude can avoid racist discourse per se—and on the contrary cast itself as a postcolonial corporation attuned to the need to preserve Indigenous culture and to encourage First Nations self-determination—while simultaneously insinuating an essentialist discourse of Aboriginality with a fixed, subordinate relation to white cultures of capital."[64] These semiotic processes develop at the material level as academic commentary, news discourse, and promotional material underscore how the wood bison at Syncrude's Beaver Creek Wood Bison Ranch are maintained by Fort McKay First Nation.

As our climate and energy futures hinge upon whether we develop good relations with the more-than-human world, the role of decolonization and Indigenous knowledges in determining this future is difficult to overstate. Despite traditional Indigenous territories comprising up to 22 percent of the planet's land, for instance, these territories host 80 percent of the planet's biodiversity.[65] And Indigenous peoples have been living in reciprocal ways with the nonhuman environment that nurture this biodiversity since time immemorial. Western scientific epistemologies, historically hostile to knowledge systems other than their own, are taking notice. Kyle Powys Whyte underscores the tensions generated by this valorization of Indigenous knowledge from institutions such as universities as they operate in the shadow of ongoing settler colonialism. For Whyte, climate change is a form of "intensified colonialism" as the twin forces of colonialism and capitalism have "produce[d] the drivers of anthropogenic climate change."[66] And Indigenous knowledges are crucial to addressing climate change. Yet the valorization of Indigenous knowledges in these settings marked by colonialism and capitalism potentially opens up further avenues of exploitation. "Of course," Whyte elaborates, "many Indigenous persons are understandably concerned that climate scientists will intentionally or naively clamor around Indigenous communities to exploit the information Indigenous knowledges might possess that could fill in gaps in climate science research."[67] As climate change deepens, the value of Indigenous knowledges and practices so integral to good planetary relations are becoming valuable to those very same forces that propel settler colonialism, which paves the way for the subsumption of Indigenous knowledges as a force of production in parallel with the subsumption of Western scientific knowledge discussed earlier. This dynamic comes to bear on how Indigenous knowledges and practices are being supported by Canadian fossil capital. Just as the architects, agents, and allies of Canada's fossil economy are now in support of the implementation of a modified version of UNDRIP, so too are they subsuming Indigenous knowledges as a force of production under fossil capital.

But if wood bison are a living barometer through which to gauge the health of a given reclamation ecosystem, an indicator of reclamation's success, the prognosis remains an uncertain one. A 2015 article by the Canadian Press for Global News, for instance, reported the death of several bison after an anthrax outbreak: "three bison from Syncrude's herd in the oilsands have tested positive for anthrax."[68] While anthrax is a naturally occurring disease in free-roaming North American bison and is a threat to their conservation, it is worth repeating that these bison are not free roaming; they are captive.[69] Despite these issues related to anthrax, the population of bison has grown since their introduction. A 2018 CBC News article written on the twenty-fifth anniversary of Syncrude's introduction of the wood bison celebrates, among other things, the boom in wood bison population from thirty in 1993 to three hundred in 2018. Then-chief Jim Boucher is quoted in the article, stating that "the herd's growth represents the success of Syncrude's oilsands reclamation," but his overall observations are notably less than celebratory in relation to reclamation efforts in general. "The numbers are very disappointing to look at currently," Boucher said. "I think we need to do a lot more reclamation to demonstrate to the world that we have the ability to reclaim the land." A subhead of the article is telling—"Bison an example for future oilsand reclamation."[70] Rhetorically embedded in much reclamation discourse are gestures to a future in which reclamation is a smooth process. Present leases that allow the continued expansion of the oil sands, which require companies to sign off on the clause of returning the land to "equivalent land capability," continue to treat reclamation as if it was an already smooth process.

Lands and waters are first rendered into Crown land through settler colonial and capitalist expansionism. Parcels of this territory are then carved out to lease to oil and gas companies for the life span of a given project. Exhausted of use value, these lands finally undergo reclamation as they are rendered back into Crown land. This circuit of extraction, again, of which only one project to date has traveled in its entirety, maintains and reproduces settler colonial and extractive capitalist relations rather than breaks from them. When land back has become a demand in Indigenous movements for self-determination, the mode of reclamation at work in Gateway Hill's Wood Bison Viewpoint is inadequate. For Anishinaabe theorists Hayden King and Riley Yesno, reclamation is not about returning an exhausted landscape to some kind of new productive state after resource extraction has halted. Instead, Indigenous reclamation involves the assertion of jurisdiction over territory whether condoned by the state or not. King and Yesno detail strategies of reclamation in which they include the reoccupation of ancestral lands and waters, citing the Tiny House Warriors housing project and the Unist'ot'en Healing Centre as examples.[71] At the center of both the Tiny House Warriors' and the Unist'ot'en Camp's reoccupation efforts are a blockade against major pipeline projects threatening their territories. Reclamation, in other words, is pursued to halt the settler colonial inertia of Canada's fossil economy rather than maintain and reproduce it.

Who and what do actually existing modes of oil sands reclamation in the present serve? Human intervention into lands and waters with reciprocal relations are integral to Indigenous lifeworlds. This historical–material truism is the kernel of Potawatomi plant ecologist Robin Wall Kimmerer's work with sweetgrass in which she details how the plant prospers when tended to in ways that Potawatomi scientific knowledge suggests.[72] So it is not human intervention as such that constitutes the problematic of extractive and postextractive processes in the oil sands. But enclosure and containment rather than reciprocity are keywords for the entire process of oil sands production in the present and the future, including in its postextractive state as reclaimed land. Referencing the final stop on her tour of the oil sands, Shukin discusses the vision of the future that Syncrude offers through its reclamation projects. In this prospective future, Shukin sees the maintenance of capitalist forms and processes that shape extractive landscapes in postextractive landscapes as well. "Real estate and recreational tourism are the two prospects Syncrude envisions for its reclaimed mine sites, prospects which pledge the land to renewed 'health' within affluent white cultures of capital," she writes.[73] And within this dynamic, the econometrics of equivalent land capability become all the more clear:

> Global capitals' fatal treatments of leased Aboriginal lands arguably forecloses the possibility of any return to use-value (trapping, hunting). . . . Ruined for anything but re-capitalization as recreational destination or "lakefront property," what oil sands capital promises to return to Aboriginal people in the region is the death of nature as use-value and the future of nature as exchange-value.[74]

Use values are depleted, while exchange values are valorized and extractive capitalism persists. This is the future on offer, founded on the same relations of the present and in service of reproducing these relations.

Such commitments to a future like the present reveal the limitations of social and ecological justice that petroturfing and other promotional ventures produce and circulate as, for instance, the agents, architects, and allies of Canada's fossil economy further subsume Indigenous knowledges in an era of reconciliation—as Suncor does in its articulation of what it calls its "journey of reconciliation," which includes conditionally "reflecting Indigenous knowledge in what we do, where appropriate."[75] What constitutes reclamation, then, is still an unfolding struggle.

Exhausted Relations

In the ecological imaginaries of the architects, agents, and allies of Canada's fossil economy, Western scientific knowledge and Indigenous land-based knowledges are subsumed not to resolve the ecological contradictions of extractive capitalism but to reproduce them. Refined as they are throughout the media of petroturfing, these social, ecological, and technological pursuits become artillery in the oil culture wars as Canadian oil is deemed green. What may seem as categorically incongruous with the development of the oil sands—conservation and stewardship—is, rather, wholly compatible with extractive capitalism in superficial ways. Petroturfing, then, serves as a vehicle through which to sustain the petrocultural environmental imaginary by employing a constructivist vision of nature that suggests human beings can reconstruct nature or return it to its previous state through, for example, oil spill cleanup. Nature and environment as such figure into the oil sands ecological imaginary only after the landscape's exhaustion of value as raw material. In reclamation, nature is simultaneously recast in terms of a material and aesthetic exchange value in which "pretty sights" and potential forestry and logging capacities or real estate prospects operate as metrics from which to judge its success. The *OED* has a number of definitions for reclamation, but one in particular jumps out in the context of this chapter, that is, "a reassertion of a relationship or connection with something; a re-evaluation of a term, concept, etc., in a more positive or suitable way."[76] Indeed, reclamation is a reassertion of a particular relationship between the human and the nonhuman, one that asserts a technoscientific mastery masqueraded as stewardship. The uneven consequences of planetary climate change as expressed in the concept of the Anthropocene are premised on a recognition of the ways in which all landscapes are now human-altered ones, and reclamation projects like Gateway Hill can thus be rendered as manufactured and artificial, as human constructed and perhaps no different from an office building in any given metropolis. After all, both sustain and reproduce a form of capital that in turn sustains the social life that bitumen extraction enables.

In my early work on reclamation imaginaries, I approached reclamation projects like Gateway Hill through Sigmund Freud's uncanny on the one hand and Jean Baudrillard's simulacra on the other hand.[77] These frameworks, however, have limits based on how they describe the effect and phenomenological experience of reclamation rather than explain what reclamation does on an economic, ecological, and, indeed, social or cultural level. Mobilizing the myth of our technological ability to rebuild damaged landscapes to "equivalent land capability," reclamation is a reinscription of settler colonial, extractive capitalist relations that see land as something to be managed from above, another form of primitive accumulation that Coulthard argues has been fundamental to historical and ongoing processes of colonization.[78] As "new ideas" inoculate discourses of ecological destruction—fossil fuel companies are now "energy" companies, pipelines are now "energy projects"—questions about the possibilities of a post-oil energy future are made visible at the level of language, discourse, and culture more broadly. Petroturfing is part of this package of new ideas.

6

FROM THE HIGHWAY TO THE LEGISLATURE

FOSSIL FASCIST CREEP

> In the climate emergency, the far right is a vehicle in which primitive fossil capital takes a seat, driving the state away from any limitations on fossil fuel use.
>
> —**Andreas Malm and the Zetkin Collective, *White Skin, Black Fuel***

In March 2021, the Canadian Energy Centre (CEC) launched an online campaign against the streaming platform Netflix, alleging that a children's film recently added to its library, *Bigfoot Family* (2020), "is spreading misinformation about the oil and gas industry" and "peddles lies about the energy sector."[1] An early campaign tied to the CEC's larger "Support Canadian Energy" initiative, "Tell the Truth Netflix!" called on visitors to "tell Netflix that their attack on Canada's energy industry is just plain wrong." Visitors could do so by sending a boilerplate email to Netflix Canada's head of communications using a prefilled form. Invoking arguments straight out of the petroturfing playbook, the boilerplate listed the economic, social, and ecological benefits generated by Canada's oil and gas industry.[2] The scene under scrutiny involves the use of explosives to extract oil from a valley, a scenario that, despite claims of misinformation, inadvertently parallels a 1959 proposal to use atomic bombs to access bitumen deposits in the Athabasca region—first called Project Cauldron and then Project Oilsand—that was considered in the 1960s.[3] National and international media attention zeroed in on the campaign due to its absurdity. Why, many seemed to be wondering, were provincially funded representatives of Canada's fossil economy going after a children's movie? Yet, like much of petroturfing and petroturfing-adjacent media efforts, the absurdity was perhaps part of the strategy. In the end, the campaign was a publicity stunt that, in many ways, has bestowed international attention on the CEC after a series of slipups during its formation, which included the plagiarism of its logo by a contracted designer as well as its use of a stock photo of downtown Toronto as its Twitter cover image rather than, say, downtown Calgary, where the headquarters of many oil and gas companies sit and the CEC itself is based. The attention generated by the campaign also resulted in a heightened viewership of the film, which led the director to thank the CEC, while confirming to CBC News that the film, including the scene in question, has absolutely nothing to do with the oil sands.[4]

The formation in the summer of 2019 of the CEC, a state-sponsored venue inaugurated for the dual purpose of circulation of pro-oil narratives across legacy and social media and an outlet for fighting what it perceives as misinformation surrounding the oil sands, was an early move in then-premier Jason Kenney's adoption of power. This move not only signaled the prioritization of the strategies, rhetorics, and discourses that underwrite petroturfing at the level of government. The CEC's formation also cemented war-based vocabularies and frameworks as a privileged mode of expression for oil and gas support. Notably, Kenney first described the initiative to press members at its launch as a "war room," and the CEC continues to be known colloquially by this name.

Demarcated in my periodization that sees Bernard the Roughneck's impassioned speech on the Parliament steps as ushering in the second wave of petroturfing, petroturfing has changed shape by following the larger ebbs and flows of the new right, an umbrella term to describe the various emergent fascisms and crypto-fascisms of the present. Such flows turned into rapids around 2016, spurned by a storm culminating in former U.S. president Donald Trump's rise to power, that is, the well-documented empowerment of the far right and alt-right online and off, which has been lubricated by the architectures and infrastructures of social media.[5] Petroturfing has followed in tandem, becoming more brazen and aggressive in its messaging, all while gaining more traction as it transformed from a largely online, social media–based effort to an on-the-ground one. Through the war room, petroturfing is now a formally institutionalized state project.

Yet, as I showed in chapter 1, association with formal political apparatuses has marked petroturfing from its inception. The relationship between figures such as Ezra Levant and the Canadian conservative scene helped establish the initial momentum through which petroturfing took shape. What reads on the surface as a tension between the state and the grassroots, in other words, has instead been a formative characteristic of petroturfing that has simultaneously undermined its own grassroots self-presentation from the get-go. Within months of its first push, for instance, petroturfing already had the ears of politicians in the House of Commons, where Levant pedaled fresh copies of *Ethical Oil.* Extractive pursuits underwrite the Canadian state apparatus, tied to bound, persistent, and formative processes of settler colonial dispossession and capital accumulation. When Canada became a major oil-producing region, the Canadian political establishment, as much as its political economy, was glossed in the oily sheen of fossil capital. For this reason, politicians didn't necessarily need to be converted into champions of Canadian oil; it was, instead, the broader public whose hearts and minds needed to be infused with an oil executive epistemology by petroturfing. A disavowal of influence and carefully constructed image of grassroots formation is a constitutive feature of petroturfing as it claims the marginalization of Canada's fossil economy as its animating condition, despite the very strategies and tactics of petroturfing itself being an integral part of Alberta's provincial establishment. The road traveled by petroturfing so far has been one of its own making by loosely affiliated actors, taking off first in the influential space of Parliament in 2010, only to end up in the Alberta Legislature in 2019.

Petroturfing first leveraged notions of balance to curate an image of political–intellectual good faith. Such good faith legitimated and then placed oil executive epistemologies on equal footing as Indigenous and environmentalist resistance to the expansion of Canada's fossil economy. Once it began to achieve this equal footing, a wave characterized by more aggressive tactics and a mobilization of a base that follow patterns and tendencies of the growing online and offline presence of a new right followed. The degrees of separation between the broader far-right and new right-wing mediascape and petroturfing have always been few to none, which speaks to the historical enmeshment between Canadian fossil capital and the far right as well as shared material–historical reinforcement through figures such as Levant and his Rebel Media empire.

Petroturfing has always been soaked in the toxic by-products of the far right; it is only as the cultural and political climate warmed to the growing new right that these by-products floated to the surface.

This chapter adopts a historical approach in the spirit of chapter 1 to explore petroturfing of the present as it articulates this shift through the notion of the fossil fascist creep, a term I develop following Cara New Daggett's and Andreas Malm and the Zetkin Collective's theorization of U.S. and global manifestations of fossil fascism. Their work on the rise of fossil fascism helps clarify the motivations, causes, and effects of petroturfing today as well as its strategies of legitimation and recruitment.[6] To provide a critical account of the fossil fascist creep in Canada at the end of petorturfing's first decade of existence, this chapter examines the contours of petroturfing's second wave by turning to two capstone events of 2019: the United We Roll! convoy from Red Deer to Ottawa and the formation of the energy "war room" in the early days of power of the United Conservative Party (UCP) of Alberta. Divided according to the material sites of the highway and the legislature, the chapter traces the bifurcation of petroturfing as a purportedly grassroots phenomenon and one imbricated in existing political settings that meet today at the Canadian Energy Centre. By turning to the more recent past of petroturfing, this chapter also details the consequences of this conjuncture on how the oil culture wars are waged now and in the future. Through this road trip from the highway to the legislature, glimpses of the future oil culture wars come into view—a future that will likely be increasingly defined by the logics of fossil fascism as the effects of climate change become more pronounced and evenly distributed. Embarking on this journey through the recent routes followed by petroturfing, however, requires a pit stop that dwells on the contours of the contemporary right-wing media ecosystem in which petroturfing is imbricated.

The Ethical Oil Wedge and the Fossil Fascist Creep: A Pit Stop

The first wave of petroturfing sought to wedge pro-oil and pro-pipeline views into mainstream public discourse on the oil sands—to shape Canadian energy consciousness in favor of ethical oil over dirty oil by appealing to liberal sensibilities of balance. Following this legitimation, its second wave represents a creep that relies on more aggressively right-wing tenets, some of which I have discussed in the previous chapters. In using metaphors of creep to describe what this more aggressive mode of petroturfing represents, I am indebted to recent theory that has detailed the spread of various forms of fascism in the twenty-first century.[7] Leaning on these metaphors of movement, thinkers who have examined the emergence of what is generally described as the "new right" in the age of social media point to how this rise has been achieved through a pipeline that enables and generates a process of radicalization. Users swayed by these ideologies can end up following this pipeline by, for instance, being progressively exposed to increasingly radical content, all of which is made possible by a given platform's algorithms, or what I have been referring to as its architectures.[8]

YouTube in particular has arguably received the most scrutiny by scholars and media activists for its role in greasing the wheels of the rise of the new right. The platform does so by targeting an audience of users most likely to cozy up to these views. A 2020 investigation into YouTube's algorithms empirically demonstrates how this "radicalization pipeline" functions in three prominent, distinct, yet overlapping right-wing YouTube communities whose presence and ideas spread across the web like wildfire over the past half decade: the Intellectual Dark Web, alt-lite, and alt-right.[9]

In the petroturfing mediascape, which exists within a media environment shaped by these new-right spheres of influence, the pipeline is a material–discursive symbol upon which political energies are focused. After all, the expansion of Canada's fossil economy through the construction of pipelines is the petroturfing project's rallying cry. In light of this growing critical attention to social media's radicalization tendencies or dispositions, petroturfing's imbrication with the contemporary right demands further examination. As I will show throughout this chapter, petroturfing constructs its own radicalization pipeline that runs parallel to the building of oil pipelines.

The new right that has emerged alongside petroturfing over the past decade is composed of intersecting and diverging worldviews. The Intellectual Dark Web (IDW) is a title self-imposed by a set of right-wing provocateurs who mobilize new and social media platforms for circulating content that furthers the ends of the political project of the new right.

Constructing identities as dangerous enough to dominant powers that these powers hope to censor or hide from view, those who comprise this network lean on the connotations of the "Dark Web" signifier in order to legitimate this identity, to infuse their views with an edge. While the Dark Web is simply a term that describes content on the internet that can only be accessed using routing software such as Tor, it carries with it a set of nefarious associations due to the illegal activities that occur over this network, such as the now-defunct drug market Silk Road.[10] Mobilizing the cultural capital afforded by these connotations establishes a countercultural image that makes their ideas seem as though they are a break *from* and challenge *to* the dominant liberal order. From the natural order–obsessed former University of Toronto psychology professor Jordan B. Peterson, who made a name for himself in a viral video taken in one of his classes ranting against a bill in Canada that would see gender identity become a protected class alongside race and sex, to the fast-talking conservative media mogul Ben Shapiro, who coined the new-right mantra "facts don't care about your feelings," new and social media have both nurtured this self-presentation and offered the material conditions for its thriving.

But the core positions that inform the new right are fashioned from the old right. Political commentator Michael Brooks offers a detailed account of the figures and ideologies of the new right by extensively cataloging and critiquing their views. Brooks also shows how the architectures and infrastructures of the contemporary internet have been effectively leveraged by the new right through, for instance, the gaming of algorithms on social media platforms.[11] As Brooks describes, the Intellectual Dark Web came to mainstream attention through a *New York Times* opinion piece by Bari Weiss, whose title invited readers to "meet the renegades of the Intellectual Dark Web." However, the freshness of the viewpoints of these figures as harbingers of a new, self-defined countercultural right, is questionable. "Crucially, in all of these areas [of social and economic relations] the IDW promotes narratives that either *naturalize* or *mythologize* historically contingent power relations—between workers and bosses, between men and women," Brooks writes, "they are old school reactionaries."[12] Upon scrutiny, the viewpoints on offer by the IDW are far from new; they're stale. But the "new" in "new right" may more aptly describe the avenues of circulation through which figures like Peterson or Shapiro gain their reach.

These figures are immensely popular and influential, particularly in online settings. A Twitter bot account that tracks the daily ten top-performing links posted by U.S. Facebook pages, ranked by total interactions, is illuminating in this regard as Shapiro and other figures of the IDW consistently appear, often several times in one day's ranking. On June 15, 2021, for instance, Shapiro occupied eight of these spots, with the other two occupied by Fox News and David Wolfe, a new-age conspiracy theorist.[13] The day before, Shapiro occupied the top five spots.[14] While trading in the performance of disrupting the mainstream, the figures of the IDW are some of the most influential today.

The form and content of this new right's media strategies are like those of petroturfing. In many ways, the petroturfing project can be viewed as a new-right media project through and through. Here, the links with petroturfing's second wave as a project of the new right in strategy and structure come into relief as petroturfing shares with the new right broader issues of concern, such as nationalism or patriotism, free speech, and, more recently in the heat of the Covid-19 pandemic, anti-lockdown and anti-mask sentiments that flirt with conspiracy theory thinking if not entirely embrace it. Of course, petroturfing has always been a project of the right in these ways, as it first took shape through Levant and others tied to the Canadian conservative political apparatus. But historicizing this shift from a more balance-oriented approach inflected by the liberal, postpolitical imagination of ethical petrocapitalism to a more aggressive, inward-looking agenda surfaces the turn petroturfing has taken in tandem with broader social and political trends that exhibit a fascist creep.

It is, perhaps, unsurprising that the figures who follow the routes of the new-right pipeline also express adoration for the fossil economy, primarily through varying forms of climate denialism and fossil fuel boisterousness. Putting pressure on these climatic dimensions of the new right's tendencies, Malm and the Zetkin Collective detail how a denialist ideological formation has taken hold over the global right from the United States to Brazil, India to Europe. Extending Althusser's influential theorization of ideological state apparatuses (ISAs), Malm and the Zetkin Collective develop the concept of the *denialist* ideological state apparatus.[15] As in Althusser's conceptualization, the denialist ISA can be found where state and extrastate actors operating alongside the state reproduce the relations of the dominant mode of production.[16] These

ISAs function in tandem with repressive state apparatuses (RSAs), which encompass the institutions that reproduce the relations of the dominant mode of production through physical and material repression, such as the police.[17] Methodologically, Malm and the Zetkin Collective's engagement with and extension of Althusser echoes my own, which I employ to articulate how the fossil economy is continuously reproduced materially and culturally across ISAs and RSAs. Malm and the Zetkin Collective focus more on the ideological dimensions of the reproduction of the fossil fuel economy without as much attention paid to these repressive dimensions.

In the face of increased criminalization of resistance to the fossil economy at the behest of industry and the allies of the fossil economy, it is important to draw attention to how the repressive apparatus restrains resistance through, for instance, legislation and, as a result, enforces the reproduction of the fossil fuel economy on these terms. Whether it is former-premier Jason Kenney's institution of Bill 1 in the throes of #ShutDownCanada in early 2020, which criminalizes any form of protest or blockade that impacts the functioning of critical infrastructure, or the RCMP raiding the Unist'ot'en Camp, Canadian RSAs often appear in full force to maintain and reproduce the fossil economy. Alongside RSAs that work to reproduce these dominant energetic relations, the denialist ISA describes those think tanks and front groups who expel great energies to synthesize modes of doubt, anticommunism, and free market valorization to maintain and reproduce the existing fossilized order.[18] The two, in other words, must be understood together. While the denialist ISA is a global phenomenon, here in Canada it has been described by those working for the Corporate Mapping Project as composed of "legitimators," or those agents and actors who legitimate dominant industry views to obscure climate science, while promoting Canada's fossil economy.[19]

Several of the prophets of the IDW are deeply attached to the climate denialist ISA through the promotion of climate skepticism. Peterson, for instance, has gone on record stating that "you can't trust the [climate change] data because too much ideology is involved."[20] And Shapiro has breathlessly challenged the climate activism of Greta Thunberg, the teenage environmental activist from Sweden who launched Fridays for Future. Thunberg helped center the voices of youth in climate change activism, eventually traveling by boat from Europe to the Americas, including a stop at a climate change march in Montreal I attended in fall 2019 that drew a crowd of roughly 500,000 people onto the city streets. This march was the largest demonstration in Montreal's history, which is no small feat in a city with strong activist roots. In a video posted to Shapiro's YouTube channel, The Daily Wire, titled "Ben Shapiro DESTROYS Greta's CRAZY Climate Change Arguments," with more than 2.1 million views, he says that Thunberg's "solutions to global warming are patently insane, yet they are propped up by everybody in the media."[21] Shapiro's critique focuses on a statement Thunberg made at the 2020 World Economic Forum at Davos, Switzerland, which was a critique of efforts that posit low-carbon economies and net zero emissions as climate change solutions, suggesting that to avoid catastrophic warming we need to implement rapid fossil fuel divestment to achieve negative emissions, or "real zero."[22] In a condescending tenor, Shapiro tells viewers that "real zero means that you actually shut down the entire economy of the world," concluding that we should not listen to children telling us to panic. "I'm not going to panic over the possible increase of global temperature of at maximum 4 degrees Celsius according to the IPCC over the course of the next century," Shapiro declares. "In fact," he continues, "what we should be attempting is mitigation. Adaptation."[23] Two streams of the denialist ISA coalesce here between Peterson and Shapiro that, in my view, we will continue to encounter as climate change deepens—one that questions the integrity of climate science and, accordingly, the urgency for solutions.

Some dismiss the use of fascism to name the politics and desires of the new right as a label too hastily applied. In this hasty application, the narrative goes, the political–historical specificity of fascism is lost, and fascism becomes a term to describe a politics not of one's own. What constitutes a fascist in the twenty-first century? It turns out that a twenty-first-century fascist is not much different from a twentieth-century one. In North America, groups such as the Proud Boys, formed in 2010 by Canadian transplant and cofounder of *Vice* magazine Gavin McInnes, employ street-level violence and intimidation tactics to further the group's crypto-fascist ends. A group exclusively for men, as of 2021, the Proud Boys have been deemed a terrorist organization by the Canadian federal government and have since disbanded.[24] Groups such as the Proud Boys were central to the August 2017 Unite the Right rally in Charlottesville, Virginia. The rally brought right-wing energies from online to the streets and, as the name suggests, hoped to establish a coalition of right-wing groups and individuals under a common cause: to protest the removal of a statue of Confederate general Robert E. Lee.[25] Historian David C. Atkinson argues that the rally exposed the traditionally far-right tendencies of the alt-right, such as white supremacy.[26] And while Charlottesville has largely been viewed as a failure for the alt-right, these tendencies have arguably been amplified in the years following.

To name a fascist of the present, then, is to name the links between boisterous masculinities and unwavering support of extractive and fossil-powered lives. This is the conjuncture that Daggett names when she articulates the mutually constituting entanglement among certain dominant, toxic masculinities, extractive relations and worldviews, and desires for authoritarianism, which together take shape as an emergent fossil fascism.[27] Carrying the torch Daggett lit, Malm and the Zetkin Collective offer a political–economic, state-oriented definition of fascism, from which they delineate their articulation of fossil fascism "as a real historical force."[28] "Fascism," they write,

> is a politics of palingenetic ultranationalism that comes to the fore in a conjuncture of deep crisis, and if leading sections of the dominant class throw their weight behind it and hand it power, there ensues an exceptional regime of systematic violence against those identified as enemies of the nation.[29]

Fossil fascism, then, can be viewed "as a conjunction of a deep crisis and dominant class interests rooted in fossil fuels."[30] The climate crisis offers one such fertile ground in which fascism may take root, and while modes of denialism inflect fossil fascism, the material consequences of some 150 years of burning fossil fuels produce uncertain futures from which growing fossil fascist tendencies emerge: "nationalist politics on the rise; deep crises afoot; dominant class interests in realignment."[31] Whether one believes in the science or not, these conditions materially exist and will only deepen, barring unprecedented change to dominant modes and relations of production.

As a new right gained steam online over the 2010s in the form of the IDW, alt-lite, alt-right, and everything in-between, so, too, did it take shape on the streets. New and social media fueled its travel by creating conditions for its spread, further legitimating the narrative that the new right challenges business as usual when it, instead, supports already dominant relations of class, race, gender, sexuality, and, indeed, environment. The fossil fascist rejoinder cements fossil fuels as the material foundation of the new right, and it is this formation's emergence and expression in Canada to which I turn for the rest of this chapter. This emergence has most prominently appeared in flash points through Yellow Vests Canada (YVC) with its dual concerns of strengthening borders and building new fossil fuel infrastructure, and the subsequent United We Roll! convoy from Red Deer to Ottawa that saw hundreds of trucks take to the highways and demand more support for the oil and gas industry by the federal government. At the confluence of the pipeline and the border, a fossil fascist creep has been set into motion.

The Oil Culture Wars Hit the Road

On November 17, 2018, a crowd clad in high-visibility vests took to the streets of Paris to protest the high cost of living and a rise in fuel prices through increased taxation, which was seen as a kind of class warfare repackaged as a measure to mitigate climate change. The sea of yellow that took over the streets on this fateful Saturday would do so every weekend for two years until spring 2020, when lockdown measures were installed in France on the heels of the Covid-19 pandemic. As is often the case in an age shaped and conditioned by the tenets of neoliberal capitalism, the antigovernment positions informing the revolts against government were in many ways ambiguous ones. At the foundation of the original *gilets jaunes* struggle, however, was an indisputable class character. And as the movement took hold over international consciousness, prominent French philosophers, theorists, and public intellectuals such as Alain Badiou, Étienne Balibar, Jean-Paul Deléage, Jacques Rancière, and Thomas Piketty all offered their own hot takes on what the movement signified as a world historical event. For Badiou, the *gilets jaunes* was doomed as a movement due to its wholly negative character latched on to a desire to merely reinstate the middle class, whereas for Deléage, the movement was an expression of class critique leveraged against "la macronie," or Macronism.[32] As varied as these readings may be, these versions of the *gilets jaunes* all reveal a markedly classed character.

Yellow Vests at Home and Abroad

Elsewhere across the planet, yellow vests were donned for right-wing ends, capitalizing on the cultural capital the movement accumulated through France on the world stage and toying with the ambiguity of its messaging. In the United Kingdom and Canada, the movement was a meeting point to surface what were previously more subterranean views, such as Islamophobia, white nationalism, anti-immigration, and, in the case of Canada, a commitment to expanding the fossil economy through the building of new fossil fuel infrastructure.

The ideological foundation of YVC is a potent blend of libertarian protectionism and settler self-interest, aggressive anti-immigration views that see strong borders as essential to maintaining order, and unwavering support for the fossil economy with a dash of a kind of green nationalism that prioritizes self-sufficiency and national ownership of energy infrastructure as an expression of energy sovereignty. Unlike the explicitly classed characteristics of the *gilets jaunes,* the motivations of the Yellow Vests Canada movement were less than coherently articulated. These demands have been most clearly expressed in a document that went viral in December 2018 through Facebook. Titled "What is Canada's Yellow Vest Protest About?" and printed on yellow cardstock paper, this "unofficial manifesto" was circulated as a photo in a Facebook post that received more than twenty thousand shares (Figure 11). This post was linked to by then editor in chief of the Canadian alt-right online news magazine the *Post-Millennial,* who made immediate connections between the Canadian movement and the *gilets jaunes,* identifying both as populist movements against certain kinds of taxation and government overreach.[33] Many recent public posts on the account peddle in Covid-19 conspiracy theories, a now-common right-wing tendency that anticipates recent online activity from Rally 4 Resources.

Localized manifestations of the movement cropped up across major Canadian cities from the Atlantic to the Pacific, but Alberta arguably had some of the most activity. Edmonton, Alberta's capital city, has been a hotbed for YVC actions. Edmonton is also where its ties to explicitly

What is Canada's Yellow Vest Protest About?

The Issues

Anti-Tax: We oppose over-taxation laws and policies, including the proposed carbon tax.

Sovereignty: We advocate for maintaining the people of Canada's complete sovereignty over Canada's borders and lands within, and call for the immediate withdrawal from the UN Global Compact for Migration

Immigration: We call for an immediate end to illegal and irregular immigration, **while promoting legal immigration in amounts that allow for successful integration into Canada's multicultural society and economy.**

Free Speech: We advocate free speech and oppose any censorship laws and measures.

Free Press: We advocate for full freedom of the media.

Energy: We advocate a complete self-sufficiency, including pipelines, opposing the import of oil from foreign states and the eventual greening of the energy supply and use.

Reform: A complete reform of the Canadian Federal political system, including the electoral system and equalization payments.

Peace: We are a peaceful movement and advocate a **No First Use** policy for violence, **but shall not tolerate** mistreatment or ignorance by authorities, individuals, or other violent groups.

In a Nutshell: We want this government and future Canadian governments to do their job, serve and look after the Canadian people, all of them. Not to treat us as tax paying, wage slaves, who they can milk to the grave!

Figure 11. A facsimile of the unofficial Canadian Yellow Vests manifesto as circulated on Facebook and elsewhere in December 2018.

white nationalist and white supremacist organizations became most clear. At rallies, known white supremacist groups such as the Soldiers of Odin appeared in support.[34] As a result of internal strife, the Soldiers of Odin have since splintered into a number of factions; according to Omar Mosleh, a reporter for *StarMetro Edmonton* who extensively covered the rise of YVC, even a former member of Soldiers of Odin was unclear as to how many groups have splintered off or what their new names were.[35] While accusations of logical fallacies have become weaponized in recent years to absolve critique in the new right mediascape—a Shapiroean gesture par excellence—guilt by association seems more apt here than it does fallacious. Mosleh's coverage of YVC demonstrations in Edmonton reveals these overlapping communities of the far right that share ideological tenets and goals. While known white supremacist groups are bad company to keep when hoping to popularize a movement among a less extreme public, when the movement treats the fortification of the fossil economy and borders with equal footing as the most significant sites for political action, an alliance with white nationalism and supremacy seems a natural fit. A placard of one Yellow Vest demonstrator in Edmonton made this clear: "Open Borders Breed Chaos."[36]

Online and off, YVC continued to enjoy growing attention and activity despite ever-apparent extremism. And as YVC enjoyed this rise, a series of convoys in late 2018 and early 2019 would play a role in defining the contours of petroturfing's second wave. In this transformation, some have broken off as a means to separate the more balance-oriented modes of petroturfing from the more extreme far-right manifestations, but cross-pollination and mutually shared ideological tenets underwrite the petroturfing project in ways that cannot be ignored, particularly in the wake of the 2022 Freedom Convoy, organized and attended by some of the same figures of United We Roll!, to which I return in the book's conclusion.

The Rubber Hits the Road and the Pedals Hit the Metal: The Convoy That Was and Wasn't

On the brisk winter's day of December 16, 2018, more than 1,500 people attended a pro-pipeline demonstration in Grande Prairie, Alberta. Participants showed up to the demonstration, which featured hundreds of towering pickups with raised suspension and big rigs, to rally against Bill

C-69, a federal act that would revise environmental assessment protocols. Participants would instead call for more support of the oil and gas industry in Alberta. The demonstration was organized by Rally 4 Resources and Oilfield Dads. A sea of Canada Action branding was on the horizon as politicians, industry representatives, and familiar petroturfing mascots, including Bernard the Roughneck, took the stage to deliver messages to Ottawa. The oil and gas industry in Alberta, Bernard declared, "puts chicken in the pot in New Glasgow, Nova Scotia. It puts a roast in the oven in Miramichi, New Brunswick. It puts tortiere on the fork in Granby, Quebec. And it puts tofu on the table in Toronto and Vancouver!"[37] Up to this point, Rally 4 Resources had, by its own account, organized thirty demonstrations across Western Canada in 2018 alone, but the turnout in Grande Prairie was more than three times what was expected. Riding the momentum, Rally 4 Resources and Oilfield Dads took to planning a cross-country convoy from Grande Prairie to Ottawa, with a series of stops in Saskatchewan and Manitoba along the way in coalition with Oil Sands Strong, Canada Action, Bernard the Roughneck, and others. Opening a campaign on the popular crowd-funding platform GoFundMe, the Resource Coalition Convoy amassed some US$11,000 in donations in one day. In the shadow of the Grande Prairie demonstration in late 2018, the convoy would emerge as a crucial weapon in petroturfing's on-the-ground arsenal to battle on the front of the oil culture wars.

But the Resource Coalition Convoy would not come to fruition. As YVC broke through as a distinct movement in concert with rising expressions of pro-oil discontent, groups like Canada Action and Rally 4 Resources were first hesitant to associate with YVC, and later distanced themselves from this movement. At the time of the announcement of the Resource Coalition Convoy, two competing convoys from Western Canada to Ottawa emerged. One of these convoys was tied to those established in the petroturfing world who organized the Grande Prairie demonstration. The other was associated with the growing YVC movement. First named the Yellow Vest Convoy for Canada, this second convoy hoped to distance itself in name only after controversy percolated surrounding YVC's extremist foundations. Renamed the United We Roll! Convoy for Canada, the convoy nevertheless maintained its ties to YVC through the convoy's organizer, owner, and operator of Oilfield

Paramedics, Glen Carritt, who was allied with YVC from the start.[38] The organizers behind the Resource Coalition Convoy established distance from what was increasingly being understood as a far-right movement with racist foundations. Eventually, the organizations behind the Resource Coalition Convoy went into retreat, canceling their convoy and refunding donators, while the competing convoy chugged along with a few stalls along the way.

A convoy is a potent material–symbolic act of combustion as global heating intensifies. And it would emerge as the tactic of choice for the pro-oil movement over the course of 2019 and again in 2022. In their oft-cited meditation on scale, consequence, and culpability in the Anthropocene, environmental philosopher and literary theorist Timothy Morton describes the act of ignition in terms of a compelled relation to the acceleration of global warming, what Morton sees as a "hyperobject," or "things that are massively distributed in time and space relative to humans."[39] "The reason why I am turning my key—the reason why the key turn sends a signal to the fuel injection system, which starts the motor—is one result of a series of decisions about objects, motion, space, and time," Morton speculates.[40] Morton's investigation into the intentions of this action unearths subterranean drivers and aftershocks of the act of ignition as evidence for reigniting critical attention to ontology in a warming world. By turning to the ignition of an internal combustion engine as the end result of "a series of decisions" whose totality of effects reshapes planetary relations through global warming, Morton provides an entry point in unpacking the political ecology of the convoy as a material–symbolic gesture of excess. In Morton's meditation, ignition is a quotidian action, an impulse that inadvertently sets into motion a chain of events with consequences that outweigh the severity of the single act. For United We Roll! and the smaller-scale pro-oil convoys that anticipated United We Roll!, however, ignition is a conscious act that fuels a politics of combustion. In burning fuel as an expression of such a politics of combustion, these convoys set fire to the flames of petroturfing as parts of it veered further right.

United We Roll! had two clear targets that echo the essential ingredients of fossil fascism: the first tied to the building of new fossil fuel infrastructure and the second to the closing down of borders. Focused primarily on Bills C-48 and C-69, which would implement a crude oil tanker ban on the West Coast and overhaul environmental assessment regulations for new energy projects, respectively, and Canada's adoption of the UN Global Compact for Safe, Orderly and Regular Migration, the energies coalescing are telling in their resonance with existing agendas put forth by YVC. Even though efforts were taken to distance the convoy from the Yellow Vests, in the melding of pipelines and borders as equally significant political targets, such distance would end up as purely semantic.

The cast of support that showed up at Parliament Hill for the convoy's arrival was a veritable who's who of Canada's fringe and establishment right. Then prime minister hopeful Andrew Scheer gave a speech to an enthusiastic audience, stating that "it is time that Canada has a prime minister that is proud of our energy sector."[41] Far-right, white nationalist, and former Rebel Media correspondent who was on scene at the Unite the Right rally, Faith Goldy, made an appearance as well. After being heckled by an Indigenous counterprotestor, she responded by saying, "If you don't like our country, leave it."[42] And Saskatchewan senator David Tkachuk raised the stakes by telling the audience he "want[s] [them] to roll over every Liberal left in the country."[43] This culminating event revealed how closely broader right-wing and far-right interests are aligned when it comes to questions of pipelines and borders.

In the lingering exhaust fumes of the convoy, United We Roll! further cemented the convoy as a premiere mode of political expression in a time inflected by the fossil fascist creep. As Winona LaDuke and Deborah Cowen note, the United We Roll! convoy was "white and masculine backlash animated by climate change denial and hyperextractivism," which "is diagnostic of a politics that has taken hold across the continent."[44] Despite one convoy's cancellation and another's identity transformation, in this fractioning and rebranding was a surface-level bifurcation of petroturfing that strengthened instead of weakened it. Where official denunciation of the fossil fascist demonstrations flowed from more well-established voices of petroturfing, more aggressive tendencies fomented in tandem with YVC. And following the election of the UCP in 2019, this former strand would become fully absorbed in Alberta's provincial governmental apparatus.

The Oil Culture Wars Take Over the Legislature

Jason Kenney's UCP officially took power while the exhaust fumes of the United We Roll! convoy were still in the air. By beating out the New Democratic Party (NDP), which consistently demonstrated allegiance to the fossil economy despite campaigning on commitments to climate action, the UCP represented a return to conservative rule. Former premier Rachel Notley proved herself to be a strong ally to industry by maintaining existing royalty rates, much to the disappointment of those who saw promise and possibility in the campaign. But just as Jim Boucher received vitriol in the face of support for the fossil economy on Oil Sands Strong's Facebook page, as seen in chapter 4, so, too, was Notley on the receiving end of bigoted, misogynist energies, some of which lifted the mantra from the United States used against Hillary Clinton: "lock her up."[45] Such was the climate in which Kenney rose to power, gaining momentum through resentment of the NDP. Those chants of "lock her up" came early in the NDP's reign, and by the 2019 election the fate of the province was all but sealed—conservatives would rule the prairie province once again, surprising few who followed provincial politics in any capacity. Anger, it was clear, fueled the rebound to conservative rule, and this anger would be mobilized throughout Kenney's reign, including in his declaration of war against those working toward a just energy transition in Canada and across the planet.

Declaring War

Launched with an annual operating budget of $30 million, which was lowered to $18 million in response to the Covid-19 pandemic, the Canadian Energy Centre (colloquially known as the War Room) operates as a provincial corporate entity. Being incorporated in this way immediately raised suspicion about transparency and accountability, as reporters were quick to note that as a corporate entity in these terms, the CEC receives public funds but is not subject to Freedom of Information and Protection of Privacy (FOIP) requests, the very kinds of requests that investigative journalists might make in order to discern how funds are being distributed and to what ends.[46] Not to raise doubts over the voracity of Kenney's party's commitments to the fossil economy, "war room" phrasing cemented war as an official framework through which government and the architects, agents, and allies of the fossil economy would shape energy consciousness in favor of Canadian oil. With the war declared, the signifier *war room* itself carries with it a legacy as a centralized command center operating during times of war. According to the *Oxford English Dictionary,* the term was coined by an advisor to Winston Churchill during World War I. More recently, the phrase is often used metaphorically to describe centers of political campaign efforts.[47] Such war-room metaphors are favored by the far right, with, for instance, Steve Bannon, cofounder of Breitbart News and former Trump aide, launching a series of podcasts under the title *War Room* in the fall of 2019.

Several components and initiatives comprise the CEC, all of which propel the process of legitimation through circulation that I have shown to be an integral formal characteristic of the petroturfing project. These layers also achieve different ends through differing means, ranging from the circulation of pro-oil content in the style of daily news articles to active online campaigning following the format of pledges and letter-signing initiatives pioneered by groups and campaigns such as Canada Action or CAPP's Canada's Energy Citizens.

First, the CEC runs a blog on its home page with articles laid out with resemblance to an online news magazine. Categorizing articles according to topics of environment, economy, community, and research, the outlet publishes short pieces on hot-button issues with opinions that reproduce dominant industry thinking and help spread oil executive epistemologies. The platform even employs the same framing as Ethical Oil from more than a decade ago—a section on what it calls "mythbusting on Canadian oil and gas."[48] These charged articles perform the basic task of petroturfing—to refine Canadian oil as a socially, economically, and ecologically progressive force. An article by Grady Semmens, for instance, makes the case that "expanding access to Canada's vast fossil fuel resources will significantly lower global greenhouse gas emissions, according to a growing body of evidence."[49] This growing body of evidence emerges from speculative projections surrounding the impacts on emissions that would occur were all coal-fired power plants across the planet to switch to Canadian liquefied natural gas (LNG). Such a position is emerging as one way to promote LNG by construing it as a bridge fuel, that is, a fuel that serves as a stepping stone to a renewable energy future.[50] Semmens relies on these accounting tricks to promote a fossil fuel as a solution to a condition produced by the burning of fossil fuels. Other articles directly engage narratives and actions of resistance to Canada's fossil economy as a means to promote Canadian fossil fuels through expressions of petrocapitalist realism. These articles seem to follow a template that introduces a basis of resistance, such as pipeline safety concerns, then claims that opponents are, for instance, ignoring our collective fossil-powered realities or being unrealistic about what is politically possible today.[51] None of this is new. These are the same strategies honed by petroturfing from its inception. But through the self-presentation as a legitimate, state-sponsored news source, the CEC creates an archive of petrocapitalist realism from which other petroturfing pursuits can rely.

CEC's Support Canadian Energy initiative is in many ways a conventional petroturfing effort. Like Canada Action's and CAPP's Canada's Energy Citizens' campaigns that call upon users to take pledges of support, which then gather user data using the features offered by the NationBuilder platform, the Support Canadian Energy campaign asks visitors to "take action" by, as pointed out in the opening pages of this chapter, sending boilerplate emails or signing petitions tied to specific infrastructures or recent events. Along with the campaign against Netflix, one of the most recent campaigns garners support to revive the Energy East pipeline. "Canada is in trouble," the write-up for the email campaign begins. The pitch continues:

> The radical anti-energy activists are getting close to their goal of landlocking Canadian oil in the west. Our oil and gas pipelines through the US [are] being targeted and closed off. . . . We can't rely on the US to transport our oil any more to foreign markets or even other parts of Canada. . . . We need an all-Canadian pipeline that takes oil from the West to the East.[52]

Closing by urging visitors to "tell your Member of Parliament to support a West to East pipeline," the page provides a template for sending an email to a visitor's MP using the generic functionality of NationBuilder. Another campaign does the same for the Keystone XL, asking visitors to "keep Keystone XL alive." The language of vitality is telling here as infrastructure theorists such as Ashley Carse and David Kneas have come to describe unbuilt or unfinished as zombie infrastructure, which identifies incomplete or canceled infrastructural endeavors that nevertheless maintain a presence in public consciousness.[53] Through these campaigns, the CEC hoards zombie infrastructure in the hopes of a revival at some future conjuncture.

Kenney's entrance into the oil culture wars through the formation of the CEC represents an institutionalization of petroturfing, while its submerged far-right undercurrents rise to the surface. And even as petroturfing is elevated to an official state discourse in the form of a subsidized symbolic war, it retains its performance of marginalization and its underdog character by positioning the battle being fought as uneven and asymmetrical against what it construes as powerful progressive environmentalist and Indigenous resistance. These claims to the marginalization of the oil and gas industry would come to the fore even before the CEC was formed, with the launch of a publicly funded investigation into the financial and ideological infrastructure of anti–oil sands campaigns, which contained in its own animating impetus a view that environmental and Indigenous activism was more powerful and influential than the oil and gas industry and its allies, which is, to remind readers, one of the most active industries in lobbying the federal government and by far the most dominant in the area of environment and resources.[54]

Inquiring Minds, Fossil Fascist Hearts

Before the formation of the CEC, the UCP launched an Alberta Public Inquiry into what it described as "anti-Alberta energy campaigns that are supported by foreign organizations."[55] Specifically, the inquiry's mandate was threefold: to investigate the role of foreign funding of opposition to the oil and gas industry in Alberta, consolidate similar research on broad questions of foreign influence on local political issues, and, finally, provide recommendations emerging out of the commissioner's engagement with the collective knowledge produced during the inquiry. Headed by the forensic accountant J. Stephens Allan, the inquiry took three years, from its investigatory phases in 2019 to the summer of 2021, with the final report being made public in the fall of 2021. While the inquiry could certainly serve as the subject of its own chapter or book, I distill some key aspects of the inquiry's major reports and its recommendations to then relate these to the larger petroturfing project.

Separate from the CEC, the inquiry has nevertheless played an important role in mutually legitimating the CEC's efforts and the broader ends of petroturfing. Both the CEC and the inquiry demonstrate priorities that Kenney and the UCP held in terms of their allegiances to Canada's fossil economy by finding new avenues through which to circulate the very narratives that petroturfing refined. Whereas the CEC plays an active, state-sponsored role refining Canadian oil in tandem with more legacy petroturfing efforts, the inquiry, particularly the set of supplementary commissioned reports, provides a kind of justification for the formation of the CEC. The inquiry might best be understood as the *rationale,* while the CEC is the *practice.*

But like my brief history of the CEC in the opening pages of this chapter suggests, the inquiry was marked by blunders that called into question the credibility of the initiative at each stage over its three-year duration. The inquiry's first publicly released report, for instance, raised the eyebrows of reporters and commentators. Written by Tammy Nemeth, who holds a PhD in history from the University of British Columbia and is currently employed as a homeschool teacher in the UK, the report is ultimately a kind of right-wing speculative fiction that constructs an alternative present in which environmental activism is merely a Trojan horse for a centrally funded global socialist agenda that hopes to topple modern ways of life. With the revealing title *A New Global Paradigm: Understanding the Transnational Progressive Movement, the Energy Transition and the Great Transformation Strangling Alberta's Petroleum Industry,* or "Nemeth Report," as it is referred to throughout the inquiry, the report argues that there is a globally coordinated effort to stoke energy transition and move from capitalism to greener economic modes, or what she terms the "Great Transformation," among a coherent, mutually funded Transnational Progressive Movement. As Nemeth puts it, the Great Transformation "is about the destruction of the modern western way of life."[56] The report is marked by conspiratorial thinking—spending around seven pages rehashing climate denialist talking points, for instance—while performing questionable analyses of activist efforts to support energy transition. Reviving the Cold War imaginary, Nemeth even claims that international support for energy transition might very well be an attempt to weaken the West. "One could make an argument that China is encouraging an energy transition within the Transnational

Progressive Movement as an opportunity to weaken the west (especially the US if possible) and assert the dominance of 'socialism with Chinese Characteristics' as a global alternative," she writes.[57]

Throughout the report, Nemeth relies on denialist frameworks and far-right watchwords, including phrases such as "virtue signaling," which is often used in alt-right circles to criticize expressions of identity politics that are construed as vacuous attempts to gain cultural capital by appearing to be accepting and considerate of marginalized identities. Nemeth considers sustainability a form of virtue signaling in these ways as she describes financial organizations as "creating an investment environment hostile to any organization or fund that cannot tick the virtue signaling boxes of sustainability."[58] Beyond these winks and nods to the alt- and far-right world, Nemeth directly cites concepts and work from known alt- and far-right figures, including Breitbart London editor James Mark Court Delingpole's concept of a watermelon, which purports that environmental activism is a smokescreen for socialism—that is, it is green on the outside and red on the inside—as well as a citation of a review of Douglas Murray's *The Madness of Crowds: Gender, Race and Identity* hosted on the climate change denial blog *Watts Up With That* to show how progressives "embody a redefined global Marxism."[59] And where many of Nemeth's most damning claims are made, no notes appear, such as when she asserts that "an extraordinary amount of money has been, and continues to be, distributed to a number of different ENGOs whose unifying cause is shutting down the oil sands and keeping it in the ground."[60] The report ultimately legitimates itself by adopting an academic tone and style replete with notes, but not all notes are created equally.

More professional in its design and presentation, another inquiry output tracks organizations and campaigns over the past couple of decades. Produced by Energy In Depth, a think tank tied to the oil and gas lobbying group Independent Petroleum Association of America based in Washington, D.C., this report investigates the role of foreign funding in activism against the oil sands. In other words, the report itself is a product of the inquiry and uses provincial funds to support a foreign organization. Titled *Foreign Funding Targeting Canada's Energy Sector*, the report argues that growing environmentalist activist efforts in Canada have been "designed to appear as an organic grassroots resistance, but they are in fact funded and coordinated by wealthy philanthropies, many of which are located outside of Canada."[61] Highlighting specific funding bodies and campaigns tied to the very pipelines discussed in this book, the report provides insight into the financial aspects of environmental activism and economic stakes of disruption for the present and future of the oil sands.

But these insights are weak, marked by a lack of understanding of the existing grassroots Indigenous and environmental activism surrounding these pipeline projects as well as an even more basic understanding of the pipelines themselves. The profiles of each pipeline are brief, and the flow of the report is only semicoherent. A proverbial smoking gun in the report is a quote from the climate activist and founder of 350.org Bill McKibben, citing an interview in which he evades a question by an antagonistic interviewer about funding sources, which is then used to cast doubt on the integrity of all funding for environmentalist groups and initiatives.[62] As the authors of the report make clear, they have pieced together the research for their analysis from publicly available information at a distance, and this distance from the actually existing material circumstances that shape the contours of Canadian pipeline politics—especially the territorial politics—produces no new, compelling, or interesting insights. Concluding its analysis, the report argues that "energy producers and anti-energy activists are engaging on an uneven playing field. The energy industry is among the most highly-regulated and heavily scrutinized. Activists and their supporters, meanwhile, are largely given a free pass by the media."[63] The agency of arguably the most powerful and influential industry in recent world history is dampened.

Alongside the Nemeth and Energy In Depth reports, Barry Cooper, a Calgary School figurehead, contributed a survey of social science research that historicizes philanthropic organizations and their funding strategies to inform a critique of "the ideological justification of contemporary environmental activism."[64] Titled *Background Report on Changes in the Organization and Ideology of Philanthropic Foundations with a Focus on Environmental Issues as Reflected in Contemporary Social Science Research,* the report clunkily participates in speculative straw manning packaged as a coherent social theory of ideology that ends up focusing a significant portion of its energies on a critique of the role of Marxist thought in the social sciences. Following Energy In Depth's claims about the unrestrained power and influence of progressive environmentalism, which in the report's view dwarfs the power of fossil capital, Cooper argues that "progressive environmentalists have nearly silenced their opponents."[65] *Nearly* and *silence* carry a lot of the discursive burden here, since fossil fuels continue to be the dominant energy source and the fossil fuel industry retains some of the most effective lobbying power in Canada and across the globe. Nevertheless, Cooper leans on Jane Mayer's concept of "stealth funding," which describes sophisticated strategies developed by conservative philanthropists such as the Koch brothers to avoid public scrutiny over where their funds were going. Following this engagement, Cooper suggests that liberal progressive environmentalists and the conservative fossil-powered right are mobilizing the same strategies with equal footing. For the liberals, this was the Tides Foundation, an organization that serves as a right-wing boogeyman that appears in the Nemeth and Energy In Depth reports as well. In fact, Cooper's use of notes seems to suggest that Mayer agrees with this assessment, when in reality Mayer was merely recounting the words of the founder of DonorsTrust, "the conservative answer to the Tides Foundation" and a key player in refining the processes of stealth funding.[66] Mayer's accounting of the founder's characterization of DonorsTrust here built up to the observation that DonorsTrust "soon had four times the funds and a far more strategic board" than the Tides Foundation.[67] So, while donor-advised funds may have been pioneered by liberal actors, they were put into overdrive by a fossil-powered right with far more political and economic resources.

Consistent with Cooper's history of climate denialism and the other reports in the inquiry, Cooper's report ultimately strengthens the denialist ISA. He argues that by taking "the hypothesis of anthropogenic climate change . . . as given," environmentalist organizations participate in silencing science and intellectually bankrupt agenda setting. In concert with fellow compatriots of the old and new right, Cooper is firmly against what he construes an alarmism that takes anthropogenic climate change as given and deems a response to that change urgent. As I first read these lines in the summer of 2021, more than one hundred active wildfires burned across BC and Western Canada while these regions were experiencing record-breaking heat waves, Montreal and Toronto were blanketed with smoke from forest fires in Northern Ontario, and massive flash flooding had taken hold in Europe. History will not look kindly on these denials of urgency as the planet continues to experience warming and burning in growing severity.

It furthermore speaks to the current ideological conjuncture that a report whose aim is to criticize movements within the progressive environmental left can rely heavily on historical and theoretical insights from a book that developed its frameworks out of an analysis of the role that the spoils of fossil capital played in reshaping the landscape of philanthropy in the United States. Cooper's use of Mayer's *Dark Money* divorces Mayer's critical insights from their historical material context, and it signals an evacuation of content consistent with the petroturfing project. Although he acknowledges that Mayer's book is a "generally critical account of right-wing and conservative philanthropy," Cooper sidesteps that it was the agents of fossil capital who were the architects of philanthropic conditions in which large sums of cash were spent to establish front groups, some of whom struck paydirt in the very industry the inquiry has sought to defend, that is, Alberta's oil and gas industry. By relying on Mayer's insights to offer a vague secondhand analysis of the funding mechanisms behind progressive environmentalist organizations, Cooper muddies the waters on who it is precisely that has pioneered what we might call proto-petroturfing, a new astroturfing that mobilizes front groups for political and self-interested economic purposes—the Koch brothers in particular, and the oil and gas industry in general.

To reveal this tension is not to defend mainstream progressive environmentalism, nor is it a defense of the progressive groups such as the Tides Foundation named in Cooper's report. As I show in chapter 1 and will return to in the conclusion, mainstream progressive environmental organizations often continue to fight in the oil culture wars in ways that, in my view, fortify impasses. Yet, by commissioning reports such as these, the inquiry is participating in exactly the kinds of far-right, fossil-powered ideological nourishment that Mayer's book sets out to challenge. In true petroturfing fashion, it is the act of inquiry itself that matters rather than what the inquiry produces—an evacuation of content characteristic of the process of legitimation through circulation in which meaning is derived from form without content.

Submitted to Alberta's minister of energy Sonya Savage on July 30, 2021, Allan's 675-page report and set of six recommendations do little to provide any clarification since they lack hard data on the role of foreign funding in the Canadian environmental movement and its activism against the oil sands. If anything, the findings undermine the hunches of the inquiry's rationale. The recommendations, however indirectly, call into question some of the claims that appear throughout these three commissioned reports, perhaps unsurprising given how Allan repeatedly points out that the reports do not necessarily represent the final views of the inquiry. Pushing against Nemeth's imagined conglomerate of the Transnational Progressive Movement, Allan admits there is no coordinated global environmental movement that shares centralized funding sources or directives. While Allan notes that there are networks of support and mutual aims, "there does not appear to have been one independent, controlling entity."[68] And against all three reports, Allan repeatedly admits that genuine motivations and concerns for the future do inform the progressive environmental movement in Canada and its resistance to oil sands expansionism.[69]

Despite the incoherence of the inquiry and its commissioned reports, when taken together, a series of key themes emerge that provide a glimpse of future narratives and discursive pressure points that will likely inform petroturfing, while also establishing base positions and views that resonate strongly with the foundational tenets of an emergent Canadian fossil fascism. Of the six recommendations made by Allan, the sixth and final one stands out: a call to "rebrand Canadian energy."[70] In the closing pages of the report that detail the rationale and potentials for acting on this recommendation, Allan decries the success of what he calls "the strategy," an umbrella term for all anti–oil sands activist media efforts, whose origins he traces to 2008. "If industry and governments wish to 'level the playing field,'" Allan writes, "then the success of the recommendations that follow will not be measured in the short term, but will require the strong leadership and financial commitment of industry and government on a sustained basis in the years to come."[71] Evaluating past and present efforts in what I call petroturfing, including Canada Action, Allan suggests that much is left to be desired in terms of these initiatives' abilities to effectively rebrand Albertan oil, yet "they may however be important partners in such an initiative."[72] Allan's solution is to

> develop, in collaboration with industry and with the direction and advice of marketing and communications experts a long-term strategy built on a vision of being a global leader in lower carbon energy and climate solutions, while emphasizing the importance of energy in creating a high quality of life and a prosperous future for people everywhere.[73]

So even as Allan empirically hedges some of the larger hunches that occasioned the inquiry, these recommendations rationalize petroturfing as a state-funded enterprise complete with a plan of action. Like the modes of lubrication that Mark Simpson described to characterize emergent forms of petroturfing, so too does this inquiry lubricate conditions for a more robust mode of petroturfing in the future.

Canadian Oil's Permanent Campaign Turns Ten

Recent years have not been especially kind to the pipelines that petroturfing took shape around to promote and realize. Out of the four major pipelines I've used as infrastructural anchors to build an account of petroturfing, only one seems to have a secure future, due, arguably, to the fact that it is now a pet project of the federal government. But a refrain I find myself repeating from the introduction is that unrealized pipeline projects often haunt the present. From the Mackenzie Valley Pipeline in the 1970s to Energy East in the 2010s, what is as good as buried remains a kind of living dead, zombie infrastructure as industry and government keep the pipedream alive through campaigns such as those pursued through the CEC. Uncertainty is a constitutive condition that both hinders and cements the inertia of the fossil economy in these ways.

It is precisely the question of *for whom* uncertainty favors that has raised the attention of the agents of the fossil economy and that has served as a recent rallying call for pro-oil activist energies. These energies have been channeled directly to policy through campaigns and demonstrations that name the bills as sites of attention. For the United We Roll! convoy, these lines of sight followed YVC's twinned concerns of pipelines and borders, rallying against Bills C-49 and C-69 and migration pacts between the UN and Canada, which in the movement's mind create social and economic uncertainty for a particular kind of Canadian. Former prime minister Stephen Harper referred to such Canadians in the 2015 federal election as "old-stock Canadians," that is, settlers who have Indigenized themselves through an internalization of the frontier narrative's settler colonial origin story packaged as nativist mythos.[74]

Legislation has increasingly become a targeted site of struggle for the pro-oil movement that follows cues of effective strategies from Indigenous and environmental activism. A CBC News article covering the decision by Conservative Party of Canada delegates to reject the inclusion of the statement "climate change is real" from its party policy book, for instance, offers a glimpse into where the pro-oil movement's material–discursive energies are being focused. Including a photograph from a pro-pipeline protest in Ottawa from 2019, the article shows an audience of mostly men, many of whom sport fresh Canada Action shirts with the iconic "I ♥ Canadian Oil & Gas" logo while holding Canada Action–branded signs declaring that "Bill C-69 = INVESTMENT UNCERTAINTY."[75] Investment climate, then, became a site around which to rally, with specific demands surrounding potential future legislation. Against an overhauling that would strengthen environmental regulations through assessment protocols, those challenging Bill C-69 cited the investment uncertainty that more stringent requirements would produce. Even after the bill's successful adoption, a Google search shows a top result from CAPP's magazine *Context: Energy Examined* that spells out dominant industry sentiment, which is that implementation of Bill C-69 "could drive away investment in Canada."[76] Here, an oil executive epistemology is on full display. While this is not to say that the oil and gas working class is not, cannot, nor should not be aware of or organize based on policy and economic conditions, investment remains the executive's lingua franca.

On the heels of the inauguration of the CEC in 2019, legacy petroturfing groups have gone into overdrive by amplifying and intensifying their presence online and off. Canada Action, for instance, redesigned its home page; partnered with a global PR organization, Cision, for press release distribution; and deployed a slicker aesthetic for its memes. Canada Action also launched a youth-focused directive called Students for Canada, an initiative that calls to mind Thunberg's Fridays for Future.

Along with this overhaul, Canada Action refashioned its origin story to stretch back to 2010 and minimize Cody Battershill's role as sole founder. A new narrative on Canada Action's "About" page uses passive voice and first-person plural pronouns to make its founding more opaque and collective. Canada Action was "founded in 2010" and "over time, we've grown into a nationwide movement."[77] On its "Who We Are" page, Canada Action visualizes this collective gesture as visitors are confronted with a series of selfies with people sporting Canada Action gear and other photos that feature branded merchandise, which load in an endless scroll.[78] No longer the brainchild of a single Calgarian real estate agent described back in 2014 as a "one-man oil sands advocate," Canada Action instead has a new origin story that suggests it has always been a collective enterprise.[79]

Oil Sands Strong has followed a similar path by redesigning its home page, expanding its merchandising, and updating its characteristic meme format with crisper branding and higher-quality images. It has become more active on YouTube, producing videos with high production quality and the promise of more. As Oil Sands Strong refined itself, the content generated on its Facebook page has become more dialogic with its followers. In the summer of 2021, for instance, Oil Sands Strong asked Facebook followers to complete the following sentence in the comments: "Anti-oil and gas people are . . ." More than five hundred comments were added, with responses such as "bought and paid for by someone," "stupid woke left wing pansies," and "sheeple."[80] A plethora of comments in this petrotrolling tone and tenor is arguably expected as part of an attempt to garner strong reactions and draw attention to the page.

Through their organizational revision and growth, both Canada Action and Oil Sands Strong have emerged all the more slick. As a supplement to the explicit fossil fascist threads of the pro-oil movement, Canada Action and Oil Sands Strong are arguably cozy with industry by design. While some of petroturfing can put forward a corporate-friendly aura in form and content, the fossil fascist creep moves forward as yellow vests hit the street.

Other legacy petroturf groups have taken a different route. Since the pandemic took hold in Canada and various lockdown measures were instituted at provincial levels in the late spring of 2020, the Rally 4

Resources Facebook page became an outlet for circulating content with a conspiratorial view of the pandemic and measures in response as much as it was about the resources from which it derives its name. The Nemeth Report's attention to the then-emergent pandemic's impact on resource politics framed lockdown measures not exactly as planned in the "plandemic" conspiracy theory sense but nevertheless emphasized how the pandemic has been framed by some as an opportunity for progressive movements to disrupt the existing economic order to force the "Great Transformation." Rally 4 Resources has repeatedly shared content on its Facebook page that feeds into this narrative. A post in June 2020, for instance, questions the integrity of data surrounding excess deaths in the first few months of the pandemic, declaring in a meme that "the cure is worse than the disease" and asking followers to "share if you agree."[81] Another congratulates Quebec for holding an anti-mask protest in Montreal.[82] Rally 4 Resources' transformation from an organization close with more established ones such as Canada Action and Oil Sands Strong into a mélange of the most eyebrow-raising characteristics of the Nemeth Report reveals the underbelly that has only become more pronounced in the face of petroturfing's self-consciously sanitized image.

In proximity with the broader program of the alt-lite to far-right media ecosystem that I examined earlier in this chapter, the petroturfing pipeline has spread as it takes shape in a distributed way, seeking to saturate the traditional and social mediascape from official corporate and state-sponsored positions *above* and allegedly grassroots, collective energies from *below.* Where slicker, corporate-friendly petroturfing outfits have expressly denied or severed relationships with what are seen as more extreme movements such as YVC, legacy petroturfing and creeping fossil fascist tendencies within the pro-oil movement are mutually informing. Comments on posts from Rally 4 Resources in the lead-up to the convoy cancellation confirm this point, as many expressed discontent with the decision by the Resource Coalition Convoy to not ally with United We Roll![83] In the wake of the much more impactful follow-up 2022 Freedom Convoy, which raised millions of dollars in donations and saw participants occupy Ottawa for weeks, the operator of the Rally 4 Resources Facebook page went rogue, rebranded as Your Liberty Project, and placed its attention on the promotion of resource extraction, protest of pandemic restrictions, and Western alienation. Oil Sands Strong also eventually endorsed the convoy, posting during the height of the convoy occupation about its own future tour to Ottawa in a modified school bus.

Combusted Futures

More than a decade after Levant's book launch on Parliament Hill, when he refigured Canadian oil as ethical oil, a further-reaching movement has emerged that followed the ebbs and flows of a new right while sharing many ideological features, such as a deep nationalism that informs commitment to the extraction, refining, and burning of fossil fuels now and in the foreseeable future. The permanent campaign petroturfing advances may have fumbled out the gate in the first half of the 2010s, but it has since taken a firmer hold above and below, which has been strengthened by the architectures and infrastructures of social media even if it remains minor. These architectures and infrastructures provide the conditions of possibility for a performance of authenticity that helps define the terms and conditions of the oil culture wars as pro-oil interests are made equivalent to those of Indigenous and environmentalist movements of resistance.

After Levant, Bernard the Roughneck's appearance in soiled high-visibility coveralls and an oil-stained face was a symbolic harbinger of the yellow vest undercurrents to the second wave of petroturfing as the oil culture wars intensified. Deeply enmeshed in the forces of a larger new right whose hold on a larger public's political imagination has been fortified through the architectures and infrastructures of social media, petroturfing's contours have been shaped alongside a growing fossil fascist creep. In a think piece written for the progressive left magazine *Canadian Dimension,* sociologist and director of the Parkland Institute, Trevor Harrison, approaches the YVC's presence in Alberta as a symptom of growing economic uncertainty and anxiety, during which calls for the construction of new pipelines are a kind of "magical solution" to economic woes.[84] "Pipelines will not save Alberta's economy in the long term," Harrison writes, "and will only provide a few jobs in the short term."[85] Harrison cautions against a dismissal of those protesting for pipelines "as right-wing troglodytes" or fascists, pointing out that for those of us committed to more equitable social and ecological futures, "a harder, but more useful task is to see beyond the rhetoric to the real human concerns of the Yellow Vest protestors for their livelihood, their families."[86] These concerns over easy dismissal graft onto the larger petroturfing project and its supporters as well, yet it is important not to downplay the fossil fascist creep at the current conjuncture, as oil executive epistemologies become common sense and underwrite a more dangerous political tendency that sees in the continued extraction, refinement, and combustion of fossil fuels a means to maintain power. To name the fossil fascist creep as such is not to demonize a working class whose livelihoods are tethered to the boom-and-bust cycles of the fossil economy but to put pressure on the kinds of authoritarian desires that manifest as a promised way out of these cycles. There remains a myopic element to the continued rejoinder that critical empathy be extended to those on the right, almost naturalizing fascist tendencies as a response to economic anxieties without confronting the dangers of the fossil fascist creep.

As trenches are dug deeper in the oil culture wars, it is more important than ever to denaturalize the fossil economy and its expression of petrocultures, which petroturfing hopes to make even more difficult. How we might we exit the deep trenches of the oil culture wars?

CONCLUSION
EXITING THE TRENCHES OF THE OIL CULTURE WARS

"Is the 'Just Transition' an existential threat to Alberta?"

Oil Sands Strong prompted its Facebook followers to answer this provocative question in the sweltering hot summer of 2021. Once relegated to grassroots environmental justice circles, just transition discourse has taken hold in more conventional political ones. Just as this discourse has been refashioned as a commitment by those in more conventional political spheres, so, too, has a challenge to its promises taken shape on the right. Such promises are those of a future in which the economic, social, and ecological inequities produced by the fossil economy past and present are absolved through energy transition. For Oil Sands Strong's part, invoking existential threats to Alberta inverts the common framing of the climate crisis spurned by the burning of fossil fuels. Here, it is not the consequences of what some call the Anthropocene that will alter or destroy the ways of life we have come to hold dear but the very efforts to avoid this future. In this formulation, existence figured within the bounds of the province is linked with the capacity to produce and consume oil, taking Matt Huber's approach to oil as North American "lifeblood" at its literal word.[1]

Despite reassurance from Commissioner J. Stephens Allan over the course of the inquiry that I examined in the previous chapter, it remains difficult to understand the modifier "anti-Alberta energy" in the inquiry's official title as anything but wielding a dual meaning. This dual meaning suggests that activism against oil sands expansionism is at once against Albertan energy (read: oil sands) and anti-Albertan full stop. Although formally stated in the inquiry's "Ruling on Interpretation of the Terms of Reference" to be merely a geographical modifier rather than opposition as "'against Alberta' or its interests in some sense," this ambiguity is a feature, not a bug.[2] If Roland Barthes has taught us anything, it is that signifiers exceed their intended meaning and, as a result, are malleable. From environmentalists to Indigenous land defenders and water protectors, belonging to province and nation has been an easy point on which to place pressure through the shaping of energy consciousness.

Under pressure is an aim to separate those pursuing a more just, equitable energy future from the fold of Albertans or Canadians and unite those whose social and political identities are expressed through a commitment to a fossil-fueled one. Who is included and excluded in these categories is mediated by one's affective relationship to oil and its infrastructures. No doubt, a different Alberta, a different Canada, and a different world would result from the kinds of transition that animate just transition visions. However, such differences are not mutually exclusive from the ideals petroculture might envision. Yet the perceived threat to these ways of life is the rationale for the conflict at the center of what I have been calling the oil culture wars. In these material and symbolic struggles, the just transition becomes a target in the oil culture wars from which to articulate the stakes of conflict as petroturfing claims another site mobilized by environmental justice movements: existence. Ultimately, the oil culture wars center on the meaning of a set of terms with shifting meanings. Who gets to define these terms holds an upper hand.

War occupies an interesting position across the political spectrum today as a go-to metaphor for naming conflicts or identifying forms of resolution. On the one hand, war has been mobilized metaphorically to describe the gravity and impact of climate change as well as the urgency and scales to provide a solution. Progressive Canadian writer and activist Seth Klein, for instance, makes the case that mobilization of state resources for addressing climate change in a manner akin to wartime is both necessary and desirable. For Klein, World War II represented the rare kind of "good war" in which resources were effectively mobilized by the Canadian state, while businesses and individuals altruistically sacrificed for the greater good. That same level of intervention, Klein argues, might be the only way to adequately change the course of climate change.[3] From a Marxist position, human ecologist Andreas Malm coins "ecological war communism" as a metaphor to quell the condition of "chronic emergency" that he views as a constitutive condition of the present and very near future.[4] Ecological war communism, for Malm, represents a distinctly more socialist expression of war than Klein's as he refashions Vladimir Lenin's formulation for the demands of the climate emergency and pandemic present. This war, Malm promises in Lenin's words, will be one against the oil barons.[5]

On the other hand, contemporary invocations of war signal a revival of the culture wars generated by frictions between a progressive left, broadly understood, and an old and new right that employ war framing to gather troops against a perceived dominance of progressive and left tendencies today. As detailed in the previous chapter, these material–discursive delineations of war form milieu on which to stoke and centralize reactionary energies, or what critical scholars of the reactionary present might call backlash. Backlash, of course, names those reactions to gains made by progressive movements primarily in the twentieth century, such as feminist or civil rights movements. From panics over the teaching of critical race theory in education systems to threats waged against drag queen story hours, a modulated echo of these earlier modes of backlash conditions the present with increasing intensity. With petroturfing, this backlash carries with it a fossil-fueled edge that, as Cara New Daggett reminds us, isn't so much an offshoot of reactionary politics but a central component to them.[6]

Yet, at the tail end of drafting this book, war did break out in ways that brought into starker relief the stakes of war framing, while calling into question the usefulness of war framing in pursuits for more equitable futures. Under the impetus of energy security, this war would be mobilized by the agents, architects, and allies of Canada's fossil economy for promotional ends. When Russia invaded Ukraine in late February 2022, a nearly immediate response by Alberta's then-premier Jason Kenney was to take to Twitter and, in the same breath as stating that "the democratic world must be united in standing with Ukraine," pitch oil and gas sanctions as an early offensive tactic: "that should begin with a hard global embargo of all Russian oil & gas exports."[7] In the days to come, news media would seize this opportunity to promote Canadian oil across the screen and page as an antidote to Russian influence, including an op-ed by the *Globe and Mail* editorial board titled "The World Needs More Canadian Oil and Gas."[8] In this war, then, is a cynical promotional opportunity for which the same questions of energy security that followed the War on Terror and helped mold Canada into the major oil-producing country it is today are redeployed. Colder, highly mediated oil culture wars are entangled with hotter, militarized geopolitical wars in these ways, and Russia's invasion has brought new life to the narratives of Canadian exceptionalism that are a cornerstone of the petroturfing project.

Throughout this book, I have also employed war framing and vocabularies. But I've done so not to reify war as a privileged condition to build either a better or worse future. As much as a war on oil barons sounds like strong praxis, aside from, say, class war, war as I understand it feeds impasse rather than moves past it. For my part, I've developed the concept of the oil culture wars as diagnosis and critique. By employing war as diagnosis and critique in these ways, I've argued that petroturfing drafts foot soldiers to expand the front of the oil culture wars.

As war carves out space for material and symbolic intervention in very particular ways that many activists and thinkers find productive, in these closing pages I want to caution against its adoption as a neutral or ambivalent grounds upon which futures both better and worse are fought. Like populism, war framing as metaphor or material carries with it historical and critical baggage that forecloses ways of intervening on the problems of today rather than generates alternative modes of engagement that the present demands. Wars such as those I outlined surrounding oil and identity benefit existing systems and structures of power. My naming of the oil culture wars throughout this book offers a critical frame to expose the promises and pitfalls of media efforts by those for *and* against the expansion of Canada's fossil economy. As chapter 1 showed in its accounting of the emergence of the dirty oil frame vis-à-vis intentional efforts by ENGOs and others, for instance, my approach does not let those groups, organizations, and campaigns off the hook. Without dirty oil, as I said in chapter 1, there would be no ethical oil, since petroturfing is a reactionary endeavor, as exaggerated as the grounds for that reaction might be.

Beyond benefiting the existing order, war framing also invokes uncomplicated notions of urgency and emergency. Such limits to this urgent and emergent setting offered by war become clearer when addressing this question by placing it in the larger context of climate change, particularly its relation to the twin forces of the fossil economy and settler colonialism. For one, the urgency through which the crises of the present are often figured continue to be challenged by Indigenous peoples whose experience of such states of exception is deeply shaped by ongoing settler colonialism. "Exception," in other words, is often anything but exceptional in these settings. Potawatomi environmental philosopher Kyle Powys Whyte makes this condition visible when he describes how Indigenous peoples faced and continue to face the very same conditions under which climate change has taken shape: forced relocation, destruction of lands and waters, and more.[9] An alternative avenue that recognizes and responds to urgency without flattening these relations is needed.

In the face of urgency, the content produced and circulated across the petroturfing mediascape evokes strong feelings among diverse audiences and in diverse settings by design. A decade into its formation, petroturfing has gained traction in large part due to these strong feelings. My experience sharing my work on petroturfing over the years reveals as much. As I was scrolling through the social media platform Reddit in late 2021, for instance, I encountered a familiar image: the "lesbians are hot" meme produced by Robbie Picard that I examined in chapter 3. The self-declared "frontpage of the Internet," Reddit is a message board on which posts by individual users are organized by a ranking function based on user inputs: upvotes or downvotes. Reddit has more than fifty million active users per day and is host to a plethora of communities organized as "subreddits." When the meme was posted to the r/Canada subreddit, discussion in the comments indicated that many were unaware of its history. I decided to offer some context based on my research. Aside from stating that I was currently writing a book on the conditions under which this meme was incubated, I did not offer any analysis or reveal the argument of this book, only empirical observations and details about the episode under question. I pointed out that the meme was created and circulated by Picard, a colleague of Rebel Media and Ethical Oil architect Ezra Levant, and, further, that the Facebook group has since changed its name from Canadian

Oilsands Community to Oil Sands Strong as a result of the controversy that followed its circulation. One Reddit user replied that those in industry don't buy the ethical oil argument, that it was disingenuous to suggest that these kinds of positions had any influence, and questioned the integrity of my scholarship on these terms.

But this user's dismissive response was not unique in my experience; as a young graduate student and, later, as a junior scholar on the academic job market, workshopping some of the ideas and analyses that would become this book, I would continue to run into resistance to this work. Something about petroturfing on the one hand and its critique on the other hand got under people's skin. As I presented this work at conferences, for instance, some peers felt as though petroturfing media were easy targets or, like the Reddit user I encountered, not taken seriously enough to warrant extensive scholarly attention. While I would never want to exaggerate the influence of petroturfing, it is the case that it is has become more influential over the past decade in ways that make attention necessary. The 2022 Freedom Convoy, staged after the 2019 United We Roll! rehearsal, illustrates this point. However, the most prevalent of these critiques has been that my analysis of petroturfing and the pro-oil movement more generally is based on a vulgar reductionism that does not account for the ideological agency of those who might find themselves supporting the oil and gas industry.

In the introduction, I accounted for some of the more formalized critiques as they appear in the little academic work that exists on what I have been calling petroturfing. Communications scholar Tim Wood, for instance, identifies what I call petroturfing as corporate grassroots campaigning, which in this formulation means it is a rational, good-faith response from the agents, architects, and allies of Canada's fossil economy as industry comes under threat from environmental and Indigenous activists.[10] Interrogating petroturfing, even if understood in the generous terms of corporate grassroots expression, is not simply a rehearsal of vulgar ideological critique that sees workers duped into a straightforward, crude form of false consciousness (as if false consciousness is ever crude). As an affective infrastructure in Kai Bosworth's formulation, part of what is appealing to supporters emerges from desperation in a setting in which many feel the uneven distribution of costs and benefits of a fossil economy that first exploits the labor, then seeks to carry on this exploitation into the day-to-day lives of oil and gas workers as it recruits foot soldiers for the oil culture wars.[11] The busts of larger political economic forces trickle down as significant impacts on the day-to-day lives of workers, like we encountered in chapter 3 in the personal narratives of workers provided through the partnership between the Oil Respect campaign and Oilfield Dads. This condition creates fertile grounds for recruitment.

When personalized, morality takes over and critique of those responsible becomes refigured as a critique of those impacted, which ends up serving the interests of fossil capital. And when material–economic livelihoods become the vector through which support for the fossil economy is garnered, oil executive epistemologies that equate the interests of industry and workers are, no doubt, attractive. Following this trajectory, my critiques of the petroturfing project are sometimes construed as antiworker. These terms for dismissal of critique are arguably by design, exhibited in the responses of devil's advocates who point to some of the truisms contained in petroturfing media or, as mentioned earlier, in accusations of my critique as dismissing the agency of the workers. As much as working-class energies are appealed to in the reproduction of Canada's fossil economy, they must also be centered in building a more equitable future beyond fossil capital, as Huber argues.[12] That workers are a threat to fossil capital is precisely why they are a main character in petroturfing's plotline that separates them from other social movements.

Let me be clear in the closing pages of this book. The petroturfing project as I understand it has *never* been a working-class project, and, for this reason, it never will be. Petroturfing is a petit bourgeois initiative that seeks to fuel impasse for the benefit of those agents and architects of Canada's fossil economy by equating the interests of the oil and gas industry with its workers. First dreamed up in the pages of a book written by a lobbyist lawyer turned right-wing media mogul and then refined by a real estate agent in the capital city of Canada's oil and gas industry's financial apparatus, the project then became an extended arm of former premier Jason Kenney's pro-oil ISA as it maintains its grassroots aura. More empirical work should be done in order to confirm a hunch of mine that has been at the forefront of my mind since the 2019 and 2022 convoys—that large and small business owners, a bourgeois and petit bourgeois class, are those most enthusiastically participating in the broader petroturfing project. The oil culture wars, in other words, seem to have been ignited not by those laborers toiling in the Patch but by those banking on Canadian oil. This is why I offer the framework of the oil executive epistemology to make sense of the ideological kernels of petroturfing in which more investment becomes the rallying cry. In one way of understanding petroturfing, the working class has become both a scapegoat and a shield, which are glimpsed in the dramas I have unfolded in this book in economic, social, and ecological settings. Hunches, of course, are not reliable data from which to form cogent theories or analyses, which is why I've saved these speculative observations for the final pages of this book.

But, of course, it is not only the working class who are instrumentalized through both their labor and their positioning to lend authenticity to the petroturfing project. As I have shown throughout this book's central chapters, women, 2SLGBTQIA+, Indigenous peoples, and the nonhuman environment are mobilized as raw materials to be refined and circulated through petroturfing's affective infrastructure. Social media is the primary means through which this refining occurs, although traditional or legacy media play an important role in mutually reinforcing perspectives among audiences with differing levels of authority, as I have shown how petroturfing relies on the authority of traditional news media as sources for claims about the economic, social, and ecological character of Canadian oil. Work from those associated with the Corporate Mapping Project on the role that traditional news media like newspapers play in shaping Canadian energy consciousness is important in this respect. Robert Hackett and Hanna Araza, for instance, reveal the influence that the interests of the architects, agents, and allies of the fossil economy have in political–economic terms of far-reaching newspaper distribution across the country on the one hand and then the cultural impact of the views circulated by those newspapers under the editorial control of Postmedia on the other.[13] Postmedia is Canada's "largest newspaper chain"; it became so through the purchase of local and regional papers, which was made possible by creditors with backing from U.S. hedge funds.[14] In this capacity, Hackett and Araza observe that "Postmedia and Big Oil share an agenda around institutional legitimacy, political influence, and economic interests."[15] Many of the op-eds I have engaged with throughout this book that were used as primary sources for petroturfing came from the Postmedia enterprise, findings correlated with empirical work by Robert Neubauer and Nicolas Graham.[16] Refining is an integral component of oil sands production today, whether in reference to the material dynamics of oil sands production or the cultural dynamics of oil sands imaginaries, that is, what the inquiry discussed in the previous chapter has described as "rebranding."[17] It may come as no surprise, then, that in the wake of the release of the inquiry's final report, in the spring of 2022, Robbie Picard of Oil Sands Strong announced on Facebook the expansion of the project, including a digital magazine, podcast, vlog, rebranding as Oil and Gas World, and more, all of which will be centralized in a studio to be built in Fort McMurray.[18] Picard also hinted on his personal page to a future collaboration with Jordan B. Peterson.[19] As the petroturfing project stabilizes its footing in the contemporary mediascape and political arenas, it begins to look even more like the ENGOs scrutinized throughout the Allan inquiry.

For all this interplay between traditional and new mediascapes, however, the architectures and infrastructures of social media—its governing algorithms and platforms—play a unique role in stoking conflict as new frontiers of an increasingly datafied social and political milieu. Media theorist Wendy Hui Kyong Chun presciently details how polarization in the contemporary digital media environment is the end result of hard-coded processes at an algorithmic level through governing principles of correlation, processes deeply indebted to a longer history of eugenics.[20] And these architectures help give shape to the form and content of petroturfing as it transitioned from a project governed by appeals to balance to garner support for Canadian oil and its infrastructures to one more interested in recruiting and training foot soldiers ready to go to war for oil cultures. Polarization, in other words, is the point. Chun's taxonomies of these hard-coded strategies reverberate with the modes of legitimation through circulation that I have tracked throughout this book in relation to petroturfing, itself subordinate to the larger media moment to which it takes cues.

As a descriptor of how petroturfing refines Canadian oil, the process of legitimation through circulation draws attention to the centrality of questions of circulation in shaping energy consciousness. I've also described this shaping of energy consciousness as occurring through a struggle waged across the contemporary mediascape both for and against the fossil economy. Circulation struggles productively capture the convergence of these energies on the web and on the ground, as if the two could be easily distinguished. Literary and cultural theorist Joshua Clover describes "contemporary circulation struggles" as occupations, riots, and critical infrastructure blockades that, crucially, "requir[e] no privileged access to the production process, unfolding in ambiguously public space policed by the state, often interfering with the circulation of commodities."[21] Historically associated with the left, the 2022 Freedom Convoy mobilized the tactics of circulation struggles for decidedly right-wing ends after 2019's United We Roll! dress rehearsal. "The circulation struggle, but make it nationalist," as Clover puts it. Expanding the concept of circulation here by situating it into the mediated settings in which petroturfing has taken shape provides further weight in describing how a parallel struggle occurs across the mediascape, in which tactics commonly associated with progressive politics and movements have been mobilized to reproduce the conditions of business as usual as if they were unusual. For Clover, the 2022 Freedom Convoy's riff on circulation struggles reveals how "tactics migrate across the political spectrum (in so far as the political spectrum is still operative, a significantly related question)," which "is inevitably uncanny."[22] That same uncanniness marks petroturfing, but as the agents of the petroturfing project accumulate more resources, this uncanniness may disappear as these resources allow for further reach. Such reach is crystallized in the fact that one of the 2022 Freedom Convoy organizers who was also involved in the 2019 United We Roll! convoy, Tamara Lich, appeared at her bail hearing in the iconic Canada Action hoodie that reads "I ♥ Canadian Oil & Gas."

Petroturfing: Refining Canadian Oil through Social Media has performed two tasks in historicizing and critiquing the petroturfing project. First, the book has provided an account of how the pro-oil movement emerged through social media over the past decade, and second, it has critiqued how the architectures and infrastructures of new and social media have been an integral component in refining Canadian oil. In these closing pages, however, I would like to conclude with some more speculative lines of thought in how to exit the trenches of the oil culture wars, that is, how to move beyond the mutually imbricated tendencies of platform and fossil capitalism operating in the shadow of the fossil fascist creep. In this pursuit, two crucial dynamics relating to our relationship to oil, social media, and their infrastructures come into view—what I've described elsewhere as ambivalence and intensity that ends up fueling the oil culture wars and the kinds of relations that Chun and others outline in terms of digital cultures.[23]

How might we exit these trenches of the oil culture wars? Materially speaking, such an exit involves a wide-scale material transition from fossil fuels to renewable ones that foregrounds more equitable ways of being. This much is certain. But as has been insisted upon by those of us working in the energy humanities and the study of petrocultures, such transitions will not be effective if they occur only at the technological level; social and cultural transitions must occur alongside and in concert with these technological ones.[24] The same, in my view, holds true for platforms as energies of dissent get extracted, refined, and rerouted, like those I describe in NationBuilder's homogenization of activism through aestheticization and datafication.[25] To address this condition, we need to generate and nurture ways of doing activism that cannot be copied and pasted by already dominant forces only to be used in antagonistic ways to undermine these actions on the one hand and stoke the kinds of polarization that permeate new and social media's political economy and ecology on the other hand.

So, too, do we need to generate and nurture new ways of living with and relating to oil and its infrastructures. The architects, agents, and allies of the fossil economy in Canada and elsewhere are correct in their assertions about the ways in which oil permeates everyday life to the degree that to imagine a life otherwise is an exceedingly difficult endeavor. But it is in the best interest of these architects, agents, and allies to be in control of how those futures are imagined and built. In fact, they're banking on being in control of it. By insisting on the cynical reason of petrocapitalist realism as a default setting of the present, control of this future is more easily secured as energy consciousness is shaped in favor of fossil fuels. But there are pathways out of this deadlock in which the uncertainty produced by impasse can serve as an opportunity for transition instead of as a rationale for further fortifying that impasse through fossil fuel expansionism.[26] Cynical reason casts a long shadow. For those of us committed to building a more just and equitable energy future, it is difficult to not feel resigned to the fates forecasted by our warming world. As is often repeated, even if the combustion of fossil fuels were suddenly stopped today, the delayed effects of GHGs accumulated in the atmosphere would carry on. Malm presciently calls these temporally confined conditions that continue to expand the "heat of this ongoing past."[27]

Oil and other fossil fuels, in other words, are here to stay. Whether in the form of residues remaining in the atmosphere, as carbon dioxide propelling climate change, or as remnants sedimented in the infrastructures built for the fossil economy, fossil fuels will continue to shape cultural, economic, and ecological life even after their status as the dominant energy source wanes, with intention or not. Recognizing the role that culture plays in shaping our energetic present and future, as this book and others do, this material and cultural condition of persistence provides the opportunity for generative action by curating alternative relations to fossil fuels rather than the more immobilizing option presented by a purity politics of fossil fuel abolitionism.

Part of the solution, then, might lie in establishing and nurturing other ways of living with these sedimented forms of oil and its infrastructures attuned to a future beyond the petrocultures of the past and present by altering how we relate to oil. Literary and cultural theorist Jon Gordon's meditation on the problematics of oil as a substance is telling here: "Oil, then, is not the problem: a philosophy that presents oil extraction as the means to the good is the problem. Bitumen extraction is a symptom of a cultural narrative, and literature can intervene to change that narrative."[28] What might be read as bad materialism is the opposite; because oil used as energy is a social relation, requiring human intervention in the form of extracting, refining, and burning, altering those relations reshapes the role of oil in social and cultural life. For cultural theorist and artist Simon Orpana, the materials and infrastructures of petroculture can be reclaimed in a Situationist *détournement.* In the closing pages of his scholarly graphic novel *Gasoline Dreams: Waking Up from Petroculture,* Orpana mobilizes the Situationist concept of the "beach beneath the streets" to argue that skateboarding is one way in which petroculture is materially refigured as generative and relational versus destructive and atomizing.[29] From the polyurethane of a skateboard's wheels to the skater's use of streets first made for automobiles, the act of skateboarding offers a glimpse of future post-oil relations in the present.[30] From a Métis line of sight, Zoe Todd makes a similar intervention by refiguring oil as kin as a way to quash what she understands as the weaponization of fossil fuels.[31] Todd's strong words are instructive:

> It is not the oil itself that is harmful. It rested beneath the loamy soil and clay of what is now Alberta for eons. Anecdotes of the Dene people's use of the bituminous tar that occurs naturally along the Athabasca river in northern Alberta to patch canoes reminisce me that these oily materials are not, in and of themselves, violent or dangerous. Rather, the ways that they are weaponised through petro-capitalist extraction and production turn them into settler-colonial-industrial-capitalist contaminants and pollutants.[32]

Taken together, these diverse approaches to oil imaginaries point to significance in how we understand and embody our relationship to oil. Gordon, Orpana, and Todd signal alternative imaginaries and relations that, I argue, must follow in tandem with the necessary political struggles and technological innovations that will make a transition to more equitable fuel sources and ways of life possible.

Put more directly, the challenge presented by petroturfing resides in the ways that it has mobilized traditional or legacy and social media to shape energy consciousness in the service of Canadian oil in particular and fossil fuels in general. How successful the petroturfing project will be on these terms remains to be seen. But the solutions to this challenge also, in part, reside here. The sooner we recognize this, the better. These speculative lessons on energy imaginaries and consciousness that aim to reshape how we collectively relate to oil and fossil fuels as praxis apply equally to fossil capitalism as they do to platform capitalism, since media are bound up with energy systems.[33] As the mercury rises and climate denialism becomes all the more difficult to mesh with the realities of climate change, public favor or, as the vocabulary of corporate governance-speak phrases it, social license will become more important than it ever has been in influencing the outcomes of newly proposed fossil fuel projects. In order to disrupt this process and avoid the fossil-fueled future put forward by the petroturfing project and the architects, agents, and allies of the fossil economy, we need to build energy and media futures beyond platform and fossil capital against the reactive pursuits that gave us both dirty and ethical oil. It's time to exit the trenches of the oil culture wars.

ACKNOWLEDGMENTS

My earliest encounters with petrocultures were at the gas pump. To say I grew up at a gas station isn't much of an exaggeration. My dad managed one in what is now called Prince George, British Columbia, Canada, and I spent around five years working at the downtown Mohawk station as a teenage gas jockey. At the station, I confronted the complexities of petroculture—its promises, its realities, and, most important, its ubiquity. If one thing united the people of that city and so many others, it's the need for fuel. This personal lineage informs my critical–intellectual position in environmental media studies, which is important to surface when writing about substances so central to everyday life like oil. It is one thing to reflect on petrocultures as consumers at the pump or as academics at conferences; it is another to have spent time pumping gas, washing windows, and changing the pricing signage by hand (prices rose from something like $0.79 a liter to $1.15 during my years of work). This book, critical as it is of the petroculture we inhabit and the political economies that underwrite it, owes much to these experiences working in a Northern BC resource town.

As acknowledgments of books often begin by stating, a book is a collective project, with first books likely standing out more in these terms. *Petroturfing* began on a lead provided in a graduate course taught by professor Kristen Guest. Another student, Devan Joneson, recommended that I check out *Ethical Oil,* which launched the phenomenon that this book historicizes and critiques: the pro-oil movement in Canada. At the time, I followed the emergent phenomenon closely. Maryna Romanets and Kevin Hutchings generously supported the modes of intellectual inquiry I found most generative to confronting the pro-oil movement then.

But it would not be until I arrived in Edmonton, Alberta, to work with Imre Szeman at the University of Alberta that this work began in earnest. Not long after arriving, I met Sheena Wilson, who became my second reader and, in many ways, a cosupervisor, at a downtown Edmonton café alongside Matt Hern, Am Johal, and Joe Sacco, who were on a research trip up to Fort Mac. Imre and Sheena provided me with immeasurable material, financial, and intellectual support as I worked under the banner of the Petrocultures Research Group, which modeled what scholars committed to building a better future do while creating space for me develop my own critical practice and voice. This is where the work that became this book first took shape, made all the stronger by the influence of Mark Simpson, Laurie Adkin, and Jussi Parikka.

The protracted life of this book brought me to many places where I wrote during travel or downtime. Milestones are revealing on these terms. I finished a first draft in Bratislava, Slovakia, where I was participating in a workshop organized by Matúš Mišík and Nada Kujundžić; here I also met Laura Pannekoek, who has since become a close collaborator and comrade. Years later I finished a revised draft at a pub in Vienna, Austria, where I was participating in a workshop organized by Ernst Logar, an artist whom I first met during the inaugural After Oil School in 2015. During my time in graduate school, many conferences, workshops, and residencies provided space to share what appears here, particularly in terms of its theoretical and methodological interventions. In 2015, I presented early ideas that form the core of this book on a panel about "Bitumen Rhetorics" at MLA, which was chaired and organized by my late friend and colleague Jon Gordon, with Darin Barney as a fellow panelist. At MLA, I met other students of Imre: Brent Ryan Bellamy, Jeff Diamanti, and Sean O'Brien. At the inaugural After Oil School, my reading and writing group established lasting relationships, especially with Darin and Bob Johnson. Here I also met Graeme Macdonald, who has been an inexhaustible source of inspiration, mentorship, and camaraderie since. In 2016, I served as a research assistant for Banff Research in Culture during a month-long residency at the Banff Centre, which opened up new ways of thinking and doing for me given the residency's mix of artists and researchers. Here, many deserve notes of thanks, including Heather Ackroyd and Dan Harvey, Frederic Bigras-Burrogano, Edith Brunette, Megan Green, Mél Hogan, Cameron Hu, Matthew Huber, François Lemieux, M. E. Luka, Chris Malcolm, Jenni Matchett, Maria Michails, Michael Rubenstein, David Thomas, and Jayne Wilkinson. After my presentation at Petrocultures 2016, the basis of chapter 5, I was approached by Jacob Goessling; we quickly bonded and formed a strong collaborative relationship. And in 2017 I briefly visited Montreal for events surrounding Lynn Badia, Marija Cetinić, and Jeff Diamanti's Climate Realism colloquium, where Amanda Boetzkes and I discovered shared ties to the BC tree-planting scene.

Fellow graduate students at the University of Alberta deserve equal recognition. Benjamin Neudorf's friendship over these years, which began with orientation, has been vital, as was my friendship with the rest of our cohort: Ana Horvat, Chelsea Miya, Sarah McRae, and William Owen, as well as then-MA students Veronica Belafi and Matt Tétreault. Collaboration with Lucie Stepanik led to a special issue of *MediaTropes* titled "Oil and Media, Oil as Media." Beyond this more immediate cohort, being introduced to curling by Stephen Webb offered much-needed off-campus camaraderie. Matt Cormier's personal and intellectual support during and after graduate school helped weather the demands of the academic job market. Get-togethers hosted by Amanda Spallacci would introduce me to peers outside my cohort. And closer to my work with Petrocultures, Adam Carlson was always available to go guitar shopping, offer advice, or give sharp feedback on writing, including on portions of this book. Relationships fostered within the Just Powers and Future Energy Systems circle were generative too, especially with Angele Alook, Jessie Beier, Ariel Kroon, Simon Orpana, and Danika Jorgensen Skakum. Thanks also to those who have worked on the pro-oil movement, whose work I have drawn on and with whom conversations were influential, especially Patrick McCurdy.

Rather than fully pursue new research under pandemic conditions, I placed most of my attention on revising this book. In spring 2020, I took up a postdoc at McGill University and joined a book-writing cluster organized by Anne Pasek alongside Zeynep Oguz and Shirley Roburn that proved instrumental in wrapping up this project. After first getting feedback from Brent in the proposal's early stages, a Zoom workshop organized through the Comparative Theory Facebook group sharpened it further, as did Michael Truscello's consistent feedback throughout writing.

At McGill and beyond, Darin's mentorship has been generous, comradely, and unwavering. And the Grierson Research Group became a site for lasting collaboration with Hannah Tollefson, Ayesha Vemuri, Burç Köstem, Rafico Ruiz, and others. Ayesha gets an amplified shout-out for recommending, after listening to my struggles with chapter 3, that I read *Terrorist Assemblages*. During this period, Pat Brodie was a stabilizing confidante as we both navigated the academic job market.

At various points in the project, I held funding from the Social Sciences and Humanities Research Council of Canada in the form of a doctoral fellowship (2015–19) and postdoctoral fellowship (2020–22), which was jointly held with one from Le Fonds de recherche du Québec—Société et Culture (2020–22). A postdoctoral fellowship with the Mahindra Humanities Center at Harvard University (2022–23) saw the project through its final stages.

Given spatial constraints, there are simply not enough words to capture the support, companionship, and care that my partner, Allisa Ali, provided for more than a decade, weathering the storm of uncertainty so endemic to academic life and work. Our late cats, Sarah and Maggie, alongside Cece, who is still with us, kept me company during otherwise solitary reading and writing sessions.

This book wouldn't have materialized without the support of the University of Minnesota Press and the anonymous reviewers. The book's editor, Leah Pennywark, nurtured the project with an infectious clarity and confidence, making the daunting prospect of a first book much less so. Christopher Breu offered this lead, and I couldn't be more grateful.

The project this book emerged from moved with me from Western to Eastern Canada, to cities on ceded and unceded Indigenous territories: unceded Lheidli T'enneh territory (Prince George, British Columbia), Treaty 6 territory (Edmonton, Alberta), and unceded territory in Montreal, Quebec, the custodians of which are recognized as the Kanien'kehá:ka nation. I hope that this book will, in however minor a way, help land defenders and water protectors here and elsewhere by mapping the contours of one expression of fossil fuel expansionism in the present.

Finally, with a project that has taken so many forms over so many years, I have no doubt missed paying some dues; my sincerest apologies to those whose names should appear but are absent.

NOTES

Introduction

1. As the Covid-19 pandemic took hold, Rally 4 Resources focused its content on the pandemic and rebranded as Your Liberty Project. All citations of Facebook posts use the former page name, but posts can still be accessed by swapping out "/rallyforresources/" with "/yourlibertyproject/." This rebranding is discussed more thoroughly in chapter 6.

2. Rally 4 Resources, "#ShutDownCanada Toronto Protest," March 8, 2020, https://archive.is/KJ0E3.

3. Rally 4 Resources, "About Rally 4 Resources," accessed July 12, 2020, https://archive.is/IEQgZ.

4. Cultural Survival, "In Memoriam: 28 Indigenous Rights Defenders Murdered in Latin America in 2019," January 28, 2020, http://www.culturalsurvival.org.

5. Rally 4 Resources, "Rally 4 Resources—The Movement—Publications," Facebook, July 14, 2020, https://www.facebook.com/rallyforresources/posts/2546552138992437.

6. NationBuilder, "NationBuilder," accessed May 25, 2020, https://nationbuilder.com/.

7. Nick Srnicek, *Platform Capitalism* (Cambridge, UK: Polity, 2017).

8. Andreas Malm, *Fossil Capital: The Rise of Steam Power and the Roots of Global Warming* (New York: Verso, 2016), 13; Bob Johnson, *Mineral Rites: An Archaeology of the Fossil Economy* (Baltimore: Johns Hopkins University Press, 2019), xii.

9. James Davison Hunter, *Culture Wars: The Struggle to Define America* (New York: Basic Books, 1991).

10. Natural Resources Canada, "What Are the Oil Sands?," July 28, 2020, https://natural-resources.canada.ca; "Crude Oil Industry Overview," March 31, 2020, https://natural-resources.canada.ca.

11. Energy Information Administration, "Canada Is the Largest Source of U.S. Energy Imports," June 5, 2020, https://www.eia.gov/todayinenergy/detail.php?id=43995.

12. Chris Turner, *The Patch: The People, Pipelines, and Politics of the Oil Sands* (Toronto: Simon & Schuster, 2017), xxiv.

13. Jane Mayer, *Dark Money: The Hidden History of the Billionaires behind the Rise of the Radical Right* (New York: Anchor, 2017), 49–50.

14. Jeffrey Jones, "Koch Industries Sells Its Oil-Sands Properties to Paramount," *Globe and Mail,* August 14, 2019; Steven Mufson and Juliet Eilperin, "The Biggest Foreign Lease Holder in Canada's Oil Sands Isn't Exxon Mobil or Chevron. It's the Koch Brothers," *Washington Post,* March 20, 2014.

15. Mayer, *Dark Money,* 281.

16. Ezra Levant, *Ethical Oil: The Case for Canada's Oil Sands* (Toronto: McClelland & Stewart, 2010); Andrew Nikiforuk, *Tar Sands: Dirty Oil and the Future of a Continent* (Vancouver: Greystone Books, 2008).

17. Levant's official lobbying history with a major tobacco company, Rothman's Inc., between 2009 and 2010 tellingly describes one of his "communication techniques" as "grass-roots communication." See Office of the Commissioner of Lobbying of Canada, "Inactive Registration: 734374-258503-1," June 23, 2011, https://web.archive.org/web/20110720200942/https://ocl-cal.gc.ca/app/secure/orl/lrrs/do/publicSummary%3Bjsessionid%3D0001AJXvq-faIVLUqQbdlh9vrY5%3A3K2HQN8TBK?_flxKy&regDec=603900&sMdKy=1262945130370&searchPage=publicSearch.

18. On extraction as a constitutive process of contemporary capitalism, see Sandro Mezzadra and Brett Neilson, *The Politics of Operations: Excavating Contemporary Capitalism* (Durham, N.C.: Duke University Press, 2019).

19. Raymond Williams, *The Long Revolution* (Harmondsworth, Middlesex, England: Penguin Books, 1965), 64.

20. *bp Statistical Review of World Energy 2020* (London: BP p.l.c., 2020), 16.

21. *The Elephant in the Room: Canada's Fossil Fuel Subsidies Undermine Carbon Pricing Efforts* (Toronto: Environmental Defence Canada, 2016), 1. All dollar amounts are Canadian dollars unless otherwise noted.

22. John C. Stauber and Sheldon Rampton, *Toxic Sludge Is Good for You: Lies, Damn Lies, and the Public Relations Industry* (Monroe, Maine: Common Courage Press, 1995), 14.

23. Stauber and Rampton, 14.

24. Philip N. Howard, *New Media Campaigns and the Managed Citizen* (Cambridge: Cambridge University Press, 2005), 99.

25. Shane Gunster, "Extractive Populism and the Future of Canada," Canadian Centre for Policy Alternatives, July 2, 2019, https://www.policy alternatives.ca.

26. Tim Wood, "Energy's Citizens: The Making of a Canadian Petro-Public," *Canadian Journal of Communication* 43, no. 1 (2018): 76.

27. Wood, 76.

28. Wood, 90.

29. Carol Linnitt, "'Grassroots' Oil and Gas Advocacy Group Canada Action Received $100,000 from ARC Resources," *The Narwhal,* June 24, 2020, https://thenarwhal.ca.

30. Naomi Oreskes and Erik M. Conway, *Merchants of Doubt: How a Handful of Scientists Obscured the Truth on Issues from Tobacco Smoke to Global Warming* (New York: Bloomsbury, 2010).

31. Wood, "Energy's Citizens," 78.

32. Johnson, *Mineral Rites,* 2.

33. Andrew Crosby and Jeffrey Monaghan, *Policing Indigenous Movements: Dissent and the Security State* (Black Point, N.S.: Fernwood, 2018).

34. Peter K. Bsumek, Jen Schneider, Steve Schwarze, and Jennifer Peeples, "Corporate Ventriloquism: Corporate Advocacy, the Coal Industry, and the Appropriation of Voice," in *Voice and Environmental Communication,* ed. Jennifer Peeples and Stephen Depoe (New York: Palgrave Macmillan, 2014), 25.

35. Bsumek et al., 26.

36. Bsumek et al., 23.

37. See, for instance, Jon Gordon, *Unsustainable Oil: Facts, Counterfacts and Fictions* (Edmonton: University of Alberta Press, 2015); Patrick McCurdy, "Fanning Flames of Discontent: A Case Study of Social Media, Populism, and Campaigning," in *Power Shift? Political Leadership and Social Media: Case Studies in Political Communication,* ed. David Taras and Richard Davis (London: Routledge, 2019), 187–201; Mark Simpson, "Lubricity: Smooth Oil's Political Frictions," in *Petrocultures: Oil, Politics, Culture,* ed. Sheena Wilson, Adam Carlson, and Imre Szeman (Montreal: McGill-Queen's University Press, 2017), 287–318; Imre Szeman, "How to Know about Oil: Energy Epistemologies and Political Futures," *Journal of Canadian Studies / Revue d'études Canadiennes* 47, no. 3 (2013): 145–68; and Sheena Wilson, "Gendering Oil," in *Oil Culture,* ed. Ross Barrett and Daniel Worden (Minneapolis: University of Minnesota Press, 2014), 244–63.

38. Caroline Levine, *Forms: Whole, Rhythm, Hierarchy, Network* (Princeton, N.J.: Princeton University Press, 2017), 6.

39. Since acquiring Twitter in 2022, Elon Musk has changed its functionality, restricted access to users with accounts, and, most recently, rebranded the platform as X. Given the timeline of my focus, I choose to refer to the platform as Twitter.

40. Nick Dyer-Witheford, *Cyber Marx: Cycles and Circuits of Struggle in High-Technology Capitalism* (Urbana: University of Illinois Press, 1999); Darin Barney, *Prometheus Wired: The Hope for Democracy in the Age of Network Technology* (Chicago: University of Chicago Press, 2000).

41. Leanne Betasamosake Simpson, *As We Have Always Done: Indigenous Freedom through Radical Resistance* (Minneapolis: University of Minnesota Press, 2017), 220–28.

42. Tzeporah Berman, "The Oil Sands Are Now the Single Largest and Most Destructive Industrial Project on Earth," *NOW Magazine,* April 10, 2014, https://nowtoronto.com.

43. Pierre Bélanger, ed., *Extraction Empire: Undermining the Systems, States, and Scales of Canada's Global Resource Empire* (Cambridge, Mass.: MIT Press, 2018).

44. Martín Arboleda, *Planetary Mine: Territories of Extraction under Late Capitalism* (New York: Verso, 2020), 5–6.

45. Shiri Pasternak and Dayna Nadine Scott, "Getting Back the Land: Anticolonial and Indigenous Strategies of Reclamation," *South Atlantic Quarterly* 119, no. 2 (2020): 205.

46. Alex V. Green, "Canada Is Fake," The Outline, accessed July 6, 2020, https://theoutline.com.

47. Frances J. Hein, *Historical Overview of the Fort McMurray Area and Oil Sands Industry in Northeastern Alberta* (Edmonton: Alberta Energy and Utilities Board, Alberta Geological Survey, 2000), 1.

48. Canadian Petroleum Hall of Fame, "Dr. Roger M. Butler," accessed July 6, 2020, http://www.canadianpetroleumhalloffame.ca.

49. Macarena Gómez-Barris, *The Extractive Zone: Social Ecologies and Decolonial Perspectives* (Durham, N.C.: Duke University Press, 2017), 5.

50. Pamela Vang, *Good Guys: A Cultural Semiotic Study of the Print Advertising of the Oil Industry (1900–2000)* (Linköping: Linköping University, 2014), 223, 253–254.

51. Ian Wereley, "Advertising an Empire of Oil: The British Petroleum Company and the Persian Khan Exhibit of 1924–1925," *MediaTropes* 7, no. 2 (2020): 19–39.

52. Mona Damluji, "The Oil City in Focus: The Cinematic Spaces of Abadan in the Anglo-Iranian Oil Company's Persian Story," *Comparative Studies of South Asia, Africa and the Middle East* 33, no. 1 (2013): 75–88.

53. Rudmer Canjels, "Films from beyond the Well: A Historical Overview of Shell Films," in *Films That Work: Industrial Film and the Productivity of Media,* ed. Vinzenz Hediger and Patrick Vonderau (Amsterdam: Amsterdam University Press, 2009), 246.

54. Patricia Yaeger, "Editor's Column: Literature in the Ages of Wood, Tallow, Coal, Whale Oil, Gasoline, Atomic Power, and Other Energy Sources," *PMLA* 126, no. 2 (March 2011): 305–10.

55. Vang, *Good Guys,* 6.

56. Elmar Altvater, "The Social and Natural Environment of Fossil Capitalism," *Socialist Register* 43 (2007): 37–59; Matt Huber, *Lifeblood: Oil, Freedom, and the Forces of Capital* (Minneapolis: University of Minnesota Press, 2013); Malm, *Fossil Capital.*

57. Louis Althusser, *On the Reproduction of Capitalism: Ideology and Ideological State Apparatuses,* trans. G. M. Goshgarian (New York: Verso, 2014), 149.

58. McKenzie Wark, *Capital Is Dead: Is This Something Worse?* (New York: Verso, 2019), 5–11.

59. McKenzie Wark, *A Hacker Manifesto* (Cambridge, Mass.: Harvard University Press, 2004).

60. Jodi Dean, *Democracy and Other Neoliberal Fantasies: Communicative Capitalism and Left Politics* (Durham, N.C.: Duke University Press, 2009), 2.

61. Jodi Dean, "Neofeudalism: The End of Capitalism?," *Los Angeles Review of Books,* May 12, 2020, https://lareviewofbooks.org.

62. Tech Transparency Project, "Facebook Ran Recruitment Ads for Militia Groups," October 19, 2020, https://www.techtransparencyproject.org.

63. Nick Couldry and Ulises Mejias, *The Costs of Connection: How Data Is Colonizing Life and Appropriating It for Capitalism* (Stanford: Stanford University Press, 2019), xi.

64. Couldry and Mejias, 138.

65. For an analysis of Trump's employment of the term *fake news* on Twitter, see Andrew S. Ross and Damian J. Rivers, "Discursive Deflection: Accusation of 'Fake News' and the Spread of Mis- and Disinformation in the Tweets of President Trump," *Social Media + Society* 4, no. 2 (2018): 1–12.

66. Kyle Powys Whyte, "Indigenous Climate Change Studies: Indigenizing Futures, Decolonizing the Anthropocene," *English Language Notes* 55, no. 1 (2017): 153–62; Kim TallBear, "A Sharpening of the Already-Present: An

Indigenous Materialist Reading of Settler Apocalypse 2020" (plenary address at Humanities on the Brink: Energy, Environment, Emergency, online, University of California at Santa Barbara, July 10–30, 2020), http://ehc.english.ucsb.edu/?p=20907.

67. M. Simpson, "Lubricity," 289.

68. Stephanie LeMenager, *Living Oil: Petroleum Culture in the American Century* (New York: Oxford University Press, 2014), 6.

69. Jordan B. Kinder, "Ambivalence and Intensity: Platform Energetics," in *Digital Energetics,* ed. Anne Pasek, Cindy Kaiying Lin, Zane Griffin Talley Cooper, and Jordan B. Kinder (Lüneburg: Meson Press, 2023), 96–120.

70. Nick Couldry and Anna McCarthy, "Introduction: Orientations: Mapping MediaSpace," in *MediaSpace: Place, Scale and Culture in a Media Age,* ed. Nick Couldry and Anna McCarthy (London: Routledge, 2004), 2.

71. On the material and metaphorical relationship between oil and data, see Sy Taffel, "Data and Oil: Metaphor, Materiality and Metabolic Rifts," *New Media & Society* 25, no. 5 (2021): 1–19.

72. Lauren Berlant, "The Commons: Infrastructures for Troubling Times," *Environment and Planning D: Society and Space* 34, no. 3 (2016): 393.

73. Kai Bosworth, *Pipeline Populism: Grassroots Environmentalism in the Twenty-First Century* (Minneapolis: University of Minnesota Press, 2022), 38.

74. Bosworth, 31, 38.

75. Gholam Khiabany, "The Future and the 'Poetry of the Past,'" in *The Future of Media,* ed. Joanna Zylinska and Goldsmiths Media (London: Goldsmiths Press, 2022), 11.

76. Khiabany, 11.

77. McCurdy, "Fanning Flames of Discontent," 190.

78. Robert Neubauer, "Gateway to Crisis: Discourse Coalitions, Extractivist Politics, and the Northern Gateway Crisis" (PhD diss., Simon Fraser University, 2017), 12–15.

79. Szeman, "How to Know about Oil," 148.

80. Jeff M. Diamanti, "Energyscapes, Architecture, and the Expanded Field of Postindustrial Philosophy," *Postmodern Culture* 26, no. 2 (2016), https://doi.org/10.1353/pmc.2016.0006.

81. Jean-Claude Debeir, Jean-Paul Deléage, and Daneil Hémery, *In the Servitude of Power: Energy and Civilisation through the Ages* (1986; repr., London: Zed Books, 1991), 2.

82. Timothy Mitchell, "Economentality: How the Future Entered Government," *Critical Inquiry* 40, no. 4 (2014): 479–507.

83. Heather M. Turcotte, "Contextualizing Petro-Sexual Politics," *Alternatives* 36, no. 3 (2011): 200–220; Cara New Daggett, "Petro-Masculinity: Fossil Fuels and Authoritarian Desire," *Millennium* 47, no. 1 (2018): 25–44.

84. Wilson, "Gendering Oil," 248–54.

85. Jasbir K. Puar, *Terrorist Assemblages: Homonationalism in Queer Times* (Durham, N.C.: Duke University Press, 2007), 4.

86. Anis Heydari, "Jason Kenney Touts $30M 'War Room' but Provides Few Details," CBC News, June 7, 2019, https://www.cbc.ca.

1. From Dirty to Ethical

1. Government of Canada, Parliament, House of Commons, Standing Committee on Natural Resources, Evidence, Meeting No. 37, 40th Parliament, 3rd Session, December 7, 2010, http://www.ourcommons.ca/DocumentViewer/en/40-3/RNNR/meeting-37/evidence.

2. Alykhan Velshi, "There Is Such a Thing as 'Ethical Oil,'" *HuffPost Canada,* September 1, 2011, https://www.huffingtonpost.ca.

3. "Pipeline News," *Toronto Star,* accessed May 28, 2023, https://web.archive.org/web/20230528011059/https://www.thestar.com/news/pipeline.html.

4. Jane Taber, "PM Brands Canada an 'Energy Superpower,'" *Globe and Mail,* July 15, 2006.

5. Randolph Haluza-DeLay, "Alberta Internalizing Oil Sands Opposition: A Test of the Social Movement Society Thesis," in *Protest and Politics: The Promise of Social Movement Societies,* ed. Howard Ramos and Kathleen Rodgers (Vancouver: University of British Columbia Press, 2015), 287–88.

6. Haluza-DeLay, 288.

7. Lindsay Telfer, quoted in Stephen Leahy, "Oil Sands: Burning Energy to Produce It," Resilience, July 27, 2006, https://www.resilience.org.

8. CEC, *Alberta Tailings Ponds II: Factual Record regarding Submission SEM-17-001* (Montreal: Commission for Environmental Cooperation, 2020), 80; Danielle Droitsch and Terra Simieritsch, *Briefing Note: Canadian Aboriginal Concerns with Oil Sands* (Edmonton: The Pembina Institute, 2010), 5, https://www.pembina.org/reports/briefingnoteosfntoursep10.pdf.

9. Robert D. Bullard, "Anatomy of Environmental Racism and the Environmental Justice Movement," in *Confronting Environmental Racism: Voices from the Grassroots,* ed. Robert D. Bullard (Boston: South End Press, 1993), 22–26.

10. Jesse Fruhwirth and Melanie Jae Martin, "Welcome to Blockadia!," *Yes! Magazine,* January 12, 2013, https://www.yesmagazine.org.

11. Jon Gordon, *Unsustainable Oil: Facts, Counterfacts and Fictions* (Edmonton: University of Alberta Press, 2015), xxxvi–xxxvii; Geo Takach, *Tar Wars: Oil, Environment and Alberta's Image* (Edmonton: University of Alberta Press, 2017), 3–4.

12. Dirty Oil Sands—A Threat to the New Energy Economy, "Quick Facts," June 27, 2009, https://web.archive.org/web/20090627020517/http://dirtyoilsands.org/thedirt/article/quick_facts/.

13. Dirty Oil Sands—A Threat to the New Energy Economy, "The Dirt on Oil Sands," June 26, 2009, https://web.archive.org/web/20090626073055/http://dirtyoilsands.org/thedirt; Andrew Nikiforuk, *Tar Sands: Dirty Oil and the Future of a Continent* (Vancouver: Greystone Books, 2008).

14. Andrew Nikiforuk, *Dirty Oil: How the Tar Sands Are Fueling the Global Climate Crisis* (Toronto: Greenpeace, 2009), 1.

15. Nikiforuk, ii.

16. Nikiforuk, 43.

17. Jennifer Peeples, "Toxic Sublime: Imaging Contaminated Landscapes," *Environmental Communication* 5, no. 4 (2011): 375.

18. Takach, *Tar Wars,* 75.

19. Lush Fresh Handmade Cosmetics, "Stop the Pipelines," accessed December 22, 2022, https://web.archive.org/web/20221221175059/https://www.lush.ca/en/stories/article_ethical-stop-the-pipelines.html.

20. Melissa Aronczyk and Graeme Auld, "Tar, Ethics and Other Tactical Repertoires: The Co-evolution of Movements for and against the Tar Sands" (paper prepared for the International Studies Association Meeting, San Francisco, April 3–6, 2013), 3–6.

21. Ezra Levant, *Ethical Oil: The Case for Canada's Oil Sands* (Toronto: McClelland & Stewart, 2010), 7.

22. Levant, 12.

23. Mark Simpson, "Lubricity: Smooth Oil's Political Frictions," in *Petrocultures: Oil, Politics, Culture,* ed. Sheena Wilson, Adam Carlson, and Imre Szeman (Montreal: McGill-Queen's University Press, 2017), 287, 296.

24. Matt Huber, *Lifeblood: Oil, Freedom, and the Forces of Capital* (Minneapolis: University of Minnesota Press, 2013), xvi.

25. Mark Fisher, *Capitalist Realism: Is There No Alternative?* (Washington, D.C.: Zero Books, 2009), 8.

26. Fisher, 16.

27. Canadian political economist Harold Innis developed the notion of the staples thesis throughout his oeuvre; the theory asserts that Canada's economy is largely dependent on the export of raw staple goods, like furs and timber, to other world powers such as Britain and the United States. For its first

full articulation, see the conclusion to *The Fur Trade in Canada: An Introduction to Canadian Economic History* (1930; repr., Toronto: University of Toronto Press, 1999), 383–402.

28. Huber, *Lifeblood,* 169.

29. Levant, *Ethical Oil,* 4, emphasis added.

30. Jennifer Wenzel, *The Disposition of Nature: Environmental Crisis and World Literature* (New York: Fordham University Press, 2020), 42.

31. Levant, *Ethical Oil,* 197–98.

32. M. Simpson, "Lubricity," 289.

33. M. Simpson, 289.

34. Levant, *Ethical Oil,* 224.

35. Levant, 224.

36. Levant, 224.

37. Levant, 224.

38. Sheena Wilson, "Gendering Oil," in *Oil Culture,* ed. Ross Barrett and Daniel Worden (Minneapolis: University of Minnesota Press, 2014), 250.

39. Wilson, 251.

40. Andrew Leach, "Fort McMurray Mayor Melissa Blake on Ethical Oil," *Rescuing the Frog,* August 5, 2011, http://andrewleach.ca.

41. Heather M. Turcotte, "Contextualizing Petro-Sexual Politics," *Alternatives* 36, no. 3 (2011): 200–220.

42. National Inquiry into Missing and Murdered Indigenous Women and Girls, *Reclaiming Power and Place: The Final Report of the National Inquiry into Missing and Murdered Indigenous Women and Girls*, vol. 1a (Ottawa: Government of Canada, 2019), 592.

43. Levant, *Ethical Oil,* 212.

44. Naomi Klein, *This Changes Everything: Capitalism vs. the Climate* (New York: Simon and Schuster, 2014), 169.

45. Leanne Betasamosake Simpson, *As We Have Always Done: Indigenous Freedom through Radical Resistance* (Minneapolis: University of Minnesota Press, 2017), 74.

46. Levant, *Ethical Oil,* 79.

47. Levant, 107.

48. Imre Szeman, "How to Know about Oil: Energy Epistemologies and Political Futures," *Journal of Canadian Studies / Revue d'études Canadiennes* 47, no. 3 (2013): 158.

49. Levant, *Ethical Oil,* 115.

50. Levant, 116.

51. Levant, 127.

52. M. Simpson, "Lubricity," 292; Szeman, "How to Know Oil," 158–59.

53. Levant, *Ethical Oil,* 179.

54. Darin Barney et al., "The Participatory Condition: An Introduction," in *The Participatory Condition in the Digital Age,* ed. Darin Barney et al. (Minneapolis: University of Minnesota Press, 2016), vii–xxxix.

55. Greg Elmer, Ganaele Langlois, and Fenwick McKelvey, *The Permanent Campaign: New Media, New Politics* (New York: Peter Lang, 2012), 3.

56. Elmer, Langlois, and McKelvey, 4.

57. The Canadian Press, "Oilsands Lobbyists Stick with Chiquita 'Boycott' Claim," CTV News, December 21, 2011, http://www.ctvnews.ca.

58. Jen Gerson, "One-Man Oil Sands Advocate, Tired of Smears against Alberta, Takes on Celebrity Activists in PR War," *National Post,* September, 22, 2014, https://nationalpost.com.

59. Emma Pullman, "New 'Concerned Citizens Group' Has Deep Pockets and Close Ties to Oil Industry," *Vancouver Observer,* April 6, 2013, https://www.vancouverobserver.com.

60. Oil Sands Strong, Facebook, April 26, 2015, https://www.facebook.com/OilSandsStrong/photos/a.1617928505094086/1626762214210715; Oil Sands Strong, Facebook, June 7, 2015, https://www.facebook.com/OilSandsStrong/photos/a.1617928505094086/1639339812952955.

61. Oil Sands Strong, Facebook, June 25, 2015, https://www.facebook.com/OilSandsStrong/photos/a.1617928505094086/1644743242412612.

62. Anis Heydari, "Jason Kenney Touts $30M 'War Room' but Provides Few Details," CBC News, June 7, 2019, https://www.cbc.ca.

63. "CAODC Member Portal," accessed September 12, 2020, https://caodc.ca/.

64. CAPP, "Canada's Upstream Oil & Natural Gas Industry," accessed March 5, 2022, https://web.archive.org/web/20220305030745/https://www.capp.ca/.

65. See Tim Wood, "Energy's Citizens: The Making of a Canadian Petro-Public," *Canadian Journal of Communication* 43, no. 1 (2018): 75–92; and Patrick McCurdy, "Fanning Flames of Discontent: A Case Study of Social Media, Populism, and Campaigning," in *Power Shift? Political Leadership and Social Media: Case Studies in Political Communication,* ed. David Taras and Richard Davis (London: Routledge, 2019), 187–201.

66. Oil Sands Strong, Facebook, August 12, 2017, https://www.facebook.com/OilSandsStrong/photos/a.1617928505094086/1942954562591477.

67. Roberto Rocha, Jeff Yates, and Andrea Bellemare, "Groups Linked to Oil Companies Funded Facebook Ads Denouncing the Rail Blockades," CBC News, March 4, 2020, https://www.cbc.ca.

68. Jodi Dean, *Publicity's Secret: How Technoculture Capitalizes on Democracy* (Ithaca, N.Y.: Cornell University Press, 2002); Jodi Dean, *Democracy and Other Neoliberal Fantasies: Communicative Capitalism & Left Politics* (Durham, N.C.: Duke University Press, 2009).

69. Tamara A. Small, "What the Hashtag? A Content Analysis of Canadian Politics on Twitter," in *Social Media and Democracy: Innovations in Participatory Politics,* ed. B. D. Loader and D. Mercea (London: Routledge, 2012), 109.

70. Barney et al., "The Participatory Condition," viii.

71. Canada's Energy Citizens (website), accessed March 6, 2019, https://www.energycitizens.ca.

72. Canada Action, "Support Canada's Oil Sands," Canada Action, accessed March 6, 2019, https://web.archive.org/web/20190630153846/https://www.canadaaction.ca/support_canadas_oil_sands.

73. Taina Bucher and Anne Helmond, "The Affordances of Social Media Platforms," in *The SAGE Handbook of Social Media,* ed. Jean Burgess, Alice E. Marwick, and Thomas Poell (London: SAGE, 2018), 235.

74. Marshall McLuhan, *Understanding Media: The Extension of Man* (Cambridge, Mass.: MIT Press), 7.

75. Daphne Bramham, "Lessons for Canada from How the Koch Brothers Hijacked Democracy," *Vancouver Sun,* September 25, 2016, http://vancouversun.com.

76. David Rovinsky, *The Ascendancy of the West in Canadian Policymaking,* Policy Papers on the Americas 9, no 2 (Washington, D.C.: Center for Strategic and International Studies, 1998), 13.

77. Marci McDonald, "The Man behind Stephen Harper," *The Walrus,* October 12, 2004, https://thewalrus.ca.

78. Alykhan Velshi, "Fraser Institute Report: The U.S. Needs More Ethical Oil," July 19, 2011, https://web.archive.org/web/20110720151454/http://www.ethicaloil.org/.

79. Richard Warnica, "Rebel without Applause: How Ezra Levant Built an Extreme Media Juggernaut—and Watched It All Begin to Unravel," *National Post,* August 19, 2017, https://nationalpost.com.

80. Jessie Daniels, "The Algorithmic Rise of the 'Alt-Right,'" *Contexts* 17, no. 1 (2018): 61.

81. Cara New Daggett, "Petro-Masculinity: Fossil Fuels and Authoritarian Desire," *Millennium* 47, no. 1 (2018): 27; Andreas Malm and the Zetkin Collective, eds., *White Skin, Black Fuel: On the Danger of Fossil Fascism* (New York: Verso, 2021).

82. Kathleen Raso and Robert J. Neubauer, "Managing Dissent: Energy Pipelines and 'New Right' Politics in Canada," *Canadian Journal of Communication* 41, no. 1 (2016): n.p.

2. Petroculture's Promise

1. Peter Zimonjic, "Trudeau Says He Will Succeed on Energy Where His Father and Stephen Harper Failed," CBC, March 10, 2017, https://www.cbc.ca.

2. Al Monaco, "2017 Canadian Energy Person of the Year" (speech, Energy Council of Canada, Toronto, November 16, 2017), 5, https://www.enbridge.com.

3. Joe Oliver, "An Open Letter from Natural Resources Minister Joe Oliver," *Globe and Mail,* January 9, 2012.

4. Carol Linnitt, "LEAKED: Internal RCMP Document Names 'Violent Anti-Petroleum Extremists' Threat to Government and Industry," *The Narwhal,* February 17, 2015, https://thenarwhal.ca.

5. Agnes Zalewski, "Petroleum in Real Life: Running Shoes," *Context: Energy Examined,* August 9, 2019, https://context.capp.ca; Holly Quan, "Petroleum in Real Life: N-95 Masks," *Context: Energy Examined,* April 15, 2020, https://context.capp.ca.

6. Enbridge, "Life Takes Energy," accessed February 22, 2021, https://www.enbridge.com.

7. *OED Online,* s.v. "promise, v.," Oxford University Press, accessed February 28, 2021, http://www.oed.com.

8. Timothy Mitchell, "Economentality: How the Future Entered Government," *Critical Inquiry* 40, no. 4 (2014): 484.

9. Mitchell, 481.

10. Mitchell, 492.

11. Anna Zalik, "Vicious Transparency: Contesting Canada's Hydrocarbon Future," in *Subterranean Estates: Life Worlds of Oil and Gas,* ed. Hannah Appel, Arthur Mason, and Michael Watts (Ithaca, N.Y.: Cornell University Press, 2015), 356–57.

12. Zalik, 369.

13. Zalik, 364.

14. Zalik, 369.

15. Patrick McCurdy, "'In the Army Now': The Rise of the Energy Citizen and Corporate Petro Nationalism" (presentation, Petrocultures 2016: The Offshore, Memorial University, St. John's, Newfoundland, and Labrador, Canada, September 2016).

16. Shane Gunster, "Extractive Populism and the Future of Canada," Canadian Centre for Policy Alternatives, July 2, 2019, https://www.policy alternatives.ca.

17. Pierre Dardot and Christian Laval, *The New Way of the World: On Neoliberal Society,* trans. Gregory Elliot (New York: Verso, 2017), 255–99.

18. Canada Action, "Taking Action for a Better Canada!," October 1, 2014, https://web.archive.org/web/20141001033538/http://www.canadaaction.ca/; Canada Action, "Taking Action for a Better Canada!," May 19, 2015, https://web.archive.org/web/20150519061003/http://www.canadaaction.ca/; Canada Action, "Canada Action," December 3, 2020, https://web.archive.org/web/20201203172749/https://www.canadaaction.ca/.

19. Canada Action, "Full Value for Canadian Resources—Support Northern Gateway—Canada Action," accessed November 16, 2020, https://web.archive.org/web/20141130211706/http://www.canadaaction.ca/northern_gateway_pledge.

20. "Support the Energy East Pipeline—Canadian Oil Should Benefit All Canadians," Canada Action, November 30, 2014, https://web.archive.org/web/20141130151531/http://www.canadaaction.ca/energy_east.

21. Canada Action, Twitter, August 25, 2013, 6:09 p.m., https://twitter.com/CanadaAction/status/371756335206891520.

22. Larry Pratt, *The Tar Sands: Syncrude and the Politics of Oil* (Edmonton: Hurtig, 1976), 17.

23. Pratt, 18.

24. Cameron Butt, "Persuasive Pictures: Advertising Northern Gateway to British Columbians" (presentation, MLA Annual Convention, Vancouver, Canada, January 2015).

25. BCProsperity, Twitter, June 19, 2014, 9:17 p.m., https://twitter.com, quoted from personal archives.

26. BCProsperity, Twitter, July 23, 2014, 7:16 p.m., https://twitter.com, quoted from personal archives.

27. Darin Barney, "Who We Are and What We Do: Canada as a Pipeline Nation," in *Petrocultures: Oil, Politics, Culture,* ed. Sheena Wilson, Adam Carlson, and Imre Szeman (Montreal: McGill-Queen's University Press, 2017), 79.

28. Ian Bickis, "Alberta and B.C. Left with Limited Options to Escalate Trade War," CBC, February 8, 2018, https://www.cbc.ca.

29. Jeffrey D. Wilson, "Understanding Resource Nationalism: Economic Dynamics and Political Institutions," *Contemporary Politics* 21, no. 4 (2015): 400.

30. Thea Riofrancos, *Resource Radicals: From Petro-nationalism to Post-extractivism in Ecuador* (Durham, N.C.: Duke University Press, 2020), 10.

31. Kevin Taft, *Oil's Deep State: How the Petroleum Industry Undermines Democracy and Stops Action on Global Warming* (Toronto: James Lorimer, 2017), 161.

32. Taft, 161.

33. Jesse Kline, "A Pipeline That's Good for Canada Is Good for Ontario, Too," *National Post,* August 23, 2013, https://nationalpost.com.

34. CERI, *Economic Impacts of New Oil Sands Projects in Alberta (2010–2035)* (Calgary: Canadian Energy Research Institute, 2011), 41–56.

35. CERI, "Our Mission: CERI," accessed October 28, 2020, https://web.archive.org/web/20201028021334/https://ceri.ca/about/our-mission.

36. CERI, *Annual Report 2019–2020* (Calgary: Canadian Energy Research Institute, 2020), 20, emphasis added.

37. CERI, 20.

38. TransCanada, *Energy East Pipeline Project: Project Description,* vol. 1 (Calgary: TransCanada 2014), 1.

39. Gerry Angevine and Kenneth P. Green, *Canada as an Emerging Energy Superproducer,* Studies in Energy Policy (Vancouver: Fraser Institute, 2013), vi.

40. Ian Goodman and Brigid Rowan, *Economic Costs and Benefits of the Trans Mountain Expansion Project (TMX) for BC and Metro Vancouver* (Vancouver: The Goodman Group and SFU School of Public Policy, 2014), 19–20, http://www.thegoodman.com.

41. Kregg Hetherington, "Surveying the Future Perfect: Anthropology, Development and the Promise of Infrastructure," in *Infrastructures and Social Complexity*, ed. Penelope Harvey, Jensen Casper, and Atsuro Morita (London: Routledge, 2016), 40.

42. Elizabeth A. Povinelli, *Economies of Abandonment: Social Belonging and Endurance in Late Liberalism* (Durham, N.C.: Duke University Press, 2011), 34–42.

43. Jon Gordon, *Unsustainable Oil: Facts, Counterfacts and Fictions* (Edmonton: University of Alberta Press, 2015).

44. Mary Poovey, *A History of the Modern Fact: Problems of Knowledge in the Sciences of Wealth and Society* (Chicago: University of Chicago Press, 1998), xii.

45. Tim Wood, "The Many Voices of Business: Framing the Keystone Pipeline in US and Canadian News," *Journalism* 20, no. 2 (2019): 292.

46. Riofrancos, *Resource Radicals,* 139.

47. Emma Pullman, "New 'Concerned Citizens Group' Has Deep Pockets and Close Ties to Oil Industry," *Vancouver Observer,* April 6, 2013, https://www.vancouverobserver.com.

48. British Columbians for Prosperity, "The Conversation: Can We Just Stop Using Oil?," YouTube, December 12, 2013, https://www.youtube.com/watch?v=LbajX-IgPiU.

49. British Columbians for Prosperity, "Check the Facts before You Make up Your Mind," YouTube, December 12, 2013, https://www.youtube.com/watch?v=UhOubA1cA9k.

50. British Columbians for Prosperity, "Can B.C. Afford to Say 'No' to 8000 New Jobs?," YouTube, May 21, 2014, https://youtu.be/kQeiIZjjMhQ.

51. British Columbians for Prosperity, "What Are the Real Benefits of Proposed B.C. Pipeline Projects?," YouTube, January 14, 2014, https://www.youtube.com/watch?v=rdBzq8xOJE4.

52. British Columbians for Prosperity, "Our Core Beliefs: British Columbians for Prosperity," 2015, https://web.archive.org/web/20150802235912/http://www.bcprosperity.ca/about-us/our-core-beliefs/.

53. Andrew Pendakis, "In Medias Res: Deleuze and the Politics of Middleness," *Stasis* 7, no. 1 (2019): 16.

54. Pendakis, 19.

55. Ngaio Hotte and U. Rashid Sumaila, *Potential Economic Impact of a Tanker Spill on Ocean-Based Industries in British Columbia* (Vancouver: Fisheries Centre, University of British Columbia, 2012), 2.

56. Gunster, "Extractive Populism."

57. Cara New Daggett, *The Birth of Energy: Fossil Fuels, Thermodynamics, and the Politics of Work* (Durham, N.C.: Duke University Press, 2019), 191.

3. Resource Hetero- and Homonationalism

1. Oil Sands Strong, Facebook, November 10, 2016, https://www.facebook.com/OilSandsStrong/photos/a.1617928505094086/1813058245581110.

2. Appearing several times throughout *Ethical Oil, gays* is Levant's preferred referent for 2SLGBTQIA+ peoples and communities.

3. Jasbir K. Puar, *Terrorist Assemblages: Homonationalism in Queer Times* (Durham, N.C.: Duke University Press, 2007), 2, 4.

4. Sheena Wilson, "Gendering Oil," in *Oil Culture,* ed. Ross Barrett and Daniel Worden (Minneapolis: University of Minnesota Press, 2014), 248.

5. Audra Simpson, "The State Is a Man: Theresa Spence, Loretta Saunders and the Gender of Settler Sovereignty," *Theory & Event* 19, no. 4 (2016), http://muse.jhu.edu/article/633280; Leanne Betasamosake Simpson, *As We Have Always Done: Indigenous Freedom through Radical Resistance* (Minneapolis: University of Minnesota Press, 2017).

6. Heather M. Turcotte, "Contextualizing Petro-Sexual Politics," *Alternatives* 36, no. 3 (2011): 201.

7. Turcotte, 201.

8. Wilson, "Gendering Oil," 244.

9. Cara New Daggett, "Petro-Masculinity: Fossil Fuels and Authoritarian Desire," *Millennium* 47, no. 1 (2018): 43.

10. Rebel News, "WATCH: Oil Industry Worker Speaks His Mind at Kinder Morgan Protests!," YouTube, 2016, https://www.youtube.com/watch?v=qwCZB97E45M.

11. Rebel News.

12. Rebel News.

13. The CAODC has since changed its name to the Canadian Association of *Energy* Contractors.

14. U.S. Energy Information Administration (EIA), "Crude Oil Prices Started 2015 Relatively Low, Ended the Year Lower," January 6, 2016, https://www.eia.gov.

15. Alberta Oil Staff, "Oilwell Drillers' Association President Remembers Life before Energy Politics," *Energy Now,* September 27, 2016, https://energynow.ca.

16. Tim Wood, "The Many Voices of Business: Framing the Keystone Pipeline in US and Canadian News," *Journalism* 20, no. 2 (2019): 292–312; Tim Wood, "Energy's Citizens: The Making of a Canadian Petro-Public," *Canadian Journal of Communication* 43, no. 1 (2018): 75–92.

17. Transcribed from Danielle Nerman, "Meet the Alberta 'Roughneck' Who Made a Moving Plea for the Oilpatch on Parliament Hill," CBC News, September 21, 2016, https://www.cbc.ca.

18. House of Commons Canada, "Petition E-216—Petitions," September 20, 2016, https://petitions.ourcommons.ca/en/Petition/Details?Petition=e-216.

19. Chris Turner, *The Patch: The People, Pipelines, and Politics of the Oil Sands* (Toronto: Simon & Schuster, 2017), 87–88.

20. Nicole Hill, Angele Alook, and Ian Hussey, "How Gender and Race Shape Experiences of Work in Alberta's Oil Industry," *Parkland Blog,* June 27, 2017, https://www.parklandinstitute.ca.

21. Gloria E. Miller, "Frontier Masculinity in the Oil Industry: The Experience of Women Engineers," *Gender, Work & Organization* 11, no. 1 (2004): 48.

22. John Hultgren, "Those Who Bring from the Earth: Anti-Environmentalism and the Trope of the White Male Worker," *Ethics, Policy & Environment* 21, no. 1 (2018): 24.

23. Sarah Rieger, "Alberta Grants Rodeos Exemptions from New Liquor Curfew," CBC News, September 5, 2021, https://www.cbc.ca.

24. Miller, "Frontier Masculinity in the Oil Industry," 48.

25. Miller, 54.

26. Miller, 69.

27. Daggett, "Petro-Masculinity," 44.

28. Velshi, "EthicalOil.org TV Ad Premieres Exclusively on Oprah Winfrey Network (Canada)," EthicalOil.org, August 29, 2011, https://web.archive.org/web/20140919102951/http://www.ethicaloil.org/news/ethicaloil-org-tv-ad-premieres-exclusively-on-oprah-winfrey-network-canada/.

29. Velshi.

30. Janice Peck, *The Age of Oprah: Cultural Icon for the Neoliberal Era* (New York: Routledge, 2008).

31. Angela McRobbie, "Post-feminism and Popular Culture," *Feminist Media Studies* 4, no. 3 (2004): 255.

32. EthicalOildotorg, "Social Oil," YouTube, 2013, https://www.youtube.com/watch?v=g_SDzXmuewk.

33. Shell Canada, "Developing the Oil Sands Responsibly: Women behind the Operation," accessed February 4, 2022, https://web.archive.org/web/20131223151441/http://www.shell.ca:80/en/aboutshell/our-business-tpkg/upstream/oil-sands/women-in-oil-sands.html.

34. Shell Canada.

35. Alix Kemp, "Why Women Could Save the Oil Sands," *Alberta Venture,* December 24, 2012, https://web.archive.org/web/20130502095718/http://albertaventure.com/2012/12/why-women-could-save-the-oil-sands/.

36. Women Building Futures, accessed September 12, 2023, https://womenbuildingfutures.ca.

37. Sean Parson and Emily Ray, "Drill Baby Drill: Labor, Accumulation, and the Sexualization of Resource Extraction," *Theory & Event* 23, no. 1 (2020): 249.

38. Nancy Fraser, "Feminism, Capitalism, and the Cunning of History: An Introduction" (Fondation Maison des sciences de l'homme, Working Papers Series, 2012), 4, https://shs.hal.science/halshs-00725055/document.

39. House of Commons/Chambre des Communes Canada, Response by Minister of Natural Resources to Petition 421-00562, September 20, 2016, https://www.ourcommons.ca/Content/ePetitions/Responses/421/e-216/421-00562_NRCAN_E.pdf.

40. Out of the Woods Collective, *Hope against Hope: Writings on Ecological Crisis* (Brooklyn, N.Y.: Common Notions, 2020), 149–58; Naomi Klein, *This Changes Everything: Capitalism vs. the Climate* (New York: Simon and Schuster, 2014).

41. Out of the Woods Collective, *Hope against Hope,* 151.

42. EIA, "Crude Oil Prices Started 2015 Relatively Low, Ended the Year Lower."

43. Anthony Heyes, Andrew Leach, and Charles F. Mason, "The Economics of Canadian Oil Sands," *Review of Environmental Economics and Policy* 12, no. 2 (2018): 246.

44. Oil Respect, "Stories," accessed December 22, 2021, https://web.archive.org/web/20220204192610/https://oilrespect.ca/hear-the-stories/.

45. Oil Respect.

46. Oil Respect.

47. Oil Respect.

48. Oil Respect, "Oil Respect Week Update April 22, 2016," YouTube, 2016, https://www.youtube.com/watch?v=pYqZILMT2FI.

49. Oil Respect.

50. Sara Dorow, "Gendering Energy Extraction in Fort McMurray," in *Alberta Oil and the Decline of Democracy in Canada,* ed. Meenal Shrivastava and Lorna Stefanick (Athabasca, A.B.: Athabasca University Press, 2015), 275–92.

51. Dorow, 289.

52. Dorow, quoted in Alicia Massie and Emma Jackson, "'Standing Up for Canadian Oil & Gas Families': Tracing Gender, Family, and Work in the Alberta Petro-Economy," *MediaTropes* 7, no. 2 (2020): 45.

53. National Inquiry into Missing and Murdered Indigenous Women and Girls, "Reclaiming Power and Place: The Final Report of the National Inquiry into Missing and Murdered Indigenous Women and Girls" (Ottawa, 2019).

54. Danielle Nerman, "Lesbians Are 'Hot' Pro-Oilsands Facebook Post Removed, Apology Made," CBC News, July 26, 2016, https://www.cbc.ca.

55. Nerman.

56. Katerina Symes, "Orange Is the New Black: The Popularization of Lesbian Sexuality and Heterosexual Modes of Viewing," *Feminist Media Studies* 17, no. 1 (2017): 29–41. For an example of how the image circulates, see a Facebook page dedicated to the two characters that seem to appear in the image, Alex Vause & Piper Chapman, Facebook, September 27, 2015, https://www.facebook.com/AlexVauseetPiperChapman/photos/a.508555875973450/527729740722730/.

57. Parson and Ray, "Drill Baby Drill," 260.

58. Parson and Ray, 262.

59. Oil Sands Strong, "LGBT," Facebook, September 12, 2017, https://www.facebook.com/OilSandsStrong/photos/a.1617928505094086/1950808428472757.

60. Kimberly A. Williams, *Stampede: Misogyny, White Supremacy, and Settler Colonialism* (Halifax, N.S.: Fernwood, 2021), 2.

61. Williams, 11.

62. Mylynn Felt and Maria Bakardjieva, "The Polite Cowboy or the Wild, Wild West: Strategic Approaches to Reducing Gender-Based Rodeo Violence through Grassroots Civic Mobilisation," in *Gendered Violence at International Festivals,* ed. Louise Platt and Rebecca Finkel (New York: Routledge, 2020), 155.

63. Panda, quoted in Jacques Poitras, *Pipe Dreams: The Fight for Canada's Energy Future* (Toronto: Viking Canada, 2018), 258.

64. Whitcomb, quoted in Claudia Cattaneo, "Irving Oil's President Says It Would Keep Saudi Imports Even if Energy East Goes Ahead," *Financial Post,* April 12, 2016, https://financialpost.com.

4. Reconciling Extraction

1. West Coast Environmental Law, "The Enbridge Gateway Pipeline: Do British Columbians Stand to Gain?," 2009, https://www.wcel.org.

2. Tim Van Hinte, Thomas I. Gunton, and J. C. Day, "Evaluation of the Assessment Process for Major Projects: A Case Study of Oil and Gas Pipelines in Canada," *Impact Assessment and Project Appraisal* 25, no. 2 (2007): 126.

3. Government of Canada, "Indigenous Peoples and Cultures," accessed September 12, 2023, https://www.canada.ca.

4. Susana Mas, "Trudeau Presents 5-Point Plan at Special Meeting of AFN Chiefs," CBC News, December 8, 2015, https://www.cbc.ca.

5. Truth and Reconciliation Commission of Canada, "Our Mandate," accessed September 12, 2023, https://web.archive.org/web/20200507215137/http://www.trc.ca/about-us/our-mandate.html. The Commission website is archived because the ongoing project is now called the National Centre for Truth and Reconciliation.

6. Truth and Reconciliation Commission of Canada, *Truth and Reconciliation Commission of Canada: Calls to Action* (Winnipeg: Truth and Reconciliation Commission of Canada, 2015), 4–6, 10.

7. United Nations, *United Nations Declaration on the Rights of Indigenous Peoples* (New York: United Nations, 2008), 16.

8. United Nations, "United Nations Declaration on the Rights of Indigenous Peoples," accessed September 12, 2023, https://www.un.org/development/desa/indigenouspeoples/declaration-on-the-rights-of-indigenous-peoples.html.

9. Judith Sayers, "Opportunities and Barriers for the B.C. Declaration of Rights Act," in *The UN Declaration on the Rights of Indigenous Peoples in*

Canada: Lessons from B.C., ed. Hayden King (Toronto: Yellowhead Institute, 2020), 4.

10. Department of Justice Canada, "Joint Statement by Minister Lametti and Minister Bennett on the Senate Passing Bill C-15, An Act Respecting the United Nations Declaration on the Rights of Indigenous Peoples," Statements, June 16, 2021, https://www.canada.ca.

11. Kyle Conway and Manjulika E. Robertson, "Oil as Solution to the Problems of Oil: The American Petroleum Institute and the Petromodern Paradox," *Environmental Humanities* 13, no. 1 (2021): 48.

12. Conway and Robertson, 46.

13. Charles Taylor, "The Politics of Recognition," in *Multiculturalism: Examining the Politics of Recognition,* ed. Amy Gutmann (Princeton, N.J.: Princeton University Press, 1994), 25.

14. Glen Sean Coulthard, *Red Skin, White Masks: Rejecting the Colonial Politics of Recognition* (Minneapolis: University of Minnesota Press, 2014), 3.

15. David Harvey, "The 'New' Imperialism: Accumulation by Dispossession," *Socialist Register* 40 (2004): 63–87.

16. Karl Marx, *Capital: A Critique of Political Economy, Volume One,* trans. Ben Fowkes (New York: Penguin Books, 1990), 877–95.

17. Coulthard, *Red Skin, White Masks,* 60.

18. Kim TallBear, "Badass Indigenous Women Caretake Relations: #StandingRock, #IdleNoMore, #BlackLivesMatter," in *Standing with Standing Rock: Voices from the #NoDAPL Movement,* ed. Nick Estes and Jaskiran Dhillon (Minneapolis: University of Minnesota Press, 2019), 13–18.

19. Leanne Betasamosake Simpson, *As We Have Always Done: Indigenous Freedom through Radical Resistance* (Minneapolis: University of Minnesota Press, 2017), 51.

20. Audra Simpson, "The State Is a Man: Theresa Spence, Loretta Saunders and the Gender of Settler Sovereignty," *Theory & Event* 19, no. 4 (2016), http://muse.jhu.edu/article/633280.

21. L. Simpson, *As We Have Always Done,* 49.

22. L. Simpson, 49.

23. Van Ginkel Associates Ltd., *Communities of the Mackenzie: Effects of the Hydrocarbon Industry* (Calgary: Canadian Arctic Gas Study Limited, 1975), 5.

24. Van Ginkel Associates Ltd., 6.

25. Coulthard, *Red Skin, White Masks,* 57.

26. Thomas Berger, *Northern Frontier, Northern Homeland* (1977; repr., Toronto: Douglas & McIntyre, 1988), 181.

27. See, for instance, Petrocultures Research Group, *After Oil* (Edmonton: Petrocultures Research Group, 2016), 15.

28. Lauren Berlant, *Cruel Optimism* (Durham, N.C.: Duke University Press, 2011), 1.

29. Sara L. Crosby and Anna J. Willow, "Indigenous-Washing and the Petro-Hero in Genre Fictions of the North American Oil Boom," *MFS Modern Fiction Studies* 66, no. 1 (2020): 82.

30. Crosby and Willow, 82.

31. Suncor, "Aboriginal Relations—Community Consultation," accessed April 15, 2021, https://web.archive.org/web/20210415105241/https://www.suncor.com/en-ca/sustainability/community-consultation/aboriginal-relations.

32. Syncrude, "Indigenous Relations," emphasis added, accessed May 13, 2021, https://www.syncrude.ca/community/indigenous-relations/.

33. Syncrude.

34. CAPP, "Discussion Paper on Implementing the United Nations Declaration on the Rights of Indigenous Peoples in Canada," April 26, 2016, 1, https://www.capp.ca.

35. CAPP, 2–4.

36. CAPP, 4.

37. Clifford Atleo, "Aboriginal Capitalism: Is Resistance Futile or Fertile?," *Journal of Aboriginal Economic Development* 9, no. 2 (2015): 41–51; Christopher Nowlin, "Indigenous Capitalism and Resource Development in an Age of Climate Change: A Timely Dance with the Devil?," *McGill International Journal of Sustainable Development Law and Policy* 17, no. 1 (2021): 71–97.

38. John Paul Tasker, "'Environmentalists Have Impoverished First Nations, Pro-Pipeline Chief Says," CBC News, December 7, 2016, https://www.cbc.ca.

39. Tasker.

40. Tasker.

41. Oil Sands Strong, Facebook, January 4, 2018, https://www.facebook.com/OilSandsStrong/photos/a.1617928505094086/2001123970107869.

42. James Wilt, "Fort McKay First Nation Fights for 'Last Refuge' amidst Oilsands Development," *The Narwhal*, January 20, 2018, https://thenarwhal.ca/fort-mckay-first-nation-fights-last-refuge-amidst-oilsands-development/.

43. Boucher, quoted in Wilt.

44. Ezra Levant, *Ethical Oil: The Case for Canada's Oil Sands* (Toronto: McClelland & Stewart, 2010), 212.

45. Oil Sands Strong, "Which would you choose?," Facebook, September 2, 2017, https://www.facebook.com/OilSandsStrong/photos/a.1617928505094086/1950787038474896.

46. Cody Battershill, "First Nations Actually Want Resource Development—If Paid Activists Would Just Get Out of Their Way," *Financial Post*, May 10, 2017, https://financialpost.com.

47. Robert Hackett and Hanna Araza, "Petromedia: How Postmedia Gives Big Ink to Big Oil," *Canada's National Observer,* April 29, 2021, https://www.nationalobserver.com.

48. Battershill, "First Nations."

49. Battershill.

50. Unist'ot'en Camp, "Action Alert—International Call to Action for Gidimt'en Access Checkpoint," accessed June 26, 2021, https://unistoten.camp.

51. Jaskiran Dhillon and Will Parrish, "Exclusive: Canada Police Prepared to Shoot Indigenous Activists, Documents Show," *The Guardian,* December 20, 2019.

52. Canada Action, "Wet'suwet'en Member Says Her People Are Being Misinformed on Gas Pipeline," February 10, 2020, https://www.canadaaction.ca.

53. Canada Action, "Hereditary Chief Helen Michelle of Skin Tyee Nation, Wet'suwet'en 'A lot of the protestors are not even #Wetsuweten. Our people said go ahead to #CoastalGasLink.' #WetsuwetenStrong #LNGCanada," Twitter, February 8, 2020, https://twitter.com/CanadaAction/status/1225990239795150849.

54. Gidimt'en Checkpoint, "She is speaking on behalf on [*sic*] the Skin Tyee First Nation whose reserve is nowhere near the pipeline route. Our hereditary chiefs made a unanimous decision in our traditional governance feast system to stand united against all pipelines proposed in the so-called energy cooridor [*sic*]," Twitter, February 9, 2020, https://twitter.com/Gidimten/status/1226582310314594305.

55. Arne Zabell, "Divide and rule (Latin: divide et impera), or divide and conquer, in politics and sociology is gaining and maintaining power by breaking up larger concentrations of power into pieces that individually have less power than the one implementing the strategy," Twitter, February 10, 2020, https://twitter.com/RuralBC/status/1226659041213964288.

56. Indigenous Resource Network, "Our Values," accessed September 12, 2023, https://www.indigenousresourcenetwork.ca/our_values.

57. Indigenous Resource Network.

58. Estella Petersen, "Opinion: I'm an Indigenous Woman Who Works in Alberta's Oil Sands—and I Can Speak for Myself," *Globe and Mail,* August 15, 2020.

59. Petersen.

60. Estella Petersen, "Indigenous Peoples in Canada Can Speak for Themselves," Canada Action, March 3, 2021, https://web.archive.org/web/20230105044238/https://www.canadaaction.ca/indigenous-peoples-can-speak-for-themselves.

61. Estella Petersen, "Have You Heard of Bill C-15, UNDRIP?," Canada Action, May 29, 2021, https://web.archive.org/web/20230105044318/https://www.canadaaction.ca/indigenous-viewpoint-bill-c15-undrip.

62. United Nations Permanent Forum on Indigenous Issues, "Media Advisory: General Assembly to Take Action on Declaration on Indigenous Rights," September 11, 2007, https://www.un.org.

63. Richard Thompson, "Trailblazer: Melina Laboucan-Massimo," KAIROS Canada, November 3, 2017, sec. Ecological Justice, https://www.kairoscanada.org.

64. Chris Turner, *The Patch: The People, Pipelines, and Politics of the Oil Sands* (Toronto: Simon & Schuster, 2017), 151–59.

65. Turner, 152.

66. TallBear, "Badass Indigenous Women."

67. Jason Hannan, "Trolling Ourselves to Death? Social Media and Post-truth Politics," *European Journal of Communication* 33, no. 2 (2018): 224.

68. Oil Sands Strong, Facebook, May 7, 2019, https://www.facebook.com/OilSandsStrong/photos/2290361514517445.

69. GreenpeaceCanada, "Oil on Lubicon Land: A Photo Essay," YouTube, 2011, https://www.youtube.com/watch?v=qz3nSscXamI.

70. Oil Sands Strong, Facebook, May 7, 2019.

71. Oil Sands Strong, Facebook, March 10, 2018, https://www.facebook.com/OilandgasworldandOilsandsstrong/posts/2031184393768493.

72. Melina Laboucan-Massimo, "Climate Justice Must Include Gender Justice," David Suzuki Foundation, March 18, 2018, https://davidsuzuki.org.

73. Tiny House Warriors, "Our Land Is Home," accessed June 21, 2021, http://www.tinyhousewarriors.com/.

74. Indigenous Network on Economies and Trade, "Standing Rock of the North: The Kinder Morgan Trans Mountain Pipeline Expansion Secwepemc Risk Assessment," October 2017, https://docs.wixstatic.com/ugd/934d11_6d9408803da54d24a2d6b650f14e6125.pdf.

75. Oil Sands Strong, "I think you need to make better life choices!," Facebook, April 4, 2018, https://www.facebook.com/OilSandsStrong/photos/2042432859310313.

76. Oil Sands Strong, "Yup this is a true story! Kanahus Manuel family owns a gas station," Facebook, July 17, 2018, https://www.facebook.com/OilandgasworldandOilsandsstrong/posts/2104707386416193.

77. Arthur Manuel, *Unsettling Canada: A National Wake-Up Call* (Toronto: Between the Lines, 2015), 73.

78. Oil Sands Strong, "This is very embarrassing for the Carleton Liberal Association," Facebook, March 26, 2021, https://www.facebook.com/OilSandsStrong/posts/2834991406721117.

79. Travis Beauregard, "Carleton Liberals Call 'Oil Sands Strong' Logo 'Racist,' Unaware That OSS Is Indigenous-Owned," *Buffalo Tribune,* March 26, 2021, https://web.archive.org/web/20220628022237/https://www.newstbt.com/post/carleton-fla-tweets-that-oil-sands-strong-logo-is-racist-unaware-that-oss-is-indigenous-owned.

80. Oil Sands Strong. "The OilSands Are the Economic Reconciliation for the First Nations!!," Facebook, December 4, 2017, https://www.facebook.com/OilSandsStrong/photos/a.1617928505094086/1988339354719664.

81. Oil Sands Strong, Facebook, July 25, 2020, https://www.facebook.com/OilandgasworldandOilsandsstrong/posts/2643588539194739.

82. Canada Action, "Indigenous & Natural Resources," accessed June 25, 2021, https://web.archive.org/web/20230104050933/https://www.canadaaction.ca/indigenous.

83. Deborah Cowen, "The Jurisdiction of Infrastructure: Circulation and Canadian Settler Colonialism," The *Funambulist* 17 (2018), https://thefunambulist.net/magazine.

5. Sustaining Petrocultures

1. OilGasCanada, "Dr. Patrick Moore on Alberta's oilsands," Facebook, November 2011, https://www.facebook.com/OilGasCanada/videos/574336350020/.

2. CBC News: The National, "GMO Advocate Says Monsanto's Roundup Safe to Drink, Then Refuses Glass," YouTube, 2015, https://www.youtube.com/watch?v=QWM_PgnoAtA.

3. Government of Alberta, "Environmental Protection and Enhancement Act: Conservation and Reclamation Regulation," Alberta Regulation 115/1993, Alberta King's Printer, Edmonton, March 1, 2023.

4. Government of Alberta, "Alberta's Oil Sands Reclamation," May 12, 2016, https://web.archive.org/web/20160512075516/http://www.oilsands.alberta.ca/reclamation.html.

5. Government of Alberta.

6. Natural Resources Canada, "Oil Sands: Land Use and Reclamation," June 29, 2016, https://web.archive.org/web/20220125191405/https://www.nrcan.gc.ca/energy/publications/18740.

7. Rob Nixon, *Slow Violence and the Environmentalism of the Poor* (Cambridge, Mass.: Harvard University Press, 2011).

8. Jodi McNeill, "Tailings Ponds: The Worst Is Yet to Come," Pembina Institute, blog, October 10, 2017, https://www.pembina.org.

9. Gillian Chow-Fraser and Alienor Rougeot, *50 Years of Sprawling Tailings: Mapping Decades of Destruction by Oil Sands Tailings* (Toronto: Environmental Defence Canada and Canadian Parks and Wilderness Society Northern Alberta, 2022).

10. Velshi, "Greenpeace Co-founder: Oil Sands Are Ethical," Ethical Oil.org, September 27, 2011, https://web.archive.org/web/20180127180300/http://www.ethicaloil.org/news/greenpeace-co-founder-oil-sands-are-ethical/.

11. Cody Battershill, "Battershill: We Need to Show the Same Passion for Pipelines as We Do for Amazon," *Calgary Herald,* November 2, 2017, https://calgaryherald.com.

12. OilsandsAction, "What is Canada's and the #Oilsands share of global greenhouse gas emissions?," Twitter, September 23, 2014, https://twitter.com/OilsandsAction/status/514506599491043328.

13. Rob Nelson, "@AKimCampbell @OilsandsAction Oilsand concerns go far beyond CO2 emissions, what about habitat destruction?," Twitter, December 10, 2014, https://twitter.com/RobNelson4/status/542715015800029185; Robert Kunzig, "The Canadian Oil Boom," *National Geographic,* January 3, 2009.

14. Brian L'Henaff, Twitter, February 18, 2017, https://twitter.com/wagondriver_75/status/833029668630458369.

15. Інна Іванівна, Twitter, July 18, 2016, https://twitter.com/CalgaryDignity/status/754863571511554048.

16. Alfred Schmidt, *The Concept of Nature in Marx,* trans. Ben Fowkes (London: New Left Books, 1971), 15.

17. Schmidt, 27.

18. John Bellamy Foster, Brett Clark, and Richard York, *The Ecological Rift: Capitalism's War on the Earth* (New York: Monthly Review Press, 2010).

19. John Bellamy Foster, *Marx's Ecology: Materialism and Nature* (New York: Monthly Review Press, 2000), ix, 155.

20. McKenzie Wark, *Molecular Red: Theory for the Anthropocene* (Brooklyn, N.Y.: Verso, 2015), xiv.

21. Jon Gordon, *Unsustainable Oil: Facts, Counterfacts and Fictions* (Edmonton: University of Alberta Press, 2015), xli.

22. Timothy Morton, *The Ecological Thought* (Cambridge, Mass.: Harvard University Press, 2010), 59–68.

23. See Gordon's discussion of these reclamation imaginaries in *Unsustainable Oil,* 54.

24. Geo Takach, *Tar Wars: Oil, Environment and Alberta's Image* (Edmonton: University of Alberta Press, 2017), 25.

25. Takach, 25.

26. Ethical Oil, Twitter, June 26, 2014, https://twitter.com/Ethical_Oil/status/482145637899595777.

27. Canada Action, Facebook, August 25, 2017, https://www.facebook.com/405377872902754/photos/a.624998014274071/1411404925633372/.

28. Don Pittis, "Branding Canadian Oil Green Would Be Good for Industry and for Climate Change," CBC News, July 24, 2017, https://www.cbc.ca.

29. Pittis.

30. Ethical Oil, "#OilSands - COSIA: Some progress made in environmental innovation, but breakthroughs will come later," Twitter, November 27 2013, https://twitter.com/Ethical_Oil/status/405724002968018944; Claudia Cattaneo, "COSIA: Some Progress Made in Environmental Innovation, but Breakthroughs Will Come Later," *Financial Post,* November 26, 2013, http://business.financialpost.com.

31. Cattaneo, "COSIA."

32. Cattaneo.

33. Cattaneo.

34. Ethical Oil, "Oil Sands Group Commits to Cutting Environmental Impact," Twitter, October 27, 2014, https://twitter.com/Ethical_Oil/status/526870898414850048.

35. Chester Dawson, "Oil Sands Group Commits to Cutting Environmental Impact," *Wall Street Journal,* October 27, 2014.

36. Dawson.

37. Isabelle Stengers, *In Catastrophic Times: Resisting the Coming Barbarism,* trans. Andrew Goffey (Lüneburg: Open Humanities Press, 2015), 29–34.

38. This is articulated in what Marxist theorists have come to know as the "Fragment on Machines," in Karl Marx, *Grundrisse: Foundations of the Critique of Political Economy (Rough Draft),* trans. Martin Nicolaus (Harmondsworth: Penguin Books, 1973), 690–712.

39. Faculty of Agricultural, Life & Environmental Sciences, University of Alberta, "Land Reclamation," accessed January 28, 2022, https://www.ualberta.ca/agriculture-life-environment-sciences/programs/undergraduate-programs/degree-programs/environmental-conservation-sciences/land-reclamation/index.html.

40. ECO Canada, "About ECO Canada," accessed January 5, 2023, http://www.eco.ca/about/.

41. ECO Canada, "Reclamation Specialist," accessed January 5, 2023, https://eco.ca/career-profiles/reclamation-specialist/.

42. Nicolas Graham, *Forces of Production, Climate Change and Canadian Fossil Capitalism* (Leiden: Brill, 2021), 2.

43. Graham, 2.

44. Jacob Goessling and Jordan B. Kinder, "Reclamation," *Environmental Humanities* 15, no. 2 (2023): 236–39.

45. Holly Jean Buck, *After Geoengineering: Climate Tragedy, Repair, and Restoration* (Brooklyn, N.Y.: Verso, 2019); Benjamin Bratton, *The Terraforming* (London: Strelka Press, 2019).

46. Ezra Levant, *Ethical Oil: The Case for Canada's Oil Sands* (Toronto: McClelland & Stewart, 2010), 4.

47. Velshi, "Mythbusting: Are the Oil Sands Destroying an Area the Size of Florida?," EthicalOil.org, July 25, 2011, https://web.archive.org/web/20120313001824/http://www.ethicaloil.org/news/mythbusting-are-the-oilsands-destroying-an-area-the-size-of-florida/.

48. CAPP, "Meet the Innovators," Energy Tomorrow, accessed Jan. 28, 2022, https://web.archive.org/web/20170930000106/http://www.energytomorrow.ca/.

49. CAPP, "Jessica Is Building Forests and Wetlands to Reclaim Mined Lands," Energy Tomorrow, accessed January 28, 2022, https://web.archive.org/web/20170929232149/http://www.energytomorrow.ca/sandhill_fen/.

50. CAPP, "Anne Is Capturing and Storing Carbon to Keep It Out of Our Atmosphere," Energy Tomorrow, accessed January 28, 2022, https://web.archive.org/web/20180115205619/http://www.energytomorrow.ca/carbon_capture.

51. CAPP, "Neal Is Using Light Oil and Steam to Reduce Greenhouse Gases," Energy Tomorrow, accessed January 28, 2022, https://web.archive.org/web/20180217011001/http://www.energytomorrow.ca/solvent_assisted_steam_assisted_gravity_drainage.

52. Stephanie LeMenager, *Living Oil: Petroleum Culture in the American Century* (New York: Oxford University Press, 2014), 10.

53. CAPP, "Anne."

54. Oil Sands Strong, Facebook, April 6, 2018, https://www.facebook.com/OilSandsStrong/photos/a.1617928505094086/2039845036235762.

55. OilsandsAction, Twitter, October 27, 2019, https://twitter.com/OilsandsAction/status/1188496896307761154.

56. R. W. Pauls, "Bison in the Oil Sands Industry," *CIM Bulletin* 92, no. 1026 (January 1999): 92.

57. Pauls, 92.

58. Tara L. Joly, "Urban Buffalo: Métis–Bison Relations and Oil Sands Extraction in Northeastern Alberta," in *Extracting Home in the Oil Sands,* ed. Clinton N. Westman, Tara L. Joly, and Lena Gross (London: Routledge, 2019), 145.

59. Nicole Shukin, "Animal Capital: The Material Politics of Rendering, Mimesis, and Mobility in North American Culture" (PhD diss., University of Alberta, 2005), 142.

60. Shukin, 142.

61. Graham, *Forces of Production,* 89.

62. Shannon Walsh, "The Smell of Money: Alberta's Tar Sands," *The Commoner,* no. 13 (2008–9): 117.

63. Shukin, "Animal Capital," 151–52.

64. Shukin, 153–54.

65. Claudia Sobrevila, *The Role of Indigenous Peoples in Biodiversity Conservation: The Natural but Often Forgotten Partners* (Washington, D.C.: World Bank, 2008), xii.

66. Kyle Powys Whyte, "Indigenous Climate Change Studies: Indigenizing Futures, Decolonizing the Anthropocene," *English Language Notes* 55, no. 1 (2017): 154.

67. Whyte, 158.

68. The Canadian Press, "Dead Bison in Herd on Reclaimed Oilsands Site Test Positive for Anthrax," Global News, August 23, 2015, www.global news.ca.

69. Dallas New, Brett Elkin, Terry Armstrong, and Tasha Epp, "Anthrax in the Mackenzie Wood Bison (Bison Bison Athabascae) Population: 2012 Anthrax Outbreak and Historical Exposure in Nonoutbreak Years," *Journal of Wildlife Diseases* 53, no. 4 (2017): 769–80.

70. David Thurton, "25 Years Later, Syncrude's Bison Herd Thriving on Reclaimed Oilsands Lands," CBC News, February 16, 2018, http://www.cbc .ca.

71. Hayden King and Riley Yesno, "Reclamation," in *Land Back: A Yellowhead Institute Red Paper* (Toronto: Yellowhead Institute, 2019), 56–59.

72. Robin Wall Kimmerer, *Braiding Sweetgrass: Indigenous Wisdom, Scientific Knowledge, and the Teachings of Plants* (Minneapolis: Milkweed Editions, 2013).

73. Shukin, "Animal Capital," 167.

74. Shukin, 167.

75. Suncor, "Journey of Reconciliation," accessed January 23, 2022, https:// www.suncor.com.

76. *OED Online,* s.v. "reclamation, n.," Oxford University Press, accessed February 28, 2021, http://www.oed.com.

77. Jordan B. Kinder, "Sustainable Appropriation: Consumption, Advertising, and the (Anti-) Politics of (Post-)Environmentalism" (MA thesis, University of Northern British Columbia, 2013).

78. Glen Sean Coulthard, *Red Skin, White Masks: Rejecting the Colonial Politics of Recognition* (Minneapolis: University of Minnesota Press, 2014), 12.

6. From the Highway to the Legislature

1. Support Canadian Energy, "Tell the Truth Netflix!," accessed June 7, 2021, https://www.supportcanadianenergy.ca.

2. Support Canadian Energy.

3. Tristin Hopper, "Nuke the Oilsands: Alberta's Narrowly Cancelled Plan to Drill for Oil with Atomic Weapons," *National Post,* August 2, 2016, https://nationalpost.com.

4. Fakiha Baig, "'It's Silly': Director of Bigfoot Movie Thanks Campaign by Alberta's Energy War Room," CBC News, March 28, 2021, https://www.cbc.ca.

5. Luke Munn, "Alt-Right Pipeline: Individual Journeys to Extremism Online," *First Monday* 24, no. 6 (2019), https://doi.org/10.5210/fm.v24i6.10108.

6. Cara New Daggett, "Petro-Masculinity: Fossil Fuels and Authoritarian Desire," *Millennium* 47, no. 1 (2018): 25–44; Andreas Malm and the Zetkin Collective, eds., *White Skin, Black Fuel: On the Danger of Fossil Fascism* (New York: Verso, 2021).

7. See, for instance, Alexander Reid Ross, *Against the Fascist Creep* (Chico, Calif.: AK Press, 2017).

8. Munn, "Alt-Right Pipeline."

9. Manoel Horta Ribeiro, Raphael Ottoni, Robert West, Virgílio A. F. Almeida, and Wagner Meira, "Auditing Radicalization Pathways on YouTube," in *Proceedings of the 2020 Conference on Fairness, Accountability, and Transparency* (New York: Association for Computing Machinery, 2020), 131–41.

10. Robert W. Gehl, *Weaving the Dark Web: Legitimacy on Freenet, Tor, and I2P* (Cambridge, Mass.: MIT Press, 2018), 2–5.

11. Michael Brooks, *Against the Web: A Cosmopolitan Answer to the New Right* (Winchester, Wash.: Zero Books, 2020).

12. Brooks, 9.

13. Facebook's Top 10, "The Top-Performing Link Posts by U.S. Facebook Pages in the Last 24 Hours Are from: 1. Ben Shapiro 2. David Wolfe 3. Ben Shapiro 4. Ben Shapiro 5. Ben Shapiro 6. Ben Shapiro 7. Ben Shapiro 8. Fox News 9. Ben Shapiro 10. Ben Shapiro," Twitter, June 15, 2021, https://twitter.com/FacebooksTop10/status/1404815323904237569.

14. Facebook's Top 10, "The Top-Performing Link Posts by U.S. Facebook Pages in the Last 24 Hours Are from: 1. Ben Shapiro 2. Ben Shapiro

3. Ben Shapiro 4. Ben Shapiro 5. Ben Shapiro 6. VOA Burmese News 7. NPR 8. The Dodo 9. Steven Crowder 10. VOA Burmese News," Twitter, June 14, 2021, https://twitter.com/FacebooksTop10/status/1404483361821708293.

15. Malm and the Zetkin Collective, *White Skin, Black Fuel,* 13–24.

16. Louis Althusser, *On the Reproduction of Capitalism: Ideology and Ideological State Apparatuses,* trans. G. M. Goshgarian (New York: Verso, 2014), 81–93.

17. Althusser, 81–93.

18. Malm and the Zetkin Collective, *White Skin, Black Fuel,* 18–24.

19. Corporate Mapping Project, "Database," accessed April 14, 2022, https://www.corporatemapping.ca/database/.

20. Quoted in John Semley, "Opinion: War of a Word: How 'Ideology' Has Been Weaponized into a Political Slur," *Globe and Mail,* April 12, 2019.

21. The Daily Wire, "Ben Shapiro DESTROYS Greta's CRAZY Climate Change Arguments," YouTube, 2020, https://www.youtube.com/watch?v=8RVooYlyl20.

22. Greta Thunberg, "Greta Thunberg: Our House Is Still on Fire and You're Fuelling the Flames," World Economic Forum, January 21, 2020, https://www.weforum.org.

23. The Daily Wire, "Ben Shapiro DESTROYS Greta's CRAZY Climate Change Arguments."

24. See Public Safety Canada, "Currently Listed Entities," Government of Canada, December 21, 2018, https://www.publicsafety.gc.ca.

25. David C. Atkinson, "Charlottesville and the Alt-Right: A Turning Point?," *Politics, Groups, and Identities* 6, no. 2 (2018): 309.

26. Atkinson, 313.

27. Daggett, "Petro-Masculinity," 27.

28. Malm and the Zetkin Collective, *White Skin, Black Fuel,* 235.

29. Malm and the Zetkin Collective, 235.

30. Malm and the Zetkin Collective, 239.

31. Malm and the Zetkin Collective, 251.

32. Alain Badiou, "Leçons du mouvement des Gilets jaunes," *Lignes* 59, no. 2 (2019): 37–46; Jean-Paul Deléage, "L'insurrection des «gilets jaunes», et après?," *Ecologie politique* 58, no. 1 (2019): 5–8.

33. Cosmin Dzsurdzsa, "Canadian Yellow Vest Movement Releases Unofficial Manifesto," *Post-Millennial,* December 18, 2018, https://thepostmillennial.com.

34. Elizabeth Hames, "Don't Dismiss Them as 'Crackpots': Who Are Canada's Yellow Vest Protesters?," CBC News, January 11, 2019, https://www.cbc.ca.

35. Omar Mosleh, "What's in a Name? Alberta's Extremist Groups Splinter Over How They Should Spread Their Message," *Toronto Star,* January 31, 2019, https://www.thestar.com.

36. Mosleh.

37. Quoted in CBC News, "'I Hope They Can Hear Us in Ottawa': 1,500 Attend Alberta Oilpatch Rally," December 17, 2018, https://www.cbc.ca.

38. James Keller, "Pro-Pipeline Convoy Overshadowed by Link to Yellow Vests," *Globe and Mail,* February 8, 2019.

39. Timothy Morton, *Hyperobjects* (Minneapolis: University of Minnesota Press, 2013), 1.

40. Morton, 20.

41. Mitchell Beer, "Convoy Mixes with White Nationalists and Delivers Toxic Message to Ottawa," *National Observer,* February 21, 2019, https://www.nationalobserver.com.

42. Beer.

43. Zi-Ann Lum, "Tory Senator Tells Truckers to 'Roll Over Every Liberal Left in The Country,'" *HuffPost Canada,* February 21, 2019, https://www.huffingtonpost.ca.

44. Winona LaDuke and Deborah Cowen, "Beyond Wiindigo Infrastructure," *South Atlantic Quarterly* 119, no. 2 (2020): 246.

45. Andrea Ross and Kyle Muzyka, "Albertans Chant 'Lock Her Up' about Rachel Notley at Rally against Carbon Tax," CBC News, December 5, 2016, https://www.cbc.ca.

46. Michelle Bellefontaine, "Incorporation of Alberta's Energy War Room Means Much of Its Operations Remain Secret," CBC News, October 11, 2019, https://www.cbc.ca.

47. *OED Online,* s.v. "war, n.1," Oxford University Press, accessed April 15, 2022, http://www.oed.com.

48. Canadian Energy Centre, accessed August 13, 2021, https://web.archive.org/web/20210728170810/https://www.canadianenergycentre.ca/.

49. Grady Semmens, "Fighting Climate Change with Canadian Energy," Canadian Energy Centre, December 5, 2019, https://web.archive.org/web/20210813191411/https://www.canadianenergycentre.ca/fighting-climate-change-with-canadian-energy/.

50. This is especially true in the European Union. See John Szabo, "Natural Gas' Changing Discourse in European Decarbonisation," in *Energy Humanities: Current State and Future Directions,* ed. Matúš Mišík and Nada Kujundžić (New York: Springer International, 2021), 67–88.

51. See, for example, Deborah Jaremko, "A Matter of Fact: Opponents of Line 5 Ignore Safety Record and Planned Improvements for Critical Pipeline,"

Canadian Energy Centre, August 4, 2021, https://web.archive.org/web/20210813211850/https://www.canadianenergycentre.ca/a-matter-of-fact-opponents-of-line-5-ignore-safety-record-and-planned-improvements-for-critical-pipeline/.

52. Support Canadian Energy, "Canada Needs a West to East Pipeline," accessed August 14, 2021, https://web.archive.org/web/20210813190639/https://www.supportcanadianenergy.ca/canada_needs_a_west_east_pipeline.

53. Ashley Carse and David Kneas, "Unbuilt and Unfinished: The Temporalities of Infrastructure," *Environment and Society* 10, no. 1 (2019): 22.

54. Maclean's, "The Top Lobby Groups in Ottawa," December 5, 2013, https://www.macleans.ca.

55. Alberta Inquiry, "Public Inquiry into Anti-Alberta Energy Campaigns," accessed July 20, 2021, https://albertainquiry.ca.

56. T. L. Nemeth, *A New Global Paradigm: Understanding the Transnational Progressive Movement, the Energy Transition and the Great Transformation Strangling Alberta's Petroleum Industry* (Calgary: The Public Inquiry into Funding of Anti-Alberta Energy Campaigns, 2020), 46.

57. Nemeth, 28.

58. Nemeth, 40.

59. Nemeth, 48, 41n98; Douglas Murray, *The Madness of Crowds: Gender, Race and Identity* (London: Bloomsbury Continuum, 2019).

60. Nemeth, 56.

61. Energy In Depth, *Foreign Funding Targeting Canada's Energy Sector* (Calgary: The Public Inquiry into Funding of Anti-Alberta Energy Campaigns, 2021), 2.

62. Energy In Depth, 7.

63. Energy In Depth, 31.

64. Barry Cooper, *Background Report on Changes in the Organization and Ideology of Philanthropic Foundations with a Focus on Environmental Issues as Reflected in Contemporary Social Science Research* (Calgary: The Public Inquiry into Funding of Anti-Alberta Energy Campaigns, 2021), 2.

65. Cooper, 11.

66. Jane Mayer, *Dark Money: The Hidden History of the Billionaires behind the Rise of the Radical Right* (New York: Anchor, 2017), 206.

67. Mayer, 206.

68. J. Stephens Allan, *Report of the Public Inquiry into Anti-Alberta Energy Campaigns* (Calgary: Government of Alberta, 2021), 596.

69. Allan, 14.

70. Allan, 643.

71. Allan, 597.

72. Allan, 648.

73. Allan, 598.

74. Moniquemuise, "'Old-Stock Canadians' Are Those Already Here, Says Harper Spokesman," Global News, September 18, 2015, https://globalnews.ca/news.

75. John Paul Tasker, "Conservative Delegates Reject Adding 'Climate Change Is Real' to the Policy Book," CBC News, March 20, 2021, https://www.cbc.ca/news.

76. CAPP, "What Is Bill C-69?," *Context: Energy Examined,* October 15, 2018, https://context.capp.ca.

77. Canada Action, "About," accessed June 9, 2021, https://web.archive.org/web/20210609211438/https://www.canadaaction.ca/about.

78. Canada Action, "Who We Are," accessed August 7, 2021, https://web.archive.org/web/20210609211025/https://www.canadaaction.ca/who_we_are.

79. Jen Gerson, "One-Man Oil Sands Advocate, Tired of Smears against Alberta, Takes on Celebrity Activists in PR War," *National Post,* September, 22, 2014, https://nationalpost.com.

80. Oil Sands Strong, "Complete this sentence . . . ," Facebook, July 28, 2021, https://www.facebook.com/OilSandsStrong/photos/2921402731413317.

81. Rally 4 Resources, "'A similar trend was observed in Alberta. For seven weeks, death counts were consistently higher than the historical baseline—but only 40 out of the 402 additional deaths are connected to the coronavirus.' #EndAllRestrictionsNow," Facebook, June 22, 2020, https://www.facebook.com/rallyforresources/photos/a.1612997935681200/2638799389767711.

82. Rally 4 Resources, Facebook, August 9, 2020, https://www.facebook.com/rallyforresources/photos/a.1612997935681200/2679021549078828.

83. Rally 4 Resources, Facebook, January 4, 2019, https://www.facebook.com/yourlibertyproject/posts/2212495829064738.

84. Trevor Harrison, "Morbid Symptoms: Alberta's Yellow Vest Movement," *Canadian Dimension,* April 7, 2019, https://canadiandimension.com.

85. Harrison.

86. Harrison.

Conclusion

1. Matt Huber, *Lifeblood: Oil, Freedom, and the Forces of Capital* (Minneapolis: University of Minnesota Press, 2013).

2. J. Stephens Allan, "Ruling on Interpretation of the Terms of Reference," appendix B of *Report of the Public Inquiry into Anti-Alberta Energy Campaigns,* by J. Stephens Allan (Calgary: Government of Alberta, 2021), para. 8.

3. Seth Klein, *A Good War: Mobilizing Canada for the Climate Emergency* (Toronto: ECW Press, 2020).

4. Andreas Malm, *Corona, Climate, Chronic Emergency: War Communism in the Twenty-First Century* (New York: Verso, 2020), 109–74.

5. Malm, 138.

6. Cara New Daggett, "Petro-Masculinity: Fossil Fuels and Authoritarian Desire," *Millennium* 47, no. 1 (2018): 28.

7. Jason Kenney [@jkenney], "Devastating to see that Vladimir Putin has now launched an invasion of Ukraine. Weakness invites aggression.," Twitter, February 24, 2022, https://twitter.com/jkenney/status/1496706075050999811.

8. The Editorial Board, "Globe Editorial: The World Needs More Canadian Oil and Gas," *Globe and Mail,* March 9, 2022.

9. Kyle Powys Whyte, "Indigenous Science (Fiction) for the Anthropocene: Ancestral Dystopias and Fantasies of Climate Change Crises," *Environment and Planning E: Nature and Space* 1, nos. 1–2 (2018): 227.

10. Tim Wood, "The Many Voices of Business: Framing the Keystone Pipeline in US and Canadian News," *Journalism* 20, no. 2 (February 1, 2019): 292–312.

11. Kai Bosworth, *Pipeline Populism: Grassroots Environmentalism in the Twenty-First Century* (Minneapolis: University of Minnesota Press, 2022), 38.

12. Matt Huber, *Climate Change as Class War: Building Socialism on a Warming Planet* (New York: Verso, 2022).

13. Robert Hackett and Hanna Araza, "The Oil Blotter: Postmedia & Big Oil's Symbiosis," *The Monitor,* May 1, 2021, https://monitormag.ca.

14. Hackett and Araza.

15. Hackett and Araza.

16. Robert Neubauer and Nicolas Graham, "Fuelling the Subsidized Public: Mapping the Flow of Extractivist Content on Facebook," *Canadian Journal of Communication* 46, no. 4 (2021): 918.

17. Allan, *Report of the Public Inquiry into Anti-Alberta Energy Campaigns,* 643.

18. Oil Sands Strong, "Cool things are happening," Facebook, April 22, 2022, https://www.facebook.com/OilSandsStrong/posts/3116087078611547.

19. Robbie Picard, "It's very rare that I'm actually starstruck," Facebook, December 13, 2022, https://www.facebook.com/photo/?fbid=8465659373504962&set=a.3168653999872219.

20. Wendy Hui Kyong Chun, *Discriminating Data: Correlation, Neighborhoods, and the New Politics of Recognition* (Cambridge, Mass.: MIT Press, 2021).

21. Joshua Clover, "The Political Economy of Tactics," *Verso Books* (blog), March 16, 2022, https://www.versobooks.com.

22. Clover.

23. Jordan B. Kinder, "Ambivalence and Intensity: Platform Energetics," in *Digital Energetics,* ed. Anne Pasek, Cindy Kaiying Lin, Zane Griffin Talley Cooper, and Jordan B. Kinder (Lüneburg: Meson Press, 2023), 96–120.

24. Petrocultures Research Group, *After Oil* (Edmonton: Petrocultures Research Group, 2016).

25. Kinder, "Ambivalence and Intensity," 110.

26. Kinder, 116–17.

27. Andreas Malm, *The Progress of This Storm: Nature and Society in a Warming World* (New York: Verso, 2018), 5.

28. Jon Gordon, *Unsustainable Oil: Facts, Counterfacts and Fictions* (Edmonton: University of Alberta Press, 2015), xxvi.

29. Simon Orpana, *Gasoline Dreams: Waking Up from Petroculture* (New York: Fordham University Press, 2021), 213–38.

30. Orpana, 213–38.

31. Zoe Todd, "Fish, Kin and Hope: Tending to Water Violations in Amiskwaciwâskahikan and Treaty Six Territory," *Afterall: A Journal of Art, Context and Enquiry* 43 (2017): 107.

32. Todd, 107.

33. See Anne Pasek, Cindy Kaiying Lin, Zane Griffin Talley Cooper, and Jordan B. Kinder, "Locating Digital Energetics," in *Digital Energetics* (Minneapolis: University of Minnesota Press, 2023), 1–14.

INDEX

Jordan B. Kinder is assistant professor in communication studies at Wilfrid Laurier University. He is a citizen of the Métis Nation of Alberta.